Read it and
be inspired!

2016

We Got Mojo!

We Got Mojo!

Stories of Inspiration and Perspiration

RAUL A. DEJU AND HIS BFF

Library of Congress Control Number: 2016911561
ISBN: Hardcover   978-1-5245-2584-2
                Softcover   978-1-5245-2583-5
                eBook   978-1-5245-2582-8

Print information available on the last page.

Rev. date: 07/19/2016

To order additional copies of this book, contact:
Xlibris
1-888-795-4274
www.Xlibris.com
Orders@Xlibris.com
732929

CONTENTS

Note: For those of you who watch NCIS on TV, these twenty rules of mine are my version of "Rules for a Successful Life," just like Special Agent Leroy Jethro Gibbs has in the NCIS show his own special rules. By the way, he has a lot more rules than I have!

What Reviewers Are Saying about *We Got Mojo!*
Stories of Inspiration and Perspiration

More reviews on the back cover

"This is an extraordinary book with important lessons for life. The book is filled with personal journeys of three dozen remarkable folks, proving that anyone born or able to find their way to the US has won life's biggest lottery. Dr. Deju shows how hard work, courage, persistence and an unquenchable desire to succeed will ALWAYS lead to success. This is the American Dream."

Douglas Doan, Founder and Chairman,
Hivers and Strivers, Angel Investment Group;
West Point and Harvard Business School Graduate

"You hold in your hands a book of stories of courage in business leadership. Just like you and me, the authors of these stories faced obstacles and crises—the sort that test your mettle and bring tears and angst to the forefront, keeping you up at night. How they overcame these fears because they *believed* in their purpose is what ultimately led them to succeed. This is a book that will help you find the courage to overcome those same obstacles all leaders must face in order to be a leader."

Drew Mendoza, Managing Principal,
the Family Business Consulting Group Inc.

"Amazing heartfelt work! This beautiful compilation of stories is a must read not only for everyone who is struggling today to find their way through life's minefield but also for those of us that have found our way through—albeit temporarily, since life's struggles are never totally behind anyone. I found the stories uplifting, yet upsetting at times, as I recalled my own struggles out of poverty. It is important to remember the circumstances that long ago lifted us from trying times and to use those memories to inspire us to become the catalyst for the success of others."

Ken Kilroy, Senior Partner, Brightstar Capital Partners;
Cofounder and CEO, Unity Investment Partners
and Trailhead Advisors; named one of the
"Power 25" top wealth managers in America

"This compilation of real stories about how to succeed in America should be a 'must read' material for all those who are determined to not just dream about a better life, but to make their dreams a reality. These stories prove that all you need is the plentiful opportunity found in this country and to have lots of "Mojo" to change not just your life but the life of those around you. Dr. Deju has mastered telling the American story of success with this book. Very inspirational!"

Lupita Colmenero, Publisher, **El Hispano News,** *and*
Executive Vice President, **Latina Style**

"Raul Deju and the contributors of his book, *We Got Mojo!* have given us something of *real* meaning. Intimate personal stories were shared throughout that provided revelations and inspiration. I was pulled from one uplifting chapter to the next! It is clear that this book was meant to serve others, and it has done so beautifully."

Dr. Tamara Monosoff, #1 Amazon Best-Selling Author
and Creator of the Author-to-Income Formula

"*We Got Mojo!* is one of the most important books you will read this year. The rich and varied stories in this remarkable volume demonstrate that the American Dream is alive and well. Each extraordinary story offers invaluable lessons on how to live a truly great life."

Dr. Anne E. Cunningham, Professor, University of California,
Berkeley; Author of **Book Smart: How to Develop**
and Support Successful, Motivated Readers

"Only an extraordinary man, such as Dr. Raul Deju, would have such extraordinary Best Friends Forever. Through this book, the reader gains 36 new BFF including Dr. Deju. All of them share their inspiring stories, their lessons learned, and their heartfelt views on life. The effect of these stories is poignant and thought-provoking and ultimately provides us with wisdom, given as only a BFF can, to improve our lives."

Dr. Debra Bean, President, John F. Kennedy University

The Authors
(in order of their chapters inside the text)

Dr. Raul A. Deju (lead author) and his thirty-five BFF

Diana Campoamor

Jacqueline P. Bhagavan

Will Martinez

Beatriz "Betty" Manetta

Dr. Daniel H. López

Patricia Moore

Deborah Peacock

Marcia Wiss

Mark C. Thompson

Tom Deierlein

Harlan P. Kleiman

Bill Hewitt

David Borlaug

Dave Hornbeck

Deborah Steinthal

Dr. Roger Werne

Mark Powell

Erica Courtney

Bill Wiersma

Dina Finta

Jill Osur

Lt. Gen. Ricardo S. Sánchez

Larry Rockwell

Phyllis Newhouse

Tom Gorham

Anne Marie Taylor

John Sánchez

Kaney O'Neill

Cecelia Lakatos Sullivan

Amber Peebles

Jennifer Schoenhofer

Mary Tuchscherer

Randy Haykin

Summer C. Selleck

Elizabeth Perlman

Edited by Cale Finta

Other Titles by Dr. Raul A. Deju

- *Regional Hydrology Fundamentals*
- *The Environment and Its Resources* (coauthored by A. P. Baez, R. B. Bhappu, and G. C. Evans)
- *Extraction of Minerals and Energy: Today's Dilemmas*
- *Nuclear Energy and the Use of Nuclear Materials* (coauthored by Harry Babad)
- *Nuclear Is Hot* (coauthored by Harry Babad and Michael Deju)
- *Planet in Conflict: Balancing Energy Needs, Economic Growth, and Environmental Quality* (coauthored by Tapan Munroe)

Bio: Dr. Raul A. Deju

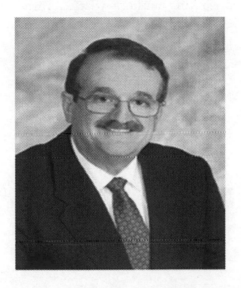

Dr. Raul A. Deju, a native of Cuba who migrated to the United States in his early teens, is the founding director emeritus and a supporter of the Institute of Entrepreneurial Leadership (IEL) at John F. Kennedy University in the San Francisco Bay Area. He is currently a senior partner at Brightstar Capital Partners, a New York–based private equity partnership, and CEO of Deju Management Advisors Inc., an advisory and consulting services firm. He has served in executive positions at the top corporate level (CEO, COO, or Division President) at multiple companies, including International Technology Corporation (now Chicago Bridge & Iron), URS Inc. (now AECOM), Waste Management (both domestically and internationally), Isadra Inc., Headwaters, and Energy*Solutions*. Dr. Deju has served as an adviser to a prior Secretary of Commerce and a prior US EPA Administrator. He is the author of six other books and over two hundred peer-reviewed articles. His first book, *Regional Hydrology Fundamentals*, was published in hardback by a major publisher in London and New York when he was twenty-five years old. He was named one of the top twenty-five Latinos in the San Francisco area and received commendations for his Latino philanthropy as well as numerous other recognitions. Dr. Deju has been involved in over $5 billion of equity capital being monetized through various liquidity options.

(Bios of the contributing authors written from the lead author's perspective can be found at the end of their respective chapters.)

To my dear kids and grandkids (Michael, Raul Jr., Lisa [daughter-in-law], Raul III, and Sofia),

I started as a scientist as the space program was being launched and have seen a half a century of unbelievable progress ever since. As I write the words in this book, the five of you are part of the next two generations that can make sure that the advances of our civilization in the next fifty years are as awesome as for the past fifty and bring mankind to a better standard of living, with great respect for one another, in peace, and carefully protecting our planet. I hope the words here guide and inspire you for all your lives. May your BFF be as good as mine are.

To my wife, Shari Lynn,

You are my partner, my best friend, my wife. I am excited and privileged to have spent most of my adult life with you, sharing the beauty of living. I look forward to a great deal more time on this fabulous ride. You are the best; you are the love of my life!

To my friends,

Since coming to America, you, my BFF, have constituted the most supportive family anyone can hope to have. To those of you who have contributed to this book, many thanks and hopefully many more years of enjoying each other. I really appreciate all your incisive contributions, your wisdom, your kindness, and the moments we spend together. To those that we couldn't include here, there is always a future book. I love you all!

The author's proceeds from this book have been donated fully to the Disabled Veteran Business Alliance to assist service-disabled veteran entrepreneurship.

Foreword

For anyone who thinks they are at a disadvantage, the book you are about to read, *We Got Mojo! Stories of Inspiration and Perspiration*, is a guiding light toward success. Dr. Deju, the lead author, has identified key traits that can give anyone the inspiration and desire to achieve many of the things they could only dream about.

Dr. Deju has chronicled from his own experience and that of a number of individual contributing authors the key traits that inspire individuals toward success. This is a book that, whether you are a disadvantaged individual or a senior executive, will inspire and motivate you to put in the extra amount of effort, to achieve positions such as president, chairman, and other significant leadership roles in any enterprise.

On a personal note, for me as a reader, he identified and helped me understand how this inner-city kid could go from being a telephone installer to becoming President and CEO of a major utility company. He has success patterns spelled out, with an emphasis on good mentoring, nurturing, and looking for success in all the right places.

Charles "Chuck" Smith
Retired President and CEO
AT&T West
Vice Chair of the Board
University of San Francisco
June 2016

Introduction

Success

So what is success? *Merriam-Webster Dictionary* defines *success* as "the fact of getting or achieving wealth, respect, or fame; the correct or desired result of an attempt; or someone or something that is successful: a person or thing that succeeds." Notice how easily in our society we tie success to money, fame, and social status. Yet many of us know wealthy or famous people who are unhappy despite their riches. Is that really success? I say no. As for me, I prefer my own definition of *success* as "having been able to take the steps to lead a happy life on this planet, with comfort, moral support, true values and a sense of accomplishment and fulfillment." As I enter my seventh decade, I can more analytically reflect on the success I have had (by my definition), with some failures or, better yet, learning steps along the way.

Friends of mine from time to time over the years have suggested that I write my biography as an inspiration to others that success is achievable even when everything is working against you. My answer has always been the same: "My bio is not that interesting, and I am not that unique." But then it occurred to me that clearly my success has only been possible because of the gaggle of friends that has helped me, guided me, set an example for me, and inspired me through the journey we call life. It is for this reason that I came up with the idea of writing a book that instead intertwines the stories from my life at various stages with the stories of some of my BFF (best friends forever) who are even more exciting and provide a more diverse framework of the trials and tribulations of life and how one can chart a course that leads to success. And this is how this book was born.

My BFF

Pretty much all my life, as an only child, I have surrounded myself with a myriad of very diverse and uplifting friends. I believe that a broad base of friends of different ethnicity, ways of life, approaches to problem-solving, background, faith, and life history provides the diverse framework that gives anyone the proper outlook to succeed in the world. My BFF who coauthored this book are truly such a diverse bunch. Fifty-four percent of them are women, and 46 percent are men. Not quite evenly split. Their ages include every age group from the thirties to the seventies. Twenty-three percent are minorities, 23 percent are veterans, and 14 percent are immigrants. Two traits that include an overwhelming percent of my BFF are (1) that over 75 percent of them extensively practice a philanthropic outlook in life (my kind of folks!) and (2) 80 percent of them came from poor or very poor families (they learned entrepreneurship early on).

One thing that is also clear from all my BFF is that they are all high achievers and have made it through awfully difficult conditions that would have stopped people with less grit and tenacity. Their adventures have ranged from escaping genocidal regimes or dictators to leaving a mostly illiterate village and migrating to the United States alone to become a world-class scientist in the area of nanotechnology, or recovering from a sniper's bullet in the Middle East and rebuilding his life after nearly two years of multiple surgeries.

Many of my BFF and I have been part of the leading innovative forces that have led to the creation of many major modern enterprises, such as a number of the Virgin brand ventures, Smule.com, Esurance.com (sold to Allstate), Interwoven.com (sold to HP), Rioport.com (they pioneered Apple's MP3 player), Appurify.com (sold to Google), Trusper.com, Telepathic.com, Digitsz.com, Box.com, Facebook.com, Pinterest.com, Waste Management, International Technology Corporation (now Chicago Bridge & Iron), URS (merged with AECOM), Energy*Solutions*, Self Health Network, Headwaters, PSC, Isadra, Shoreline Pacific, the first made-for-pay-TV movie and the first interactive pay-TV series, MTV, Nickelodeon, Yahoo!, RECON, Overture, NetChannel, AOL, Electric Minds, Outlook Ventures, Charles Schwab and Co., and Haykin Capital, to name just a few.

My military BFF include the General who led the coalition forces for the Iraqi invasion, the first female graduate as an Army Scout Helicopter Pilot, an enlisted member of the US Navy who is now the CEO of her own roofing company in the Midwest despite her significant disability (she is a quadriplegic), and a number of Army, Marine, Coast Guard, and Air Force veterans, all of whom I consider the salt of the earth.

Analyzing Success

What we did to frame this book was to ask thirty-five of my BFF to provide us a blog-size four- to seven-page story of their life that gives the reader an idea as to how they dealt with success and failure and how they got their mojo to make it through. We used the *Merriam-Webster* definition of *mojo* ("a power that may seem magical and that allows someone to be very effective and successful") and asked each contributing author to give the readers their recipes to successfully put their mojo to work.

Thirty-five of their chapters are included here, together with four chapters that define four periods of my life. Each chapter is self-standing and written in the personal style of each of my BFF. They all provide insightful points as to how they succeeded and what they learned from their failures. Some of the chapters cover an entire lifetime, while others focus on specific parts of each of my BFF's road trip through life that were particularly important to each of them.

The book is structured into six sections in order to present the stories in an organized fashion. Section 1 deals with those stories from my immigrant friends and me. Section 2 highlights the role of education in my own story and the role it played in some of my BFF's lives. Section 3 covers ten mojo secrets that my BFF and I uncovered through our lives. Section 4 deals with how to ignite your passion, while section 5 covers the role of leadership and tenacity and provides a framework for dealing with adversity. Finally, section 6 includes the stories from some of my BFF who have established meaningful and effective charitable giving entities.

In 1937, Andrew Carnegie, the successful industrialist, met a journalist named Napoleon Hill, who interviewed over five hundred rich industrialists and wrote a best-seller titled *Think and Grow Rich.* This book became, for years, the guide as to how to succeed and become rich, based on the principles that Hill derived from his interviews. Well, we have included in each chapter of our book the pointers that each of our coauthors feels to have been responsible for keeping their mojo up so they could succeed, not necessarily become monetarily rich, but instead morally and emotionally complete. Then, we analyzed all the data from all our BFF, and in the last section of this book, we have included twenty rules to keep your mojo and lead a successful life. These rules combine my own rules with those of all my BFF, all put into one list. For those of you that watch *NCIS,* the popular TV series, the main character, Special Agent Leroy Jethro Gibbs, talks about his list of rules for life; and in many episodes of the series, you see him mention one rule or another. Well, we will give you *our rules* at the end of the book. I urge you to make our twenty rules for success your own. They will make a difference.

We hope you enjoy our stories. I expect they will inspire you through all the drops of perspiration we have shed in our collective lives.

Dr. Raul A. Deju
June 2016
San Francisco, CA, USA

Section 1

Assimilating into a Nation of Great Diversity

*The land in America flourished because it was fed
from so many sources—because it was nourished by
so many cultures and traditions and peoples.*

–President Lyndon B. Johnson

Significant Reflections on the Benefits of Immigrants Coming to Our Shores

I had always hoped that this land might become a safe and agreeable asylum to the virtuous and persecuted part of mankind, to whatever nation they might belong.

—President George Washington

America was indebted to immigration for her settlement and prosperity. That part of America which had encouraged immigration most had advanced most rapidly in population, agriculture and the arts.

—President James Madison

Everywhere immigrants have enriched and strengthened the fabric of American life.

—President John F. Kennedy

What we need to do is to have a sensible approach to immigration. It needs to be open. It needs to be non-dogmatic and non-bigoted. We need to be firm but reasonable in the way we deal with the problem of illegal immigration. And we need to try to get as many of our immigrants who want to do so to become citizens as quickly as possible so that the American people will all see that this is a part of the process of American history, which is a good one for our country.

—President Bill Clinton

Chapter 1

Peter Pan Went to Neverland, but Pedro Pan Brought Me to the United States

Raul A. Deju

Cuba—the 1950s

In the early 1950s, I led a peaceful life in my hometown of Havana, Cuba, where I grew up sheltered by a loving family and friends. As most children of the Cuban professional class were, I was isolated from the turmoil of government corruption and brewing revolutionary forces. In 1951, when I was five years old, I had no idea that a budding revolutionary named Fidel Castro was already attempting to overthrow a dictator on the nearby island of the Dominican Republic. Instead, I was focused on starting kindergarten in a Catholic private school run by nuns, just two blocks from my home.

By the end of the second week in kindergarten, the Mother Superior came to our classroom and asked every kid to say what they wanted to be when they grew up. This was the first time anyone had asked me that question. After all, I was only five, and unfortunately, I was the first kid to have to respond to the Mother Superior, and the only thing that came to my mind was that I wanted to be a "garbage man."

As a child, I would see the garbage trucks driving down the street with a guy walking on the sidewalk side by side with the truck, throwing the garbage cans to another man in the open bay of the truck. Heck, it looked like fun! What I was unprepared for when I answered the Mother Superior was the response that came next. It was like a category

3

5 tropical hurricane hit me. She grew irate and told me I had no ambition and that I needed to focus on becoming a doctor or a lawyer and not a garbage man.

She then sent me to a side blackboard and asked me to write the word *ambición*, which is Spanish for "ambition," twenty times and called my mother for a chat after school. At age five, that was quite a shock. In fact, I could barely write my letters, and *ambición* was a totally foreign concept to me, as was thinking what job I wanted to have some day. Ugh! I didn't even know I would have to work someday. On top of that, when she saw I was left-handed, she had me try to write the words using my right hand. That failed miserably, and of course, I am still left-handed.

When my mother came with my father to talk to the Mother Superior, I promised all of them I would work hard for my future, which I certainly did. After finishing kindergarten, I attended first grade before skipping second grade and moving on to third, fourth, and fifth grade and eventually skipping sixth and seventh grade to move on to high school, where I earned straight As. What no one, including myself, knew at that time was that by age twenty-six, I would publish a book (my second one—I did the first book a year earlier) in New York called *The Environment and Its Resources*, which in part discussed how to properly deal with the management of garbage and other wastes, and that by age forty-one, I would be serving as president of Chemical Waste Management West, part of Waste Management, the world's largest garbage company. I must have had garbage in my veins already when I told the Mother Superior that I wanted to be a garbage man. The Mother Superior, if she lived today, would probably be smart to read Bill Wiersma's chapter in this book (chapter 23), as she truly flunked professionalism, but let's not deal with that for now. For sure, she sparked my mojo when I was five. From then on, I have always known the importance of making commitments and listening to others.

While I was skipping second grade, Castro was already fighting in the eastern hills of Cuba and had started the July 26, 1953, revolution. However, few in Havana gave him much attention. Meanwhile, I was totally focused on school, swimming, baseball cards, friends, and family.

As I entered high school, the Castro revolution became more visible. Revolutionary supporters began to throw Molotov cocktails and various incendiary devices in the middle of theaters, churches, and social events to disrupt day-to-day life. On a couple of occasions, at late afternoon events, we were surrounded by revolutionary sympathizers and had to slip out through back doors and run away. Terrorist events began to take a toll on the life of Havana, essentially destroying the tourism, entertainment, and shopping industries.

Five years later, as 1958 came to a close, we were not shocked when the government of President Fulgencio Batista collapsed and was replaced by the revolutionary forces of Fidel Castro, his brother Raúl, and the legendary Marxist Che Guevara. Still, as 1959 started, I could not conceive the personal impact that Castro would have for me and for my family.

As Castro took over the government of Cuba in 1959, change became radical and rapid. People deemed "antirevolutionary" were tried, and many were convicted to die in a firing squad only days after their trial. It is estimated today that over eighty thousand people were killed in the firing squads over various years. Food shortages were the order of the day, and Block Guardians, who worked as snitches for the revolution were sanctioned by the new government to guard against those citizens that could have democratic ideas, and were thus called worms.

Students in private schools were generally deemed unworthy and were routinely harassed. For example, if we wore our school uniforms to travel on a public bus or attend an event, we were often yelled at or called *gusanos* (worms). Many churches were shut down, and entertainment centers and restaurants were also closed, as food was in short supply.

It was in the middle of this turmoil that the US government, in coordination between the CIA and the Catholic Diocese of Miami, began to evaluate some options to allow young Cuban students to come to the United States to complete their education. The program would eventually be called the Visa Waiver Program but was informally known as the Pedro Pan program. From December 1960 to October

1962, around fourteen thousand Cuban minors arrived alone in the United States by way of weekly flights, the largest recorded exodus of unaccompanied minors in the Western Hemisphere. The Pedro Pan program was a one-way ticket with no return.

My parents became aware of the option to have me be part of this program and worked with a family friend, David Berenguer, who was the president of the Coca-Cola Company in Cuba. He knew Mr. James Baker, the headmaster of Ruston Academy (an American school in Havana), who had organized a network of Cubans and expatriates to help get children to Miami. When children arrived in Miami, they entered the care of the Catholic Welfare Bureau, which was created by Father Bryan Oliver Walsh, a young thirty-year-old priest. Minors were relocated with remote family and friends who were already in the United States or were cared for by the Catholic Church and various nonprofits in thirty states.

When I was finished with eleventh grade in Cuba, my parents finally told me that over the past two months, they had received permission for me to be part of the Visa Waiver Program. They prepared me to travel to Miami, where I would be provided a new start away from the revolution with the help of the Catholic Church, as well as the help of our close friends, the Mendez family and the Dargelo family. My parents also assured me that they would come to Miami at the first opportunity, but they had no idea if they could come to the United States or when.

I was beyond shocked; my foundations were rocked. I was a young teen who had never been away from home, and now I was going to leave and go to Neverland where there was no return, just like Peter Pan. I spoke very little English and had no parents to live with in the United States, just family friends. Furthermore, my grandmother, whom I was very close to, was dying in Havana.

A few weeks later, we were notified that my date of travel would be fixed and could not be changed. I now had all my exit papers from Cuba and flight reserved in just a couple of weeks. I was scared but did not show it. Amazingly, my grandmother passed away seven days before my scheduled departure. She was buried, and two days later, I left Cuba and have not returned since.

As a Cuban colleague of mine, Carlos Eire, who wrote a book entitled *Waiting for Snow in Havana: Confessions of a Cuban Boy*, once said, I am waiting for snow to fall in Havana before I even consider visiting my homeland in the future. I still want to remember it as it was and not as it is now. The firing squad still evokes nervousness on my part.

The few days before my departure from Cuba, I was a zombie, in total shock, but I recognized the need to adapt and not complain. As we drove to the airport in Havana, it dawned on me that this was the first flight I would ever take and that it would be the first night I would sleep away from my parents. I boarded the DC-8 Pan American Airlines Super Constellation, a super noisy four-engine plane, for a short flight to Miami, where I would be processed by the US government and the Catholic Welfare Bureau. As I shed a flood of tears, I was committed to not let this bring me down. I would succeed no matter what.

I would find my purpose. I had mojo! I did not know it then. Little did I realize that the fourteen thousand plus Pedro Pan kids would be the beginning of the Cuban exodus of over one million Cubans who would migrate to the United States from Cuba over the next quarter century, nearly one in five of the island's residents at that time.

Landing in America

Upon landing in Miami, I was cared for and nurtured principally by family friends, Catholic nuns—who taught me English—and by some of my high school teachers. My playbook was simple: (1) learn English so I could thrive in America; (2) finish high school, as I had only one school year to go; (3) find a college that would take me; and (4) get my parents to the United States. This was my plan, and now I had to execute.

My first eleven months away from Cuba were spent in Miami, and I truly learned the power of friends. Many people helped me by giving me rides, making calls on my behalf, teaching me English, and giving me clothing and shelter. To all of them, I am deeply indebted. I will never forget them. My successes are shared with them. My mojo carried me through. I also learned the importance of having some short-term goals that would allow me to see the direct results of my actions. Finally, I learned the importance of accepting that drastic things happen in our lives that we can't control and that we must be ready to charge ahead rather than wasting time sulking and complaining. In a later chapter, you will see the same comment from Richard Branson when he talked with Nelson Mandela (refer to chapter 12 by Mark Thompson). Crying for things I could not control stopped for me. Instead, I learned to always move forward, mostly unafraid.

I did learn English, although it took a couple of years for me to truly feel comfortable with my abilities to write and speak the language. I immersed myself in a language lab at Barry College in South Florida (now Barry University) and read in English as much as I could.

I finished high school in a nine-month school year, despite my language shortfalls. In fact, I signed up for physics, calculus, and advanced biology plus four other classes when I first registered for my senior year. By the second semester, however, some of my family friends were suggesting that I should take typing and shop instead of calculus and physics so I could have a job when I got out of school. But Mr. Kowalchuk, my physics teacher, went to the principal and told him that I had the highest score from the previous semester on the physics class and that there was no way I should drop physics. Then, Mr. Kowalchuk and two nuns from Barry College in South Florida contacted a physicist they knew, who happened to be president of the New Mexico Institute of Technology, Dr. E. J. Workman. Together they helped me apply to and obtain a scholarship and a spot in the work-study program at the Institute in Socorro, New Mexico—a place I had never been to and was 1,960 miles from my closest friend or relative. Whew! It also helped that by the end of the fall semester in high school, I was able to score in the ninetieth percentile on the English portion and in the ninety-eighth percentile on the mathematics portion of the college entrance exams. Not too shabby considering that just a year before, I spoke hardly any English.

While I was in high school in the United States, I began the process of bringing my parents to the United States as the revolution was tightening their noose on the Cuban population. I wrote letters to Florida Congressman Dante Fascell and others and applied for visas for them to reunite with me. However, by that time, I was committed to head to Socorro, New Mexico, and my parents were eventually able to settle in Miami, Florida, when the lengthy paperwork was finally approved. Congressman Fascell may be remembered by others for his anti-Vietnam stand, but I will always remember him for being the politician that personally sponsored my parents to ultimately immigrate to the United States while he was a member of the House Foreign Affairs Committee.

On to College

The day after my high school graduation, I left for New Mexico so I could enroll in summer college classes. I took the second plane ride in my life from Miami, Florida, to Albuquerque, New Mexico, and then traveled on a Continental Trailways bus to the school in Socorro in Central New Mexico, about an hour and a half south of Albuquerque. As we rode past desolate areas, I wondered what else could be in the cards, but indeed, I was confident that I could survive and thrive no matter what. The family setting I grew up with in Cuba was broken by the Castro revolution, but the family bonds were still there and grew stronger with time. My principles and my character kept me moving in the right direction.

So how did I survive in America and get through college? Well, when my plane landed in Albuquerque, I had twenty dollars in my pocket. I took a five-dollar taxi ride to the Trailways station downtown and hitched the next bus going south, which went to Socorro with a stop in Belen, New Mexico. Upon arrival in Socorro, the school sent someone to pick me up, and I wound up being assigned to a dorm, along with a roommate and a work-study program, but it was clear I did not have enough money to survive. By the time I made it to campus, I barely had five dollars. The answer to my need was simple: I had to do extra work to make the money I needed to live. There was no time to waste. I was then a family of one in Socorro.

Fortunately, in Socorro I met a lot of great people who let me do odds and ends for them and taught me many skills. I routinely did various tasks for Sheriff Apolonio Pineda, house-cared for Mayor Holm O. Bursum, babysat for faculty members, mowed lawns, and so on. These friends who hired me or helped me became my extended family.

The sheriff helped me learn to drive (I was a bit too young, but he saw the commitment in my eyes!). Driving helped me in many ways and allowed me to carry out various jobs. The college faculty members I dealt with over the years were terrific, helping me as I took as many classes as possible. I aimed to get a mathematics and physics degree. I was intrigued by mathematics as a language of science and engineering. In physics I was particularly intrigued by just what every teenager thinks about: space physics and stellar dynamics!

To succeed and have enough money to live, I reinvented myself as "a student who was willing to take on almost any research chore I could be handed." Today we call that "creating a Blue Ocean" (see chapter 11), but back then, I just called it survival.

I was, in fact, on a work-study assignment to the New Mexico Bureau of Mines to take measurements of what is known as Isoelectric Point of Charge, which in those days involved very tedious microscope work that nobody liked doing. Instead, I redesigned the equipment so that instead of looking in the microscope, I was counting the movement of reflections of light from particles in a fluid. Not only did my professors like the approach, but I was able to write a professional peer-reviewed paper on the subject (still available on Amazon Books today—work done in 1963–64, published in 1965), which pretty much assured me a continuing job in the laboratory for the rest of my bachelor's program. On top of that, I served as both a math and physics tutor, and by the end of my sophomore year, I was able to buy myself a brand-new car and install an air conditioner in it. In those days, air conditioners were an accessory you installed under the dashboard, but in Socorro, air conditioners were really a necessity. I also had fun at campus parties, always dating slightly older women as I was only sixteen or seventeen, and the girls were generally between nineteen and twenty-three. I was two months shy of my eighteenth birthday when I bought my first car with the cash I had earned and a tiny loan in my name.

At the end of my junior year at New Mexico Tech, I had received acceptance at the summer program on space physics and stellar dynamics at the Institute for Space Physics at Columbia University, and I started a concentrated advanced physics program in New York City—quite a change from Socorro. I moved from a town of barely five thousand people to a city where five thousand people lived within two blocks of my dorm. By then, I was fearless. I was taking an advanced program while I was finishing the last year of my BS degree in Socorro. I studied at Columbia under Professor Robert Jastrow, a world-class physicist that made physics understandable to the masses, and one of the major proponents of the US space program. At the time I started to study under him, I was nineteen and he was beginning work on a book called *Red Giants and White Dwarfs*, which he eventually published in 1967. This book has been described by experts as a masterpiece of science and one of the most significant works ever written. His thinking challenged me and took me into a stage where I devoured every astrophysics book I could get.

In my senior year back in Socorro, I presented and published two peer-reviewed papers at international meetings, created a statewide mathematics symposium, and began teaching the first Fortran computer language class at New Mexico Tech, having self-taught myself the early computer languages. I recall on one evening after the symposium, I sat at a table at the Capitol Bar in downtown Socorro, talking math with Dr. Stanislaw Ulam, who was the guest speaker at the symposium. He was then working on the hydrodynamic calculations to predict the behavior of the explosive lenses that are needed by an implosion-type nuclear weapon. Dr. Ulam was one of the mathematicians that had developed the mathematical basis for the hydrogen bomb. We sat there, and as the evening went on, he was telling me about Monte Carlo methods, which could be used to simulate systems such as fluid motion, which have many coupled degrees of freedom. Little did I realize that I was sitting with a world-class physicist and mathematician on par with Albert Einstein. I was fearless, and my mojo was boundless.

As I was immersed in hydrodynamics and stellar dynamics, I also befriended a professor named Dr. Mahdi Hantush, who was a hydrologist, scientist, and great teacher. He convinced me that instead of going into math and physics under a Bell Telephone scholarship and returning to New York City, I should move into the doctorate groundwater hydrology program he had created, where he was specializing in the application of mathematics to the solution of groundwater flow problems. He was not only a fine researcher but also a practicing and practical hydrologist, and he convinced me to make the switch.

The switch, however, meant that I would have to take many undergraduate classes in areas where I had never taken a single class. Well, another challenge. I worked three jobs, completed a myriad of classes, did my dissertation, and passed my PhD exams in the record time of under three years. I had my mojo and was ready for the world. I had a myriad of friends helping me along the way and filling in for parents that could not live close to me during my late high school and college years, and I knew that I would not succumb. In the end, I made it, and now it was time for a job and for spending time with my parents, who were by now in the United States.

Bottom line, no fear! If you have a problem, you engineer around it. You find or build a Blue Ocean. I will tell you how later in this book, but then suffice it to say it helped me to survive. When you make mistakes, you accept them as learning experiences and move on. My friends were no different than family—in my case, they became my family, and my trip to Neverland had a happy outcome.

My family was part of over one million Cubans who migrated to the United States and were able to proudly call this nation their own. While not all immigrants had the happy outcomes I experienced, I believe my success was in part a result of my passion, flexibility, and hard work. The path included making mistakes along the way, but I tried to learn from these and not get flustered.

My friends and I got mojo, and hopefully, this book will give you examples of why you can too. Not all of us came here as immigrants, but many of us have had to deal with traumatic circumstances in our early years that fully changed our life path. Some of my BFF in the next few chapters had worse trips into America than I did. Jackie Bhagavan had to come through jungle terrain while escaping the genocidal regime of Pol Pot in Cambodia in the time of the Killing Fields, and Will Martinez had to transition from life in a Peruvian village to the hectic pace of the Molecular Foundry in Berkeley, California. We were all scared. However, our mojo carried us, our values shaped us, and our passion led the way.

Our mojo, as the famous author Marshall Goldsmith (a reviewer of this book) defines it, is that special power or influence that we have, perhaps our unique talent or ability to make things happen, influence others, or get things done. Mojos seem magical, and take passion, commitment, a bit of an attitude, and never giving up. You also have to reinvent yourself in a way that employers want you, and you can indeed contribute to bettering our world. In following chapters, you will see how a gaggle of my BFF dealt with their lives and used their mojo to their advantage. I will also tell you in later sections a bit more about my life's road and the twists and turns along the way.

Brace yourself for a journey that will include some laughs, some celebrations, and quite a few sobs!

Chapter 2

Finding Our Common Humanity

Diana Campoamor.

Part of the fun of childhood is to dream what you may do when you grow up. In my case, the journey has helped me to understand that. As the Buddha said, "The future is always other than you imagined it." My journey has offered terrific opportunities, but also many critical challenges. Along the way, I've come to understand people who are different from me and have developed a sense of us.

I've always been a dreamer—and a planner. Both identities proved to be helpful in the process of managing the unexpected. I learned to loosen up, to become more agile, and to enjoy change and see its silver linings. I can identify with people going through similar experiences, being an immigrant, a woman, part of an ethnic minority, and a person who spoke a different language. All that helped me figure out that I can control my intentions, but not the outcomes. My intentions, and the values that guide them, eventually keep me on the right path.

My example certainly won't work for everybody. But as I grew up, I learned to choose people that I could depend on at crunch time. And there have been many people who have stepped up to help me when things really weren't going well.

My parents were the first. Roberto and Margot Campoamor were comfortably middle class when the Cuban Revolution happened just before the dawn of the 1960s. We lived in Havana, just like Raul Deju and his parents. My father had been sent to the United States to learn

English during a previous time of political instability in Cuba. So it was logical that almost two years after Fidel Castro's forces toppled the Batista dictatorship, my parents decided to take me and my older brother to the United States. Along the way, they thought it would also be important that we learn English. We left our penthouse overlooking the Havana skyline and flew to New Orleans in August 1960 for what my parents thought would be no more than a couple of years. In reality, they never were able to return to Cuba.

The shock of moving from a Havana penthouse to a small bungalow in the southern part of the United States in the '60s was huge. Once in New Orleans, at my uncle's small bungalow with my aunt and three cousins, my family settled into a life of looking for work and getting the children off to school. Although my dad had been an architect in Cuba, in New Orleans he only was able to find a job as a draftsman.

We arrived in the Deep South at a time when the horrors of racism and racial segregation were in full force. In order to enroll me in elementary school, my mother had to produce an affidavit to the effect that I was white. Once in school, I faced other personal challenges. I was the only foreign student, and I didn't speak English. I felt very out of place. But the teacher, Ms. Marie, seemed to understand, even if I couldn't. She had a way of drawing me into what she was teaching with her piercing green eyes. She often made eye contact and was wonderfully patient.

I had managed to find a group of friends and had started to speak English with a New Orleans drawl, but my father was offered a job in Minnesota, and we moved. When winter came and it started to snow, it seemed as if it kept coming down for nine months straight. This is tough for those of us with Cuban blood who were used to a Caribbean climate.

The beautiful lakes froze over, and after many, many falls, I learned to ice-skate. At Capitol View Junior High School in Roseville, Minnesota, my drawl took on the flat pronunciation of Midwestern American English. I was able to make friends. It was a palpably progressive place, without the race and class divisions of New Orleans. But before the fourth winter blew in, my mother decided that she had had enough of the very harsh climate, the lack of cultural affinity, and the inland Midwestern landscape, and we moved. Minnesota was just too far removed from our native tropical island and our people. My mom and my dad decided it was time to go to South Florida. My father found a new job, and in 1965, my family moved to Miami, which was by then awash with Cuban refugees.

When I went to Miami Beach and saw the ocean, I had a tremendous sense of coming home. But by then, I had lost my easy fluency in Spanish, and it took a couple of months for me to start dreaming in Spanish again. I had to get reacquainted with my native language and culture. I made friends and again learned to fit in at Coral Gables High School and Miami-Dade Community College.

Also, I learned what it felt like to be singled out as a minority and how to stare down ignorance and bias. I remember standing in line, waiting to get to the cash register with my mother at a store in Miami Beach. We were chatting in Spanish when the cashier yelled, "Speak English!" Our teachers in school also insisted that we speak only English, and a popular bumper sticker of the time said, "Would the Last American to Leave Please Bring the Flag!"

I then went on to reinvent my life at the University of Florida in Gainesville, where I made many lifelong friendships and met my husband. The university had about thirty-five thousand students, of which maybe only one hundred were of Cuban descent. There were few African American students and hardly any Asians or South Asians. We Latinos probably became closer than we might have, had we been at a more diversified university.

My husband and I returned to Miami after graduation and very soon after moved to Madrid. The Vietnam War was raging. We wanted to try new places. We each had a grandfather who had been from Spain, and we had some family connections there. But once there, we still felt too out of place, and we couldn't see ourselves staying there for the rest of our lives.

We returned to the United States, had a son, and eventually got divorced. I then became a US citizen in 1981, and as I completed all my immigration forms, I realized that I had accumulated twenty-two different home addresses over the years since I first came to the United States from Cuba.

Some years after my divorce and becoming a citizen, I also realized and accepted that I was a lesbian. At that time, this was a major revelation, as acceptance of lesbians in the United States was not even close to today's level. This triggered a whole cycle of emotions while stressing over the uncertainty of making my life possible as a lesbian single mother with a mortgage to pay. It was at a time and in a place of great taboos around homosexuality, let alone the idea of child rearing by gays. Even as I write this, Florida and some other states still prohibit adoptions by gays. Nevertheless, that uncertainty also helped me embrace change. However, the economic times were tough, and I was unemployed for two years in the 1980s. By then, however, I had a partner whose daughter was two years younger than my son, and at least I had someone to help me and who understood my challenges.

When a friend told me of an advertisement for the position of communications director of the Mexican American Legal Defense and Educational Fund (MALDEF), I quickly pulled together a request for an interview and sent off my snail mail packet virtually overnight. I thought I would be a long shot candidate, especially considering that the job was in San Francisco.

I went for an interview to the city I knew mostly because my brother and his family lived there. I remember that it was a gloriously warm July day in the San Francisco of the mid-1980s. I walked to Ghirardelli's for chocolate and looked around at the people and at the mountains across San Francisco Bay. It looked to me like the most beautiful place in the world—after Havana, of course.

Could I move there? My parents had no other children to care for them in Florida. It would mean uprooting my partner and our two children, finding a new home and schools, managing a move, starting a new job, and working in a new culture. But I was happy to find exciting new work, and everything else eventually fell into place. I even managed to negotiate a deal for a house two doors away from where my brother still lives.

When I started at MALDEF, I didn't need to look very far to find out what I didn't know. There were frequent immigration raids at local factories, and people who couldn't prove they had a right to be here were being unceremoniously tossed out of the country, regardless of whether they had spouses and children waiting for them to come home from work.

My job gave me an opportunity to see what had been happening—and still happens—in the Mexican-American and Latino communities around the United States. It was quite an eye-opener. As a Cuban exile, I realized that I had received far better treatment in being welcomed by this country.

When MALDEF moved its headquarters to Los Angeles a couple of years later, I jumped to a job in philanthropy with the Shalan Foundation. At age forty, I switched to a field generally populated by wealthy people where I hoped to leave my mark as an advocate for the not so rich.

By then, I had learned to engage professionally with people who could mentor me, and I had acquired resilience, along with my willingness to take risks. But throughout those early years of yearning to fit in, I never lost sight of who I was and where I belonged. That confidence—and a bit of entrepreneurial spirit—helped me to navigate the main part of my career.

When I started working at Hispanics in Philanthropy (HIP) in San Francisco, it had been founded a few years before to promote greater diversity in the US philanthropy scene and promote Latino nonprofits working to help underserved communities that were trying to get ahead. With a lot of help and encouragement, I worked to grow HIP from a one-person office into the national advocate for Latino leadership, voice, and equality that it is today.

As a national nonprofit leader, I travel a lot for work. But the truth is, I love opportunities to engage with the life of new places and to connect with the people who live there. I don't mean sightseeing like a tourist. In Chiapas, Mexico, for example, I learned how families with eight or ten children make a life for themselves out in the countryside. They can grow coffee but also learn, through programs, of new techniques for harvesting honey to supplement their incomes. They are devoted to their language and their culture. I am humbled to, in some measure, be able to act as an instrument for their financial stability.

My work provides me with such rare opportunities to connect with people who are the social entrepreneurs, community leaders, and new persons on the block wanting to help their community. It leads me to learn new things, to meet new people, and to see how these people can also help one another to get ahead. I try to help, too, where I can. I like to think of it as finding our common humanity.

I certainly never planned to have a career in philanthropy. But philanthropy has allowed me to connect and to have a life of meaning that is constantly fed by the examples of people who are solving problems big and small. In section 6 of this book, there are some chapters covering the stories of others involved in philanthropy.

Some of you may find experiences from my life story that apply to your situation. The keys in my life that have taken me to who I am today are accepting change in all areas of my life, enjoying new experiences, and most importantly, having a moral compass on my values that provided me the anchor for my past ventures and will most certainly guide my future. The beauty of my job is that it allows me to give back to the culture I came from and to the nation that took me in.

I am ready to keep dealing with new challenges in my profession and in my personal life, and I plan to continue to work for the betterment of myself, my family, and my adopted country. My exposure to racism, lack of resources, and my acceptance of who I am have prepared me well for whatever the next chapter of my life is.

Biographical Comments by the Lead Author

When Diana was eleven, her family left their penthouse in the heart of Havana's revolutionary political and social turmoil and migrated to a very troubled New Orleans, which was still in the throes of desegregation. It wasn't the first time she bore witness to the fault lines of social injustice. Years earlier, as a young child, the plight of poverty-stricken rural children in Cuba had moved her to write a letter to three wise men that, in her child's eye, were more powerful than any superhero today. In the letter, she appealed to the Three Kings to provide presents and resources for the children of rural Cuba. You might consider it this future fundraiser's first grant request. Although never complacent about injustice, she learned to adapt and rise above conflicts and to fend off defeat with optimism and a can-do attitude. Slowly, a social entrepreneur emerged. The experiences fueled her curiosity and determination to make things right, to listen to people's stories, and to find everyday Buddhas, everyday people who could cause enormous positive change and lead their communities. She has enjoyed a philanthropic career that spans over twenty-five years and became the President of Hispanics in Philanthropy, a national nonprofit that advocates for greater Latino participation in philanthropy. She is a member of the Boards of International Planned Parenthood for Latin America and Futuro Media Group. She also has served as a trustee of the Council on Foundations, Independent Sector, and Horizons Foundation. She was editor of Nuevos Senderos: Reflections on Hispanics and Philanthropy, *published by Arte Público Press in 1999. Her family in the San Francisco Bay Area now includes, in addition to her son, a Chinese-born daughter and two biracial granddaughters. Over the years, Diana and I have shared ideas about the world of Hispanic philanthropy, and even though we live in the same area, our travels complicate getting together, yet we enjoy from time to time some great conversation and San Francisco area food—not quite our Cuban fare, but it will do. Diana's heart is in the right place, and no one works harder for the Latino community than she does. She is the real thing, and I am proud to count her as my BFF.*

Chapter 3

Breaking Through the Storm:
A Sunrise to Success

Jacqueline P. Bhagavan

Escaping to Thailand from the Genocidal Khmer Rouge

People often ask me what my story is. What made me think as a plain small Khmer (Cambodian) refugee girl with learning problems that I could become a beauty queen? I laugh and tell them I am still that plain small refugee girl who skips words while reading and writing and often jumbles them up.

I simply decided to not just play at being a queen, as little girls do, but to become one. I had to make the conscious decision that life was not going to beat me. I may fail at some things, but nothing will stop me from conquering my dreams, and I have great dreams. I have dreams not just for myself but also for my children, my husband, my family, and my children's children. My ultimate goal is not just to be known and recognized. My ultimate goal is to create a legacy that will pass from generation to generation.

I want to reach out and touch the hearts and souls of everyone that comes in contact with me. I want to deliver a message through the stories from my life and my experiences. That message is of hope and triumph in this land we call America.

My story really began in 1975 in Cambodia during the rise of the communist regime called the Khmer Rouge. In an instant, my family was separated, and many of us were killed. The Killing Fields were not just a movie for me; they were reality. Although I was a kid, I was put in a labor camp with my parents and siblings. After many attempts, we finally escaped over the Thailand–Cambodia border. My father carried me to safety in his arms, through a minefield, while my mother carried one of my sisters.

I am the fourth of a total of seven children. I have two older sisters and one older brother, as well as three younger siblings, one of whom was born in the refugee camp in Thailand, while one was born in the United States when we lived in Houston, Texas.

Thanks to American and international aid, we were able to eventually leave the refugee camp in Thailand behind us and migrate to the United States. With the birth of my youngest brother, my family of nine lived in a one-bedroom apartment. Not ideal, but we were together. We were alive. To us it was a mansion. We had to be on welfare for a while, but those meager meals were a feast after having nearly died of starvation on the journey to our new home in the United States.

Education was always paramount in my home. My father had to start college again when he came to America, as he had no proof of his educational training since most of our documents were lost or destroyed while fleeing Cambodia. He worked several different menial jobs to make ends meet, but when he passed away from cancer in 1999, he was by then working as a social worker.

My mother had chosen to stay home to raise and support the family. With our large family and our very limited resources, this was a daunting task, but she made sure we were clean, that we were fed healthy food, and that we went to school. Our schoolwork was always done. I was put in the gifted and talented program after we moved to Stockton, California, even though I had a learning disability that would be diagnosed as dyslexia years later!

When people look at me today, they don't see all these struggles that I have gone through along the way. They see the flawless makeup, not the scars from the branches and brush left from walking barefoot on the way to safety. To this day, I still have the scars from the escape on both my right leg and my stomach. They see the designer clothes, not the mental and physical scars I carry as a result of escaping through the jungles of Cambodia.

They see only a strong, willful entrepreneur, not the small child who witnessed atrocities like that of the two guides whom we paid to help us escape that eventually turned on each other. One shot the other on the left ear, sending him falling face-down on the ground. He made it back up on his feet but then was shot in the forehead in broad daylight by his partner. I saw this interaction take place in front of my eyes. No young girl should have to see this. Such horror should never be witnessed, but these events were part of the blueprint of my journey and how I came to be. Most people don't see my past; they see what I represent today. They see accomplishment and success. However, there is so much more to me than that.

I can think of three specific things that have catapulted me to this point in my life. They have helped me develop my self-confidence to pursue my own success and happiness, regardless of what life dishes out to me. They have helped me understand that I can't let problems control my life, but that I instead must seek solutions to these problems. I also learned to be able to openly tell my story with great cathartic values.

My Mother: My Idol

For me, the first lesson in surviving was the constant mental image of my mother. She has been so strong to have brought a total of seven children into this world and to have fought every day to help keep us safe. I would watch her get up early in the morning in the refugee camp and prepare snacks, noodles, and other foods to sell inside the camp in order to earn a bit of money to help us stay alive.

I learned from her the meaning of being an entrepreneur and that to survive, one must think out of the box. I learned that success is not only about how academically smart one is but also about how creative one can be with what resources they have. She is very smart and is more courageous than any woman I know. I still draw strength and ingenuity from the memory of her working in the tropical heat in the far-from-safe conditions of the camp. Alongside my father, my mother was working in the refugee camp to keep hope alive for her family and to maintain support for her husband, who had led us through so much to reach safety.

I learned early on what it was to care for your family, and I now apply that in my own life. I cherish my family, not just my husband and children, but my human family. I love everyone. I cherish my interaction with others, and I try to help humanity, as I know we are all family in our hearts. I want my family to be happy, healthy, and well. I work to share myself with the world.

If it had not been for people caring for others outside their immediate circle, my family might not have ever been able to escape from the Khmer Rouge communist regime. Without the compassion shown to us by complete strangers, I might not have gotten the food, shelter, and medical care that allowed me to survive the ordeal that my body went through at such a young age. This is the kindness and compassion I pay forward to others as often as I can.

Watching my mother throughout our ordeal also taught me that it takes determination and ingenuity to be successful. I learned that no matter the circumstances in life, one should never make excuses. If one way doesn't work, you must try another. I learned that you draw from your resources and do your best. My mother gave birth to my second-youngest brother in a refugee camp, but there was no such thing as maternity leave. She worked selling food right after giving birth to keep her market share of the food business in the camp.

My mother is not only a strong woman but also a wise businesswoman. In the camp, she had to do the math and budgeting to get the most out of her inventory of supplies while making sure her customers were able to afford the food she was selling. She had to know marketing to make sure that what she was offering was wanted by those who had the resources to pay. She found a way to exceed expectations where others would have seen no way. This is why she still advises me on almost everything I do, even to this day.

I Learned That Not Everyone Is Nice and That One Must Count on Inner Strength to Succeed

I learned my second lesson on survival when we were traveling on the roads to escape the Khmer Rouge. I was only five years old. It was a long walk. My mother carried my younger sister, and even though I was able to walk, my father often carried me, as I was very small for my age. Eventually, we all found ourselves walking beside a cart pulled by an ox. My father held my hand as we walked beside it, one of the few times he was resting from carrying me. There was an old man driving the empty cart. I asked him politely, "Please, sir, may I ride in your cart?" The old man looked down at me and simply told me, "No, there's no room for you, girl."

That was a hard but important lesson for me. In that instant, on that hot road, tired from walking so long and so far on my spindly legs, having eaten hardly anything, I learned that the world and the people in it can be cruel and selfish. I also learned that I cannot count on the kindness and sympathy of others, no matter how politely I may ask. I learned that regardless of age or how a person looks on the outside, it's the inside—the heart—that matters. It made me decide that I would not be like this man. I decided that when I grew up, I would be kind to my world family. I would be generous with my heart. I would be generous with my forgiveness and let go. Even now, though I remember the old man's cruelty to a little starving refugee girl, I have forgiven him. This ability to forgive and let go has allowed me to remain free—physically, mentally, and emotionally.

I also believe that not every no or every rejection is a final answer. Many "nos" are really "not now" or "not yet." I have learned patience. All things will come in due time. No, I did not get that immediate relief of a ride on the ox cart, but yes, I reached my destination in America.

Patience, the ability to deal with rejection, and the ability to forgive have helped frame my character and shape my life.

I Learned That It Takes Hard Work to Achieve Big Goals

Three years ago, happily married with two great kids, I entered the competition to become Mrs. California. Entering the competition taught me that it is fine to fail. Many do not know that I competed for Mrs. California twice. The first time, I was awarded the Outstanding Married Woman award but did not win the title. It was great; however, I was not satisfied. I knew that my message—my true mission—was to show that a Cambodian refugee could overcome all her flaws and become a beauty queen in America. That is why I entered again in 2015 and won. I then went on to compete in Las Vegas in the Mrs. America competition and won the Fabulous Face award and made it to the finalists. This was a huge journey for the small girl escaping from Cambodia forty years earlier to get away from one of the most genocidal regimes ever in the history of civilization.

What Now?

I am now a business owner, an actress, a writer, and a winner of Mrs. California, and in America today, a woman like me can accomplish anything her heart desires. She just has to believe in herself no matter how many people say the goal is impossible. Anyone who reads or hears the story of my journey must learn that achieving what they want is not impossible. Their dreams must make them shout "I'm possible!" Nothing that happens in life, good or bad, is wasted when you learn and grow from it.

Weather professionals name hurricanes and major winter storms. The storms of my life have names too—names like Prejudice, Hunger, Hate, Despair, Loneliness, Loss, Fear, and Failure. Yet just like rays of sunshine that fight to show through the clouds of these storms, there is also Love, Friendship, Joy, Happiness, and Accomplishment to light the path for me to make strides forward.

My purpose in life is to encourage the people that may hear or read my words to realize that storms pass, but the sunshine is always there to shine through and continue shining after the storm has passed. Hold on to that warmth and light in your life. Be the warmth and light to others so that it can never be extinguished. By keeping it going even when you are not experiencing a storm at the moment, it will be there when you need it.

Doing what I do gives me the opportunity to impact what it is the world sees. I learned to make possible the things that seem impossible in life.

Finally, my story has had an unexpected turn in 2016. This last January, forty years after my escape from Cambodia, as the reigning Mrs. California, I was invited by the royal family of Cambodia and was photographed in the stairs of the royal palace with the Queen Mother of the country I had to leave. It is ironic that after escaping Cambodia, I could become the Fabulous Face in America and ultimately return to my homeland to shake hands with the queen in peace, but now as an American. What a ride! Then in March, I was invited to meet President Obama during one of his visits to California.

I want people to know what I have gone through so that they are able to go after their own crown, to have it raised over them, and to have it placed on their heads in victory. I am here to share where I have been on my road to now. Only in America can such a story have the happy ending that it has had for me, but the ride isn't over yet!

Biographical Comments by the Lead Author

Jacqueline was born in Cambodia. Her childhood ended early at the time when in her country the Khmer Rouge practiced some of the most heinous torture, famine, and genocide ever in the world, killing over 1.7 million people. Through her family's tenacity, they escaped the regime and embarked into a difficult and treacherous trip to America after spending time in a refugee camp. While she suffers from dyslexia, she went on to major in communications at California State University, Sacramento. Having watched her mother's entrepreneurial abilities while selling chicken, rice, and snacks in the Southeast Asia refugee camps, Jacqueline developed that same entrepreneurial spirit. After graduation, she started her own skincare line, Lavanya, and has established a well-respected online show, Complexion Kitchen. *On her show, she demonstrates ways for her audience to achieve beauty, both internally and externally, through sharing recipes, beauty tips, and mental wellness activities. A wife and mother of two, she was crowned Mrs. California in 2015. She went on to compete in the highly competitive Mrs. America competition in Las Vegas, Nevada, where she won Fabulous Face and was one of the fifteen finalists. The irony of her journey is that a little girl that escaped Cambodian genocide is now the Face of America. It has been my pleasure to be Jacqueline's friend and mentor. I have worked with her on business plans and, in a small way, served as a sounding board for some of her ideas. We routinely talk and visit as we live in neighboring towns. Her delicate tenacity has surely taken her where many have not gone and will assure her success and set an example for others to follow.*

Chapter 4

From Survival in an Andean Village to Survival in Silicon Valley

Will Martinez

My Roots

As an immigrant who came from an Andean village in rural Perú where the large majority of the population is still illiterate, it is a genuine pleasure for me to contribute my story to this book. My desire is that it can inspire others in similar settings and let them know that yes, we can be lifted out of poverty through education and sheer perseverance. The anecdotes that I will share with you in this chapter have carried me through the hardest and most difficult times in my life, and I hope that you can find in them a source of encouragement and inspiration, particularly in the very dark moments of despair that we all will face.

It was a very unusual January evening in Lima, Perú. On January 20, 2015, my dear father lay very ill on his bed, gasping for air at every breath, as we prepared to say good-bye to each other. I was getting ready to leave for the airport and fly back to San Francisco with my wife. The window was open, and a cool breeze was blowing on his pale face as he held my hand with the strength that characterized his personality. His body, severely weakened by the pulmonary fibrosis we were unable to treat or cure, lay covered with a blanket he had picked up many years ago in his beloved home village of Araypallpa. At this point, Daniel, my father, weighed less than eighty pounds, certainly the thinnest person I had ever seen in my life.

As I told my father of the severe difficulties I would need to overcome to keep my start-up company alive in California, I realized that any problem I was facing with my company was so small in comparison to my sense of despair at not being able to help him. As he held my hand, and as we watched the clock approach nine in the evening, we both knew this would most likely be the very last time we had to share and treasure each other's presence together. I knew I had only five more precious minutes to touch him, to hug him, and to tell him how much he meant to me and how grateful I was for every sacrifice he had made. I wanted to tell him that without his sacrifice to give me an education, I would never have had a shot at starting a tech company in the United States. He looked me in the eye and we had this final dialogue, punctuated by his determined breaths for air:

Dad said, "All I wanted in life was to raise good children, devote myself to them, and give them the education I could never have. And it makes me so happy and proud to have accomplished that."

"Yes, Dad. We did. You did it indeed!"

He looked back at me and said, "You keep looking ahead, no matter what happens. You keep forging ahead."

With tears in our eyes, we hugged for one last time, and my dear wife and I headed to the airport, with palpable sadness but with the knowledge that my dad's happiness had been fulfilled.

This was the last time my father and I spoke to each other face-to-face before he lost the strength to speak or stay conscious, and he passed away a few months later. These events, and others before it, have marked my life, and people like my father—the humble household man—have shaped my life and chiseled my character. Here is my story.

A Brief History of My Road from the Andes to Berkeley, California

Both my father and mother were born in rural communities high in the Andes Mountains near Cusco, and each carried a deep pride in their home and its traditions despite migrating to Lima at a young age. This is why I consider Araypallpa, my dad's village, my home. This community did not have complete access to potable water and electricity until 2005. The hardships of needing to work and fend for himself from age twelve made it impossible for my father to attend high school as he moved to Cusco and later to Lima. My mother was the youngest of nine, and even after moving to Lima as a teenager, she was not able to complete her high school education.

This is the reason why when my brothers and I were born, my parents made it their priority to ensure we would receive the best education they could afford. My father's job as a miner technician at a copper mine in southern Perú gave my parents the opportunity to place us in a school funded in large part by the mining company. From first grade, I fell in love with math. Later on, I became enamored with physics, chemistry, and biology. They intrigued my mind and captured most of my afternoons. By eighth grade, I held the valedictorian record in my school. Beyond academics, the mining village was a fortunate haven. At that time in Perú's history, terrorist guerrillas of the Shining Path Marxist movement were rampant; however, their criminal acts had limited reach in the very south part of Perú. This made my childhood particularly safe and joyful under the protection of my parents.

Those fun years didn't last very long. As I entered ninth grade, my parents' marriage faced a major crisis, and it created a very difficult emotional time for my brothers and me. My grades fell sharply, and for some reason, school didn't seem to matter much to me anymore. As my parents separated and my father struggled to raise us, my grades continued to suffer. Those were the hardest days of my youth, and my teachers noticed the abrupt change with concern. Martha, my English teacher, pulled me aside one morning toward the end of ninth grade and asked me to not give up.

She helped me understand that although I didn't have any control over the future of my parents' marriage, I indeed had control over how I chose to react to it. She showed me how much my father's work and sacrifice mattered and why it was important that I continue to embrace the education I was receiving in school. She encouraged me to apply to a scholarship program to travel to New York and spend a summer in an international youth leadership program called Camp Rising Sun (CRS). Perhaps knowing I needed a goal (and my competitive bent), she told me that hundreds of students would enter the contest to win a place at CRS and that I would need to study very hard and commit to prepare myself for the program.

Over fifty students from my school entered the competition, which was sponsored by the mining company, and the two winners from our school competed with the winners of seven other schools in the southern region of Perú. At the end, only one boy and one girl would be selected as winners; the odds to win were probably less than one in a hundred. Undaunted, I spoke with past winners and prepared every afternoon for three months. When the vision crystallized in my mind of traveling to New York, visiting the United States for the first time, and taking part in the program, studying became a joy again.

When we hit very low points in life and somehow need to find the strength to get up again, the encouragement from individuals we respect is absolutely essential. In my case, many of them have been women: teachers and mentors like Martha, and professors and advisers later on. I am incredibly grateful to them. I ultimately won the competition, and my experience at Camp Rising Sun in the summer of 1995 forever changed my life.

It was during my time at CRS that the desire to study engineering at an American university really grabbed my mind and heart. There, I met students from over thirty countries who were eager to get ready for college. We were visited several times by alumni of the CRS program who were then in college or graduate school. The journey, however, would not be easy. After returning to Perú, I began to research the possible ways I could achieve my goal of going to college in the United States. Even though my father could not contribute much to this dream with his limited income as a miner, his emotional support and some financial help enabled me to study English as a second language. This was a critical cornerstone of my preparation process, but a long and uneven path lay ahead.

It was very clear to me by now that the harder you work, the luckier you will be. I graduated from high school in 1996, and it took me an additional three years of sheer persistence to be able to apply to multiple scholarships and finally find one that would sponsor me for the entire college journey.

In late 1997, the mining company needed to reduce personnel, so my father was let go. This was a difficult time for my father and was perhaps the most challenging financial time we ever had to endure. By May 1999, my father—who was by then in his late fifties—grew incredibly worried after eighteen months of unemployment. Even though my older brother Alfredo and I were in college in Arequipa, Perú, we were both considering putting school off for several years in order to work full-time and help support the household. Most low-income families in Perú face this hardship and ultimately have to give up their college education. When there is no bread on the table, someone needs to go and get it.

Everything changed for me on May 2, 1999, when a phone call from the Colorado School of Mines (CSM) notified me that I was selected as the winner of their 1999 Andes Scholarship. Within three months, with my father's emotional support, I left my studies in Perú and immersed myself in the materials engineering program at CSM. A new chapter in my life had begun. The three years of extra work to learn English and apply to scholarships had finally come to fruition in this unprecedented blessing.

The Andes Scholarship at CSM allowed me to receive outstanding engineering education and practical training. Within two years, my aspirations grew from becoming a metallurgical engineer at a copper mine to researching and building new and innovative products. Beyond my coursework at CSM, this was really the result of engineering internships at GE Global Research, where I was exposed to the wonders of nanotechnology, modern materials, aerospace super alloys, and medical devices. Being surrounded by innovative minds and great engineers gave me the confidence that I could someday become one of them. We all need role models and mentors to give us a vision and to show us what it takes to get there. For me, it was performing day-to-day tasks with PhD-trained engineers that convinced me I could also reach that level of education and performance.

In 2005, I went further and obtained a degree in materials engineering from UC Santa Barbara and specialized in electronic materials and sensors. A new great blessing came to my life as I joined Innovative Micro Technology (IMT) in early 2006. My journey there empowered me with hands-on engineering roles as a development engineer. After three years, I was leading a team of technicians and junior engineers to ship product on time to meet strict engineering specifications. However, in 2010, the desire and ambition to start a company gripped me strongly; I felt ready. What I needed was to find a significant unmet need. A new hunting and searching process began. In mid-2011, I left IMT to pursue an entrepreneurial journey and learn what it takes to build a technology company.

In February 2012, I moved to Silicon Valley to immerse myself completely into this process. As a newcomer to the area, the journey ahead would be the equivalent to climbing Everest for me. As most entrepreneurs would tell you, it would become a journey of 10 percent inspiration and 90 percent perspiration, and it would test every aspect of my prior training and challenge me in ways that I had never been tested before. Nanotech Bio, my company, is now based in Berkeley, California, and is transforming the way modern medicines are discovered and developed to treat the most fatal types of cancers and neurodegenerative diseases.

Now that you know my story, I want to share with you five principles that have helped me shape my journey, as well as some thoughts as to how they fit in my life.

1. Stay humble. Never forget where you came from.

When you have a grand vision, you can succeed, but you can also fail spectacularly. The key is to find a critical and compelling unmet need. As you navigate the process of immersing yourself into the business world and make your product or service to provide a solution to a problem, you will transform from a humble dreamer into the leader of an organization. Always remember where you came from and how you got to where you are. Clothe yourself with humility. Seek the opportunity to remain connected to your home community, and let your background become a source of encouragement.

2. There is no such thing as the self-made man.

It is very clear to me that I would not be leading an innovative organization if it was not for the support and encouragement of my family, teachers, professors, business mentors, coworkers, and board members. Their help and desire to see Nanotech succeed has no limit. This is why I am always mindful that everything we have achieved or get to achieve is really the product of the tireless work and the support of the people who chose to trust our core team and follow my leadership. This clearly includes the customers and partners that choose to embrace our product and our solution.

3. Educate your heart, not just your brain.

During the hardest times in my life, the education I received helped me move forward, but most importantly, the passion for advancing and fulfilling a heartfelt vision is what has constantly stayed true to me over time. Ideas can develop, approaches can change, teams can change, and markets can change, but your heartfelt vision will remain steady to guide you forward. Give it some time, think, plan, and execute, but above all, listen to your heart.

4. Innovation is climbing Everest.
You can't solo Everest.

Because I was born at about eleven thousand feet elevation in the Andes of Perú, I have a great deal of respect and admiration for mountaineering and high-altitude climbers. In fact, I find mountaineering very analogous to the journey of starting and leading a biotech/nanotechnology company. In 1953, British mountaineer John Hunt formed an expedition to Everest that included Edmund Hillary and Tenzing Norgay, who ultimately became the first two men to reach the summit of Mount Everest. At 29,028 feet, the Everest summit is nearly three times the altitude of the villages in Perú where I grew up. The mountain itself had defeated previous expeditions, and in the summer of 1953, John Hunt's team was close to making it. Hunt had learned from the successful expeditions by others to the North Pole in 1909 and the South Pole in 1911 that if he was going to conquer Everest, which is sometimes known as the Third Pole, it would take a team to get there. He also knew that all possible things that could happen had to be considered and planned for. Well, plan for them he did, and he had, behind Hillary and Tenzing in the lower camps, more than one hundred people who carried forward supplies and supported their summit attempt. In the end, Hunt's team did it, and the history books reflect it.

Similarly, if your dream is to build an innovative technology product, you will need a talented team to support and execute your company's "Everest" vision. There will be numerous obstacles along the way, and others might have already failed, so you will absolutely need to find and hire the best and brightest. An organization and its products are only as great as its people.

5. No great success is possible without learning from failure.

Most founders and entrepreneurs will admit that perhaps the biggest teacher of all will be failure itself. If you have failed before, you will learn to tackle the possibility of failure. You will learn to assess risk, and you will learn to thrive in the presence of uncertainty and the unknown. You will learn to minimize the moving pieces, and you will learn to focus on reducing the biggest risk factors. Failure is nothing to be ashamed of, but it is indeed a path to becoming better. Striving for excellence is a great thing, but striving for perfection is demoralizing. When you get depressed about a failure in your business, you must think of Bill Gates. When Bill dropped out of Harvard, he started a business with Paul Allen called Traf-O-Data—terrible name and bad business model, but it led the way to the global behemoth today called Microsoft.

And What Is Next?

By telling you my story, I hope you will find encouragement and inspiration from it and from the other wonderful stories shared in this book. To me, education has been truly the most genuine platform to help me find myself. Education, coupled with my drive for self-improvement, brought me from a village in the Andes to our home in Berkeley, California. Education also allows young people to intersect their strengths with their passions. It is truly the most genuine gift an ambitious young individual can receive. Innovation, then, is the fruit that emerges when educated individuals recognize unmet needs and decide to create a unique solution for that need. Education and innovation together create a magnificent virtuous circle that can lift millions of people out of poverty. It certainly has given new meaning to my life, for which I am grateful, and it is the key to my everyday drive to focus my company on developing a sensor technology that would improve humanity.

Biographical Comments by the Lead Author

Will is the Founder and CEO of Nanotech Bio, a smart sensor start-up that is revolutionizing the biotech industry by accelerating the process to discover and develop modern medicines. Nanotech is based in the San Francisco Bay Area. In 2003, he was the Founding President of the Engineers Without Boards (EWB) chapter at the University of California–Santa Barbara; EWB has now grown from two chapters in 2001 to over one hundred chapters nationwide by 2016, supporting hundreds of development engineering projects in more than thirty-five countries across the globe. Will's industrial R&D, manufacturing, and commercialization experience for over ten years, coupled with his expertise in nanomaterials and biosensors, became the cornerstone of Nanotech's breakthrough sensor technology. He has previously served in dynamic R&D teams at GE Global Research and Innovative Micro Technology (IMT), where he held research and engineering positions. Will holds US patents in advanced materials, and he is the inventor on multiple patents pending for graphene-based devices. He earned his BS degree in metallurgical and materials engineering from Colorado School of Mines and his master's degree in materials engineering from the University of California–Santa Barbara in 2005. Will was born and raised in the southern Andes of Perú by a caring but very poor family. His drive and his exceptional engineering skills have led him to where he is today. Will and his wife were married in the Andes in Perú, and they now live in Berkeley, California. Will enrolled in one of my early entrepreneurship graduate programs at John F. Kennedy University, and it has been my pleasure to advise him for a number of years at a number of points in his entrepreneurial growth and to have participated in his start-up board. I saw him get his first funding and go through the many roads one has to travel to succeed launching a company. He has done his parents proud, and I am happy to count him as a BFF.

Chapter 5

Turning Human Energy into Accomplishments

Beatriz "Betty" Manetta

Looking back over the years, I know that without the potholes in my journey, I would not be the person I am today. And as far as energy goes, the challenges, triumphs, people, and experiences continue to provide me with a wealth of energy to press on in my own unique way.

My parents came to the United States in the early 1960s, a time of much unrest. Coming from Argentina and not knowing the quirks of the South in those days, we nearly got thrown off a bus from Miami to New Jersey because my father offered a seat to an African American woman. My father was criticized for not understanding English well and also for not understanding the rules in the South. Luckily, there was a man on that bus who spoke Spanish and instructed my father to sit. In Argentina, male chivalry toward women was more important than race. We thought, "What a strange world are we in, and what have we done!" Thank God we eventually landed in Elizabeth, New Jersey, where racial tensions were bad, but nothing like the segregation of the South. This cultural experience of injustice reaffirmed my resolve to become a strong woman and to always be an advocate for diversity and women.

If you ask me where my mojo comes from, I am not sure I can tell you. My high energy level probably was inherited from my mom. It impacts how I do business and my business success. As immigrants to the United States, my parents instilled a strong work ethic in me. My mom worked two jobs. She would walk to the Singer plant nearby in Elizabeth, come home to make sure we were fed and completed our homework, and then proceeded to her night job cleaning up after people. My mom walked fast, talked fast, cleaned fast, cooked fast—she was a four-foot eleven-inch speed machine! That seems to have rubbed off on me. But my parents were also strong proponents of the power of education. They came to America and insisted their children reach for the American dream. I took the lesson to heart, but the road was not always easy. I wanted to be independent, own a business, and succeed in my own way. But who doesn't when they are young and looking toward the future?

I believe the success I have achieved is directly related to my focused energy level and learning to play the cards life has dealt me. Energy can catapult your plans from an idea to reality. As one of my friends would say, "Energy can put legs on those dreams."

Most people who know me know I have a high amount of energy: I am constantly researching, reading, evaluating, and collaborating to find new and more prosperous ways to move my businesses and others forward. More precisely, working strategically harder and smarter can make the difference between a temporary setback and a glowing, thriving business direction. If I have learned anything in my journey so far, it is that life is always changing and that you must learn to adapt to the changes—good or bad.

So let me tell you five Cs that have governed my life thus far.

Your Core Competency Points Your Direction

I guess I must have always had a desire to own some type of business. I didn't call it entrepreneurship because I didn't even know what that meant. What I did know was that I wanted to be able to buy clothes, drive the car I liked, feed myself, and enjoy life. I knew my parents couldn't afford to give me everything I wanted. I focused on earning enough money myself. My parents energized me and created a drive in me that has lasted my entire life. Therefore, I found myself doing all kinds of odd jobs and odd businesses. I always had more than one thing going—just in case the first one didn't quite work out or because it couldn't supply all my wants (there was that mojo working again).

When I was young, I ran an ice cream truck, handled concessions at the Englishtown Raceway selling T-shirts and beer, and even ran a nonprofit dance company. Before starting my current companies, I owned a construction company. Many times I worked two jobs (just like my mom) or went to school and worked or raised my family and started a business.

In addition to my entrepreneurial endeavors, while going to school, I also discovered I had a knack for leadership. I was chosen class president, co-captained the cheerleading squad, and held several other positions, including class clown! I have always led teams and had a supervisory role (softball, secretarial pool, associates team, etc.).

I didn't really take education seriously in high school. However, a few months working at the local Woolworth's store made me appreciate again the value of a good education. I knew Woolworth's was not going to help me create an independent life. Upon graduation from high school, I went on to earn a bachelor of science degree in accounting and marketing from Rutgers University and a master's of international studies from Seton Hall University.

My corporate career began with a job as a secretary at AT&T. I spent twenty years in corporate America where my drive eventually led me to the position of Director of International Sales. I managed sales in Latin America and the Middle East. I was not on the path to business ownership, but I did develop my leadership skills, my technological know-how, and my business acumen.

Sometimes you just fall into a career path or business. Other times the challenges of life direct your path. What I do know is that I was reasonably good at leadership, learning, and collaborating with others, and all these core competencies led me to the tech-centric businesses I own today.

Whatever your core competency happens to be, embrace it and put your energy in that direction. Too many people are always trying to fix their weaknesses when they should be honing their strengths. Find your strengths, and then do all you can to utilize them to achieve your goals. Then shore up your weaknesses through collaboration with other people skilled in those areas.

Challenges Make Us Stronger

Just as we have to take a stand for what is right, I learned in high school that all decisions have consequences that can either take us down or force us to rise above them. I was kicked out of my Catholic high school during my senior year—something about being caught smoking (more than once)! Needless to say, it did not go over well with my parents.

At that time, I did not comprehend the sacrifice they made to pay for my schooling, and now they were putting me in public school. Certainly it was a rude awakening but a valuable lesson. This experience taught me two things: (1) all decisions directly or indirectly impact others, and (2) we have to take ownership for consequences of our decisions. At first, I contemplated dropping out, but then I realized I needed to redeem myself to my parents. If I didn't finish school, my school friends would think that I was a loser. I accepted responsibility, dusted myself off, and got right back in the race. I graduated with a whole new set of friends. Today, I go to two high school class reunions where I have very dear friends. Over the years, I've introduced them to one another and collaborated with many.

Trials and tribulations are what define us. What makes leaders is a decision to own the results of the cards that life deals us. While in corporate America, I returned to work from maternity leave. My old job was not available. So I was asked to support the Middle East country desk! I'm an immigrant from Argentina who grew up in New Jersey. What do I know about the Middle East? I'm a Latina, why not Latin America? Well, the only job available was the Middle East country assignment. I decided, "I can do this." I became very good at this assignment. I made many new international friends. I learned that outside the group persona, business overrides cultural norms and stereotypes! To this day, my Middle Eastern friends and lessons are still with me, and some of the people I met in those days have collaborated with me in my current businesses.

Fast thinking, good planning, and preparation always overcome fear. As my corporate career began to take off, the worst thing happened. Corporate downsizing left me facing the unemployment line. Like my high school struggles, I shrugged it off and decided to make a go at being an entrepreneur. That's right—no money, no employees, and no system—nothing but an idea.

I bounced the idea off my previous boss and asked if he would support me. I didn't want handouts but opportunities to bid on projects. He said yes, and Argent Associates was founded (currently I have two companies, Argent Associates and Asociar). I worked hard and saved my money so I could expand the business. I worked from my home on a pool table that served as my desk and conference table. I had two small children and still managed to be a cheerleading coach. My daughter asked me to start the program as I was launching my company. How could I say no!

As I look back over my life and my career, I find that without these pivotal life events in my journey, I would not be who I am. Sometimes, failure is part of what makes us resilient and gives us a thick skin, which is what entrepreneurs need to excel in business.

Continuous Learning Keeps You Fresh

Never stop learning. It is one of the key mantras I strongly believe sets my businesses and me apart from our competition. In the fast-paced world of technology, you can quickly lose ground if you are not moving forward. I have spent my fair share of time in classrooms, but I also soaked up all I could in every corporate assignment. Whether I was in the secretarial pool or leading engineers and salespeople internationally, I was constantly learning and growing. I took the time to understand and incorporate new ideas and lessons into my business direction.

During my time in the corporate world, I had an assignment related to quality and quality control. I learned how important it can be to the process of satisfactorily delivering a great product and good service. When I began Argent Associates, one of the first things I did was to make sure our firm was quality certified (ISO 9001 and ISO 14000). Quality compliance can be a strong differentiator, especially in the technology and telecommunications industries.

I still am a voracious reader and researcher. If you ask me where my energy is best utilized today, I will tell you it is in the area of continuous learning about my industry and technology. The people I work with will tell you I may read too much. I am constantly sending them articles about new findings within our industry. But this is how you adjust to keep up with the direction of the future.

Learning comes from all types of sources—books, seminars, panels, industry data, competitors, customers, and the Internet. In my field, we must constantly pivot to stay ahead of the competition. Who could have told us ten years ago how important a smartphone would be, or how cloud computing would take over our day-to-day computer center operations? Who could have predicted the impact a global economy would have on how we buy and sell products and services?

In my current businesses, software development is becoming much more important than the hardware solutions historically used to provide services. How we compete on a global basis with international wage scales versus our US-based developers is critical to the future direction of my businesses. Do we use homegrown researchers, or do we figure out how to manage a global workforce? Space travel is another industry fast becoming more internationally driven. Will the innovative ideas for interstellar travel come from our US efforts, or through collaboration with other nations?

Staying abreast of the future through continuous learning is critical for the success of any business or industry today. It is where innovative ideas emerge and innovative products and services are produced. Make continuous learning a priority, because it combines knowledge and wisdom, which is knowing when and where to apply the knowledge.

A Collaborative Network Pays Off

"No man [or woman] is an island" is a quote from English poet John Donne. This rings truer than ever in the world in which we exist today. Collaboration is how we learn, create, produce, and succeed in today's world. You can't do it all by yourself and hope to succeed. To begin with, you don't have all the skills necessary. Secondly, no matter how much energy you have, you won't have enough to continue the process to its ultimate payoff. And third, you won't have much fun or know you've succeeded without others by your side.

Steve Jobs had Steve Wozniak to help create the iPod. Henry Ford was encouraged by the famous inventor Thomas Edison to continue on his dream to build affordable automobiles. Olive Ann Beech, cofounder of Beech Aircraft Corp., with her husband, Walter, founded and developed Beech Aircraft Corp. into a multimillion-dollar aerospace firm before selling out to Raytheon in 1980.

Collaborative growth means leaning in and strategically interacting with people. It takes energy and fortitude to establish and nurture a network of people you can count on. I include my family, friends, coworkers, suppliers, customers, and God in my powerful network. I met and worked with my chief operating officer while working in the world of corporate America. We worked together on several projects and had a chance to observe each other's abilities. I have also had the opportunity in my two companies, Argent Associates and Asociar, to have brought as employees associates I had known from my prior employment elsewhere. When in doubt, your strategic network will always be there for you.

Perhaps the most exciting part of collaborative growth is the opportunity to keep defining and redefining your network with new thought leaders and skilled people. My network never stays stagnant and is energized each day with new people, new organizations, and new introductions.

You may actually want to do some homework and find people in your field you'd like to align with. Figure out organizations and the causes they champion. Determine how you can meet them in their places of interest, whether it is within your industry, at the local food bank, at the theater, or in community organizations.

I used to think politics was a waste of time; however, laws, regulations, and rules are driven by government. In order to have a voice in an area that can and does impact my businesses, I have been more actively engaged in politics. My drive in this area landed me on the President's Export Council for President George W. Bush, which helped mold policies on international trade matters and their impact upon small, minority, and women-owned businesses.

Remember, you never know who can help you and your career. Try not to burn bridges, and be nice to everyone you meet, including your competitors. Talk, listen, and collaborate strategically with others.

Community Involvement Energizes You

Perhaps the one thing that has most impacted my business and career has been my involvement in community activities and with organizations working to better the lives of others. That one incident on the bus traveling from the South to New Jersey instilled in me a drive to help make life a little fairer for those left out of the status quo loop. And I knew from my upbringing and culture that there are amazing people and talent in all cultures and races. The diversity of the people involved, the opportunities to reach beyond the norm, the unbelievable impact upon our future—this is where we get to share our dreams, struggles, and successes. This is where we reach back to help, leave our own mark on life, and define our purpose.

With two successful businesses that continue to grow, redefine themselves, and deliver, I find that my real pleasure comes from being able to support several causes near and dear to me. These include mentoring young woman–owned and minority-owned businesses. It includes being able to provide college scholarships to grow talent in the STEM fields. The boards I sit on and the organizations I belong to allow me to share my experiences and perhaps be a beacon for others to succeed.

In addition, I have made sure my companies look like the demographics of America. I am proud of our diverse workforce and the diverse collaborative network I have built. They reenergize me each and every day.

I have won numerous awards with my businesses, but nothing compares to the chance to mentor a business that succeeds or to see a young person attend college because of a scholarship you helped contribute. Acknowledging, encouraging, and helping the next generation of leaders is a most rewarding experience.

If you need to energize your vision or energize your being, there is nothing more refreshing than learning to give back to others. It will rock your world and make it much more satisfying than anything else you can do besides raising your own family. Plus, it will add to that collaborative network in ways you can never dream of.

Don't Lose Your Confidence

The final C is all about confidence. Energize your supporters and toot your own horn. Everybody loves a winner! Execute your plans and continue to update and alter them as your industry and market changes. Don't be afraid to change, pivot, or even start over. Thomas Edison once said, "I have not failed 10,000 times—I've successfully found 10,000 ways that will not work." The key here is, there is no failure. It's all a learning experience, and it's dependent upon what you do next. The other element of learning is Thomas Edison tried ten thousand times. His brain, his thoughts, and his actions were energized enough to try over ten thousand ways to make something work.

My companies, coworkers, and I have had the pleasure of winning numerous awards for our business acumen, success, community involvement, and more. That would not happen without submitting our information (you can't win if you don't play). These awards give us even more confidence to succeed, and they have turned out to be a great way to market our companies. We have people coming to us to discuss who we are and what we do. We have met and done business with some amazing companies because of it. And we have expanded our collaborative network with talented individuals in other fields.

Lastly, in terms of confidence, where many businesses falter is in creating and energetically delivering their "thirty-second elevator speeches" about their businesses. It's one of the coaching moments I like to give young and new entrepreneurs. If you've put all the other Cs together, then being able to confidently tell others in a concise manner what you do and who you are is imperative. I believe in pumping that energy into those thirty seconds. If you ask me what Argent Associates is all about, I will enthusiastically proclaim that we are an award-winning tech-centric systems integrator and technology innovator delivering an ecosystem of solutions to Fortune 100 companies across a number of technologies and at various stages of product life cycle.

Energy is important. Your mojo will keep you going even in tough times. I'd probably sum it up by saying I just work harder than most! I am an entrepreneur on a mission to fulfill my purpose in life as God continues to hand me a new set of cards. Life oftentimes calls us to take a stand. We either embrace it or leave it to someone else to take our place. Ultimately, we will realize that we are all the drivers of our own destiny!

Biographical Comments by the Lead Author

Betty emigrated from Argentina to Elizabeth, New Jersey, when she was a young girl. Her parents came to America to follow the American dream and better themselves. They were factory workers who knew the importance of an education but were unable to pay for it. They also felt they could better themselves in America more so than in Argentina. Betty would not give up reaching her dreams for lack of money, and instead she earned both of her degrees while maintaining a full-time job. She completed her BS degree in marketing and accounting from Rutgers University, and she holds a master's degree in international studies from Seton Hall University. After college, she worked in corporate America for twenty years. The knowledge, skills, training, and assignments in human resources, sales, technical support, quality management, and her focus on both national *and international assignments were great tools for her to graduate into the world of entrepreneurship. She has now created two companies. Argent Associates launched in 1998, and Asociar, in 2012. Argent Associates' mission is to offer innovative supply chain solutions that deliver real-time information, introduce process efficiencies, and deliver high-quality products and services to its customers while protecting the environment. Today Argent has $1.2 billion in assets under management. Asociar, her second company, provides technology integration on multivendor platforms to provide innovative solutions to support business growth by accelerating speed to market.*

Betty has an impeccable reputation in her business dealings. Her work ethic is always to exceed customer expectations. As an immigrant who has worked very hard to succeed, she takes social responsibility very seriously. She strongly believes that education and economic prosperity are the keys of the American dream. Betty has received numerous awards from local, state, federal, corporate, and nonprofit organizations for her leadership and commitment to community. She also sits on numerous boards that support efforts she is passionate about. Betty and her family live in New Jersey but also maintain a residence in the Dallas metro area. It has been a pleasure for me to mentor Betty and to work with her to grow her companies beyond imagination. Over the years, Betty and I have established a close friendship, and I have met the rest of the family. I have an enormous respect for what she has accomplished, but believe me, she is not done yet! Our only area of disagreement is who is the best professional baseball team, the New York Yankees or the San Francisco Giants?

Section 2

Opening Doors through Innovation and Education

Innovation distinguishes between a leader and a follower.

—Steve Jobs

Famous Comments on the Role of Education and Constant Innovation on Our World

Education is the most powerful weapon which you can use to change the world. Education is the great engine of personal development. It is through education that the daughter of a peasant can become a doctor, that the son of a mine worker can become the head of a mine that a child of farmworkers can become the President of a great nation. It is what we make out of what we have, not what we are given that separates one person from another.

—Nelson Mandela

Education is not the learning of facts, but the training of the mind to think. Logic will take you from A to B. Imagination will take you everywhere.

—Albert Einstein

Live as if you were to die tomorrow. Learn as if you were to live forever.
—Mahatma Gandhi

The function of education is to teach one to think intensively and to think critically. Intelligence plus Character—that is the true goal of Education.

—Martin Luther King

Dreaming is one of humanity's greatest gifts—it champions aspirations, it spurs innovation, leads to change and propels the world forward.
—Sir Richard Branson

It is important in creative science not to give up. If you are an optimist you will be willing to try more than if you are a pessimist.
—Stanislaw Ulam

Chapter 6

Which Road to Take in School?

Raul A. Deju

As you learned from chapter 1, most of my college education was at New Mexico Tech, sprinkled with an astrophysics detour at Columbia University. Without my college education, my life would have been very different than it has been, and for that, I am utterly thankful.

When I went to college in my mid-teens, my options were limited. I had applied to one college and was accepted into one college. Fortunately, I received a tuition scholarship and a coop work-study program that paid for basic necessities but required that I work outside the program for extra income. I also found that I needed to take a loan, as I could not count on any family income since there wasn't any to be had.

When I began my college career, I had to quickly figure out what I wanted to be so as not to waste my precious and meager resources. I was back to needing to answer the question the Mother Superior asked me when I was in kindergarten, only now it seemed to have a greater urgency. Of course, how many sixteen-year-olds know what they really want to be when they grow up? This was a bit daunting.

As I started, my approach was to focus on mathematics, truly a language that could be applied to any of the sciences, and then focus my minor on a science that interested me. After all, I was in a tech college, and all careers were science and engineering based.

In the '60s, America's space program was burgeoning. On May 25, 1961, President Kennedy had called for an ambitious space exploration program that included not only putting astronauts on the moon but also launching nuclear rockets for deep space exploration, weather satellites, and other space projects. I saw this program not only as an intellectual challenge but also as a ticket for future employment. So my decision was to study physics combined with math. Wow, it was an easier decision than I thought!

However, in the interim, I had to work to support my college education, and the best job I could muster was in a chemistry and metallurgy laboratory at the New Mexico Bureau of Mines, which was not in my primary area of study. I also did math and physics tutoring, but that paid little. My main lab job, however, provided me a backup learning platform in the areas of chemistry and metallurgy, which I continued to use in my academic growth, and the pay minimized my need for loans that I would have to later repay. Unbeknownst to me at that time, my chemistry research proved highly valuable in balancing the knowledge base that allowed me to complete my PhD in record time.

If I were to go to college today, the number of opportunities accessible to me would probably be greater. Kids can go to four-year schools or to excellent and much cheaper community colleges and even programs that allow you to take college classes while finishing high school. Unless someone has very large financial resources or amazing scholarships, I personally recommend for most people the community-college-plus-work option to minimize costs and get as much of the base of courses needed before relocating to a more expensive four-year college. Some state universities are also tied to specific community colleges and guarantee admission to a four-year program for those achieving certain standards at the end of their two-year associate programs. However, for me, the one college selection process proved to be absolutely perfect. Sometimes everything works out the way it is supposed to. Good karma or someone upstairs looking after me!

There are two big decisions to make when you select a college career, and I intellectually went through the process even though I did not know I was doing so.

First, you should choose a career that you like and where there appear to be opportunities for employment. Since my time in school, engineering, science, nursing, technology, teaching, and medicine are professions that have never experienced periods in which employment opportunities were lacking. These are true professions, and opportunities are more prevalent than in other softer-type degree programs. Today, computer science has joined the rank of true professions.

Second, be prepared to change step as life goes on. This I call the "be nimble factor." Make "change" your new normal. Let me explain.

When I was finishing my bachelor's degree, the computing revolution had begun. Even though the first computers were huge and had limited capacity by today's standards, their computational capacity was phenomenal by the standard of the 1960s.

When I was in college, my physics studies were in the field of stellar dynamics and hydrodynamics. In fact, I worked on a project to mathematically define the outer boundaries of stars. This project required either monumental all-night sessions with a calculator and NoDoz Maximum Strength to keep you awake or more computing power. Not wanting to work inefficiently, I learned the early computer languages, such as FORTRAN (FORTRAN II was available in the early 1960s, and FORTRAN IV was launched in 1966), to save my nights for sleeping. I basically became an innovator, though I did not even know it.

Once I had done that, I became valuable to anybody whose research involved solving hydrodynamic equations, or complex equations for that matter. In the mid-1960s, the Clean Air Act was also passed, and the road was paved for the passage of the Clean Water Act, which provided research funds for those studying the movement of air masses, groundwater, and pollutants underground. These studies required the type of computational skills that I had developed, and I was able to make a ninety-degree turn into getting a PhD in hydrology, focusing on the movement of groundwater instead of going to New York City to complete a space physics PhD and looking at planets and stars. I basically chose the option closer to earth. Who knows what I would have done if I had gone into planetary physics as a career?

Working in the field of groundwater hydrology led me to writing two books. *Regional Hydrology Fundamentals* was published in New York in 1971 by Gordon & Breach Publishers (now Taylor & Francis Publishers), and *The Environment and Its Resources* was published in 1972 by Ann Arbor Science Publishers, both mainstream science publishers. Both of these books, along with my PhD, represented an educational background that was well suited for the environmental revolution that effectively began in the late '60s as I was completing my college education. I was now twenty-six, had completed a PhD three years earlier, written two books, and repaid my student loans. My capabilities were clearly defined by my work and academic credentials. I was in a position to easily get a job in a field I enjoyed. This education, combined with my zest for innovation, placed me in high demand with employers as few people then combined the backgrounds that I brought together.

My suggestion to anyone wanting to begin a successful career is simple. Get a true career you love where you can find real jobs with real future. Work your way through school, as you will get additional skills and respect the importance of a job. And finally, make sure you stay nimble and grow with your profession, or take side detours like I did, moving into other fields, such as management, private equity, teaching, and entrepreneurship, that continue to make you ever more valuable and continue to keep your mind active. Become an educated innovator. Lose your fear.

Finally, it is essential as you begin to succeed that you not forget the needs of others. I am sure in your life's road you will encounter friends and mentors that care enough to be of help. Do the same when you have an opportunity! You will get a lot out of doing so. My BFF and I have gotten more out of helping others than out of helping ourselves. Be a role model. Keep that mojo going! My BFF featured in this section surely have never forgotten to keep innovating and learning. We'll get back to more of my life in the next section.

Chapter 7

From the Texas Fields on to Saving Lives

Patricia Moore

Empowered by Poverty

Growing up, being homeless was just my way of life. As one of six Hispanic children, life in South Texas was hard. It was even brutal at times, watching my father struggle for work in the cotton fields, taking odd jobs just to put food on the table. He dictated that my mother, Irma, adhere to Mexican culture and remain home with my brothers and sisters and me. Home to us was eight people sleeping on a large mattress on the floor in a laundry room, or *cuartito,* in my grandparents' tiny house.

Dad was a very talented carpenter. For over two years after working in the brutally hot cotton fields, he built our first house with his own two hands. Finally, we had a roof of our own over our heads! But tragically, it was short-lived, because soon after, it burned to the ground with no known cause. Homeless once again, our 1967 station wagon became our only shelter.

Dad focused his sights on the Northwest, as there was an abundance of fieldwork available there at that time. Driving over fifteen hundred miles, we settled in Stanfield, Oregon. We were like a fly in the ointment! We were the only Mexican Americans there.

Stanfield Municipal Park turned out to be an okay place to live! It was summer, and there were dozens of trees that offered shade. The water fountain provided us with cool, clean water, and the working toilets in the park served as our bathroom facilities!

It was actually better than we ever had it in Texas, and we could sleep under the stars and play and bathe in the windy river nearby. It was a welcoming place to return to after we all had a long, exhausting day working in the fields. Even my little five-year-old sister worked picking strawberries, as there was nowhere else for her to go.

It was the best of the worst of times of our lives! At least that was the view through a child's eyes, until fall, when it started to get cold and work ended. The money stopped coming in, and food was limited. It was back to eating cold bologna sandwiches, and to this day, I cannot even stomach the smell of bologna.

When it started to get cold outside, we helped my parents wash clothes at the twenty-four-hour Laundromat in downtown Stanfield. We always went late at night so we had a place to sleep that was warm—the floor of the Laundromat!

Eventually, lack of shelter and work pushed my father to the brink of mental illness. Fear and anxiety overwhelmed me as the situation seemed hopeless that we would ever recover as a family. My father became physically abusive and mentally unstable. State child welfare workers came to the park where we were living and tried to separate us from our parents. For the first time in my life, I was terrified of what was going to happen to us.

One Sunday, the Chief of Police came to the park to talk to my dad. The entire community knew of our plight, and Chief Tom McCann came to invite us to church services that morning. Dressed in tattered clothing, we went to church services and were greeted by an abundance of arms and loving people. They had, unbeknownst to us, collected clothing, food, and household items and offered us a place to live! We'd never received such kindness.

Our new home was an old white two-story abandoned hotel. It had a hard, cold cement floor, a small sink, and no phone or refrigerator as we couldn't afford it. Again, we all slept on one large mattress on the floor. We soon adopted a gold stray cat (or maybe he adopted us). We named him Legs, because he only had three. Legs, however, was proficient at catching mice and the cockroaches that lived with us, despite his disabilities.

Being the first Mexican-American family in the area was a challenge, to say the least. Enduring name-calling and racial slurs like "beaner" and "wet back" was a daily assault. But what really broke my heart and my spirit was when some teachers, and in particular my high school principal, showed themselves as openly racist and cruel.

Not everyone was mean to us. As I said, the church members helped us, and my coach Mrs. Flemmer, a tall thin woman with long blond hair, was very kind to me. In fact, she chose me to represent the school riding a float in an annual parade. She even bought the outfit I wore. For the first time in my life, I felt good about myself. Coach Flemmer was kindhearted, and she helped my family often. To this day, I remain in contact with her through social media.

By age fifteen, after years of working in the fields as a child with my family, I got a summer job of my own, working for the US Department of Agriculture. My shift started at 5:00 a.m., and somehow I was there on time the entire summer! I was absorbed by the agricultural processes of wheat agglutination and mitosis and by things like cell membranes. Science sparked my interest while working this job, and I found my motivation in life. For the first time, I had an idea of what I could become. Education was my key tool. I had to learn as much as possible. Innovation was needed for me to get out of the poverty that overwhelmed us.

Education Was the Key

Back in school, now in my junior year, weekends were spent working at the Lamb Weston potato factory on the cleanup crew while still applying myself in school and playing sports. By now, we had moved into a three-bedroom house with a yard. Then, one night, an electrical wiring malfunction engulfed our home in flames once again, this time nearly claiming all our lives. I was grief-stricken from losing our family kitty in the fire and the realization that we were homeless once again.

My parents had marital difficulties along the way, and soon their relationship totally deteriorated. My dad moved out of our house and was living in his car. I hated the thought of my dad being alone, and on occasion, I would visit him and read a book to him. Although he preferred I read in Spanish, he welcomed my attempt to teach him English. I enjoyed my visits with my father but also felt embarrassment when kids would bring it up at school. I felt ashamed when I should have been stronger. After all, he was my father.

I quit after-school sports and worked instead to help with family expenses. Stress consumed me, and I suffered a debilitating outbreak of herpes that spread lesions over half my face, nearly blinding my right eye. I suffered through months of pain and humiliation, and the cruel comments from other students only made it worse as my salty tears stung my face.

It was early one morning while on the cleanup crew at the potato factory that I met a boy who helped me mop the floors after what was a particularly messy day. He was a little older than me and a senior at another high school. He was very athletic and played football and ice hockey. We quickly but quietly forged a close friendship over the next two years, as it was strictly forbidden by my father for me to cross ethnic boundaries. But I was sixteen years old, and I thought that I knew everything. Mark became my boyfriend. He was the most genuine and honest person I had ever met! He was real, and I loved him.

Mark enrolled in community college forty-five minutes away in Pendleton, Oregon, to study engineering, while I began my junior year in high school. A romance bloomed, and I became pregnant a year later at seventeen. I was disowned by my family and kicked out of school during my senior year, and I sought refuge with Mark's family. Fully emancipated, I found myself needing state assistance to maintain a healthy pregnancy. I was horribly embarrassed and ashamed, so I would drive to the next town to buy groceries with my food stamps.

Our son Scott was born in 1984. Mark and I married two years later, and soon after, with a lot of faith, all three of us moved to Portland, Oregon, where Mark would fulfill his career dream to complete his engineering degree.

At twenty years of age, I returned and graduated from high school while working a full-time job, and I wondered after all that I had been through, "Is this finally going to be normal?"

When shortly thereafter, Mark's mother's life was cut short due to a motor vehicle accident, it was devastating to both of us. Elaine, Mark's mother, had endured multiple fractures from the accident, and her suffering was obvious. The image of her in the intensive care unit supported by numerous life-saving measures will never leave my mind, but in hindsight, it has given me the tools to help grieving families today through empathy. Elaine, a schoolteacher, had a major influence on my life by empowering me to see the glass half full. She was always there for us to help out, and she clearly enjoyed spoiling her only grandson. Elaine was my cheerleader and believed in me, and her untimely death made my drive to succeed even greater. Realizing that life is short, I reconnected and found that forgiving my parents was the only way to move forward in life.

In May of 1989, I was accepted into nursing school in Longview, Washington. At the same time, we welcomed our second son, Brent, into the world. The two-hour commute to and from Longview was extremely hard with a newborn baby. The daily separation from him broke my heart, but it was a sacrifice I wanted to make in order to better all our lives.

Those years paid off, especially in instances such as when I sat for my board exam and passed it on my first attempt! I had finally accomplished something from start to finish, all on my own! But without the support, love, and confidence of family, the challenges would have seemed a greater task. Life was happy and perfect. Mark and I had thriving careers and a lifestyle that we both worked hard to accomplish. The continual innovation I had to accomplish while growing up, combined with my nursing education, would serve me well from then on.

Following graduation, I joined a hospital in Hillsboro, Oregon, and floated to a variety of nursing floors where my bilingual skills were readily utilized in a now predominantly Hispanic community. I, however, decided to find a day job closer to home after a nurse practitioner was murdered while driving home from her shift. I also decided that I wanted to specialize in nephrology, working with patients who were on dialysis. I loved the patients and their tenacity for life, despite the hardships that are a side effect of dialysis. But Mark's thriving career relocated us three more times before we settled in the small upper middle-class community of Eagle, Idaho.

Our eldest son, Scott, had the most difficulty adapting and soon began to have behavioral issues that caused turmoil within the family. Our efforts and tenacity as parents to not give up on our son would prove to be rewarded, as he has since become the man we knew he could be. During our family crisis, I scaled back at work and transitioned to a day position that offered flexibility in my schedule to be home more, especially when Mark was required to travel for his job.

Following Scott's crisis, I was emotionally drained and working on a cardiology floor when I decided to return to school. I was convinced I needed more education. Online programs were just beginning, but skepticism in quality was a concern, so I enrolled at Oregon Health Science University, since they had a stellar reputation. I would have to commute again, which was a big concern as I did not want to be away from my boys. But once I completed my bachelor's degree in nursing, opportunities followed.

While having a busy life, I did not spend much time with my parents. By 2007 my father had chronic health issues, but he made amends with my mother and moved back with her prior to his death. My father was a good but tortured man, and now I realize he did the best he could under the circumstances while being tortured by mental illness and poverty. Yet after his death, I learned that he had left me a lifelong reminder of what hard work is. He left two thousand dollars of cherry- and strawberry-stained bills, rolled up and secured by a rubber band just for me. My father passed away five days after his seventy-first birthday.

I still have a lot to learn about life, but the platform that my parents gave me and the incessant poverty and hunger I endured as a child are the reasons I am who I am today. They were simple folks but taught me love; they were poor and showed me pride. When they had nothing, they worked harder. When times were tough, they prayed and found solutions and motivation to change, to innovate. Their love for God and goodness stuck with me. Seeing their hard life and living through my life challenges offered me resilience to get out of poverty and grab the opportunities for success that came along my way.

I share my story as a reminder that having success despite obstacles takes perseverance and perspiration to go around roadblocks. I've never played the victim, nor did I want to be treated as one. Today, I encourage those who struggle as I did to dig deep and to find personal investment and tenacity to never give up on your dream! I used education to my advantage, and in fact, I am still going to graduate school at Gonzaga University to get even more proficient in my chosen career. I am living proof that success is achievable in our great nation. Yes, it can be done.

Biographical Comments by the Lead Author

Patricia Montes (now Moore) was twelve years old when her Texas family migrated to the Northwest, searching for crop work. Patricia worked in the fields of eastern Oregon and helped her family meet the necessities of life since her early teens. In 2006, she completed her bachelor's degree in nursing from Oregon Health Science University. Throughout her nursing career, she has acquired numerous certifications in her field and participated in a worldwide recruitment campaign for Saint Alphonsus Medical Center in Boise, where she lives. She is actively involved with community volunteering opportunities, including championing and chairing various committees to improve the care and outcomes of the critically ill. Today, with the support of her husband of thirty years, she is continuing her education toward becoming a nurse practitioner. Patricia is my cousin by marriage, and she and her husband, Mark, have routinely vacationed with us. Despite the distance and our mutual commitments, we socially visit each other regularly. Patricia and I love to talk about our lives and how continuing to learn has reshaped both of us.

Chapter 8

A Serendipitous Journey

Dr. Daniel H. López

I was born with an innate curiosity about the world. Riding one of the ranch horses on any given day, I'd bathe in the warmth of the morning sunrise and watch the setting sun set the sky ablaze with the flame-like colors of northeastern New Mexico's desert skies, and my imagination would soar with questions and musings about what it all meant and how a mere mortal fit into the great scheme of things. Remember that my early childhood was still years away from the first lunar landing, so the moon and the sun were still infinite mysteries to a daydream believer such as me, a middle child among a dozen siblings growing up on land my father homesteaded and worked on, along with other lands his family had farmed and ranched for generations.

Over the years, I found myself in the role of buffer between my older siblings and my younger brothers and sisters, always watching and wondering why people behaved the way they did. Because of my position among my siblings and my own thirst for knowledge, I learned to listen to people, to read between the lines, a trait that has served me well during what has been a serendipitous journey in search of self.

This journey began seventy years ago on a ranch near the village of Puerto de Luna, which translates to "pass to the moon," apropos to the start of this tale, as rural New Mexico in those days might just as well have been the moon, as isolated as it was. But our home was filled with classic literature and even a set of encyclopedias, which I devoured in my great thirst for knowledge. My passion was fueled by a need to understand people, to learn why they did the things they did, their inspirations, and their motivations. Following my father's lead, I learned not just to listen but also to hear what people were saying behind their words.

There were other lessons. Eight years of Catholic schooling taught me how to please my teachers, even when I did not agree with what they were teaching. Actually, this was my first course in diplomacy! I was never satisfied with the age-old standard of "Because I told you so." That attitude never worked for me. The greater my understanding of what made people tick, the more positive strides I was able to make in consensus building, which is so vital to running an organization and in working with state legislatures and presiding governors.

For example, I was in my early twenties when I wanted to experience firsthand the workings of government at the national level. I wrote a letter to the then US Representative Manuel Lujan, a Republican, by way of an introduction, but received no response. Undaunted and with little money, I nonetheless caught a ride with a friend to Arkansas, from where I took a bus to Washington, DC, where one of my sisters lived. I prowled the hallways of the US Capitol until I met an aide to then New Mexico Senator Clinton Anderson. His aide, Lorraine Maestas, helped me get a summer job with the Small Business Administration (SBA), where I reported to the director of legislative affairs. The lesson here was very basic: I did what I needed to do to secure an introduction, and I was willing to take chances to talk with an assortment of people until I found someone willing to open a door for me. Once I was inside, the rest was up to me. The next two summers, I worked on a US Department of Labor (DOL) project, a job I secured through friends that I had made during the previous summer.

Those summer experiences gave me access to members of Congress and their staffs, as I listened to testimony and reported back my findings as part of my job. Later on, as part of my Department of Labor job, I provided "disadvantaged youth" (that was the term used at that time) with training in leadership skills by exposing them to cultural experiences they might otherwise never have. Frankly, the lessons I learned about navigating the mazes of the federal bureaucracy were as important to me as the program experience was to the students. More important, insight into how the legislative process worked at the federal level proved invaluable years later in my lobbying of Congress on behalf of higher education. You might call this experience the practicum version of Federal Politics 101. The lesson for me was that to achieve certain ends, I had to learn to build and use networks to attract the attention of decision makers. I also had to be willing and able to deal with rejection and to learn from it. Thin-skinned entrepreneurs need not apply!

Following my second summer in DC and a stint with Uncle Sam, I returned to the college classroom to complete my studies, graduating from the University of New Mexico (UNM) in 1982 with a PhD in political science and anxious to get involved with a high-level political campaign in my home state. Toward that aim, I wrote a treatise on factors that drive voting behaviors, in other words, looking at how people vote and why. A bell curve emerged, along with a theory that the more successful office seekers avoid extreme positions, choosing to align themselves with a more moderate stance.

I sent out letters outlining my findings, to no avail, until the day that then New Mexico Attorney General Toney Anaya (1975–1978) contacted me. Soon I was off on yet another unplanned journey, working behind the scenes in several high-profile Democratic political campaigns, including Anaya's. I ended up taking a six-month leave of absence from my job to work full-time for the Anaya campaign. In 1978, Anaya lost his bid for the US Senate against Republican Pete Domenici but rose from this defeat to run successfully for governor in 1983. New Mexico's new chief executive then tapped me for his cabinet, first as Secretary for the Department of Labor and later as Secretary for the Department of Finance and Administration. Working with these agencies enabled me to hone my skills in finance and human resources, vital experience that served me well later in my career.

Meanwhile, Pete Domenici, at that time a rising political figure in New Mexico politics, was well aware of my political activity. Even though Pete, the future chairman of the Senate Finance Committee, and I didn't always see eye to eye on political issues, I knew he would become a powerful national figure as I watched his rise. I also knew that our paths would likely cross many times. Over time we developed a mutual respect with the knowledge that we both loved New Mexico and that regardless of our political leanings, we each had the state's best interests in mind, and today I count the senator as one of my good friends.

Working with the New Mexico legislature was and remains a central focus in my life. It began in earnest in 1972, when seasoned legislative leaders took me in and schooled me in political protocols. I discovered that the legislative leaders of that time left their political battles on the capitol floor at the end of the day and were able to socialize after hours as individuals working toward what each believed to be in the best interest of their constituents and not as divisive political opponents unwilling to give an inch toward compromise and consensus. I see very little of that today, where too many politicians cloak themselves in the political rhetoric of their respective parties, too foolish or proud to drop their party masks in favor of the democratic principles on which this nation was founded.

How does one build consensus? Well, it is critical to understand individual interests, to be willing to work with people with diverse views and to maintain civilized social relationships with everyone. For me, this goal often meant telling people things they didn't want to hear but doing so respectfully.

In 1987, my life took a dramatic turn when I arrived on the campus of New Mexico Institute of Mining and Technology (New Mexico Tech). I had agreed to spend up to one year as Associate Deputy Director at the university's Energetic Materials Research and Testing Center (EMRTC) division. My job was to resolve a series of management issues that had evolved into a mire of Equal-Opportunity employment complaints and a class-action lawsuit. I put my negotiating skills to work and was able to resolve most of the issues through promotions or monetary reimbursement, before winning the majority of the handful of cases that did wind up in litigation. The powers that be recognized and rewarded this success by promoting me to Vice President for Institutional Development at New Mexico Tech, where I served for the next six years.

Never did I entertain the thought of one day becoming a college president. That goal was not in my foreseeable future. I am fairly safe in saying that had I not been asked to take on the assignment in Socorro, I never would have sought the top job outright. Nonetheless, I found my mojo, my great passion, at this prestigious science and engineering research university.

When Laurence Lattman announced his retirement as university president, I was encouraged to apply as his successor, an idea I hadn't considered. But once the idea took hold, I vowed to do whatever I could to secure the position, including writing a letter of interest outlining what I considered to be the major needs of the school. The Board of Regents chose me as the university's sixteenth president on a split vote, and the rest, as they say, is history.

Barriers, well, I had my share of them. Not everyone agreed with the regents' decision to appoint me as college president at New Mexico Tech. Undaunted, I showed up at my first meeting of the faculty senate, which I was told not to attend, and made my case based on my proven skills as a consensus builder with experience with the Board of Educational Finance and the Commission on Post-Secondary Education, as well as a decade of experience as an adjunct professor at both UNM and New Mexico Tech. One detractor went so far as to write a letter to the editor published in the *Albuquerque Journal* before he resigned. I proved myself to the faculty and staff through personal interaction, opening lines of communication, and listening to individual interests and needs. State leaders already knew me as a man they could trust to lay it on the line, and that trust became a vital element of my success.

And I am grateful to my mentors. Among those who counseled me are the late State Senators Ben Altamirano and Joseph Fidel and former State Representative Kiki Saavedra, gentlemen all, who taught me the art of staying the course, the knowledge that incremental changes over time become major transformations. I also watched and listened to a man named Howard M. Cowper, an extraordinary person when it came to human relations and the tools necessary to build consensus and trust.

However, it was my parents who set the foundation for any success I have enjoyed. From my mother, I inherited a lifelong love for books and knowledge; from my father, patience, tolerance, and the fine art of looking for and recognizing the value of each individual, the insight into understanding what makes people tick, and the conviction to stand up for my beliefs—if you see something wrong, try to right it; if you see something right, try to advance it. The values of my mother and father, as well as their passionate beliefs, were inspiring to a young man with fire in his soul. They taught me the value of hard work and persistence—to never give up.

These sound principles are just as valid in today's world of social and economic upheaval. The political landscape, as evidenced by the 2016 race for the White House, is radically different today than it was thirty or more years ago. Today, we see political polarization on virtually all issues. We need to recognize that our nation was founded on principles of political diversity and that individual freedom and dissent is part of that equation; however, while individuals may take opposite political views on any given issue, these views should not contaminate all issues. Closer to home, the political atmosphere also has grown more partisan.

What worked for me may not work for you, but it could. Think of mojo as the spirit that fuels your passion, the call of the siren, the voice of inspiration. Listen with your heart. Don't be afraid to take chances. And remember, dreams aren't carved in stone. Keep learning all your life. Keep fine-tuning your moves. Innovating on yourself and always absorbing knowledge will keep you young and mentally fit. Education and innovation are a lifetime-long process that creates the key to personal success.

Biographical Comments by the Lead Author

A strong family work ethic, core educational values, and a love for reading and history nourished the ideals of Dr. Daniel H. López, one of twelve siblings raised on a farm and ranch in the small community of Puerto de Luna, New Mexico. As a young man, Dan López recognized that education would pave the path for a lifetime of discovery. Early on, he chose a course of study tied to governmental financial and administrative issues, primarily in the public sectors of state government and higher education. A summons to military duty delayed his graduation from the University of New Mexico, which granted him a PhD in political science in 1982. A US Department of Labor–sponsored program in Washington, DC, where López provided leadership training for minority students, served as early training ground for the man who would spend forty-four years of uninterrupted employment in public service—and where he would continue to champion for educational opportunities for minorities. In 1987, his career brought him to NM Institute of Mining and Technology in Socorro to help the school's oldest research division get back on its feet. He then served as the school's Vice President for Institutional Development before being named the sixteenth President of the Institute in 1993. López retired in 2016 as the university's longest-serving chief executive with twenty-three years of service, leaving a rich legacy of success in improved student services and scholarship support. He and his wife, Linda, enjoy travel with family and friends. The NM Institute of Mining and Technology is my alma mater, and Dr. López and I have become friends as we are both heavily interested in the future of this fine institution. I was proud to receive in 2014 recognition from Dr. Lopez during the commencement exercises. Diversity is one of our common causes. We are also looking forward to vacationing together at a warm spot very soon.

Chapter 9

My Journey from Mining to the Moon and Back

Deborah Peacock

I was blessed with an idyllic childhood. I grew up with four siblings and happily married schoolteacher parents. We had little money, but there was lots of love, support, and humor. My siblings played school with me, teaching me reading, science, and math. My grandfather, upon greeting us, would give us math problems to solve on the spot—asking questions like how much 622 × 33 was, or how old Methuselah was (and we always had to know or find the answers). We were also a musical family, and I learned to play the piano (we now know that there is a correlation between music and improved math skills). My parents constantly told me that I could achieve whatever I wanted, and that support and understanding has helped me throughout life. I got my mojo early on with this highly supportive environment during my childhood.

Early on, outside my family, I started hearing the cries of "You can't do this." In junior high, in the 1960s, I was told, "You can't take woodshop because you're a girl." I appealed to the teacher, then the principal, and finally the school district; I prevailed and was allowed to take woodshop with all the boys. In high school, in the early 1970s, my high school counselor told me, "You can't attend Colorado School of Mines [CSM] because you're a girl." I knew at that point that I loved math and science, and so I not only applied at CSM, but I also received a full scholarship and ultimately became an engineer. I learned that persistence and a passion for what I wanted to do allowed me to open doors and achieve my goals.

At nineteen years old, my father died suddenly, just three days before I got married. I'll never forget the priest at the wedding saying, "Yesterday we buried Deborah's father—and today we are here for Deborah's wedding." This was one of the most challenging times in my life because I was truly on my own financially (no more support from my family for college), and much of my emotional support was from my father. Then there were the challenges of marrying my high school sweetheart at such an early age. This marriage didn't work out, ultimately leading to a divorce. To make ends meet during college, I worked two jobs, took a full course load, and graduated in four years with highest honors with a BS in metallurgical engineering. I had a passion for my education and a persistence to keep going, and I wanted to achieve my goal of working in the mining industry.

During one summer as a student at CSM, I went to Australia to work at a tin mine. I had a wonderful professor, Rex Bull, who placed twenty of us in mining internship positions throughout Australia for our summer employment. Dr. Bull had a particularly hard time placing me because I was a woman (as this field was a male-only field at that time). He did find a mine manager who was willing to accept me in Zeehan, Tasmania.

Upon arriving in Tasmania, the mine manager informed me he was leaving in three days and that there would be a new mine manager from the UK. When the new manager arrived, he asked others, "What the hell is she doing here?" He refused to talk with me or allow me to go into the mine. I couldn't figure out how to even get in the door to communicate with him. A week into his new employment, there was a welcoming party for him with dinner and dancing afterward. I'm a fairly shy person but decided to ask him to dance with me. He refused over and over, but then everyone egged him on, and he did dance with me. It broke the ice, and everything was fine between us after that. I was allowed to work in the mine, and nothing more was said about me being there. What a learning experience that was! I had to get up the nerve to ask him to dance, knowing it could make things even worse (but how worse could things be?). This was a great mojo builder for me, learning that there are different and unconventional ways to get things done.

After graduating from CSM, my first job was at Kennecott Copper Corporation, Utah Copper Division, in Salt Lake City. I was the first woman there since World War II (when women ran the mine). It was a time when companies were embracing equal opportunity, but they didn't quite know what to do with me. I was one of six new engineers, and the five men were immediately placed as frontline foremen. They asked me to go to the research lab instead.

Knowing that I was being treated differently and really wanting to be involved in operations, I requested that I also become a frontline foreman. I persisted with my requests over a couple of months, and they finally placed me in my first frontline position as "coarse crushing foreman." My instructions were "Go kick 'em in the butts," which could work for some, but not for a five-foot-two, ninety-five-pound woman in her early twenties with a tiny voice. Knowing that management technique wouldn't work for me, I summoned my inner mojo and used my own style, something comfortable to me. I had a genuine interest in my crew, asked about their lives and family, and had them teach me how to run their equipment.

I learned how to drive diesel and electric trains, drive a Caterpillar D9 bulldozer, operate the crusher, do welding to fix equipment, and pitched in at all times when there was a problem, even shoveling hundreds of pounds of ore back onto the conveyor belt. Respect had to be earned over time with lots of physical and emotional hard work. My shift production numbers climbed, and everyone was surprised (including me)!

That job was not without its frustrations. One day while driving behind another truck, I was mooned by three guys. I was angry and reported it, but then the joke became "Can you identify their butts? We'll bring everyone in for a line up." I learned a very valuable lesson— laugh at these things and don't turn them into a major drama.

Another night, we had a migration of tarantulas over the property. They were everywhere—like a moving blanket. For weeks after that, I found tarantulas strategically placed in my locker, my lunchbox, my shoes, etc. At first I was really ticked off, but then I also laughed at these things, particularly when I looked around and realized it wasn't just my locker, lunchbox, or shoes. Everyone was teasing everyone—it wasn't solely directed at me.

Many women leave science and engineering because they don't like the work environments. I look back at how my experiences could have led to me leaving, but my mojo includes being able to laugh at myself and enjoy the fun and pranks around me. Guys often love to play jokes on each other in a different way than women do. Plus, I had a passion for mining, and I wasn't going to let any of this get me down.

There were challenges after challenges, such as, "You're doing well on day shift, but you will never get along with the night shift crew." Moving to night shift, then as a general foreman, I had a particularly interesting crew, with some notorious characters, one who had served jail time after running over his wife with a car, and another who had served time for rape. I was told to avoid them unless there were other people around. I decided to carry a gun in my boot for my drives around.

One day I was called into the mining superintendent's office, and he said he understood I was carrying a gun and asked if I knew that was against the company rules. I acknowledged it was against the rules, fearing at this moment that I would be fired, and explained what I had heard about the crew. I was surprised when he said, "I'm glad you are carrying a gun, and make sure to be careful of that night crew." I knew what I was doing was keeping myself safe, and I learned that sometimes it's best to bend the rules a little.

My passion was mining, and I always wanted to stay in mining. However, in 1982, there was a terrible decline in the mining industry, and the mine closed down. We were all laid off, and it was such a discouraging time for me. Fortunately, I had already planned to attend law school (at the request of Kennecott Copper Corporation in order to advance my mining industry career). I had applied at the University of Utah Law School, and a very special admissions counselor—unlike my high school counselor—looked at my records and told me I could attend any law school I wanted, including the Ivy League schools.

Having attended public schools my entire life, something like this had never occurred to me. I applied and, to my delight, was accepted into Harvard Law School.

At this point, I was thrust into another career path. I worked throughout law school to make ends meet, even though it was "prohibited" during my first year—again bending the rules a bit this time for survival. Kennecott found me a job with a patent firm in Boston, a field I had never considered before, and I started writing patents. I had a wonderful patent attorney mentor who helped me start my intellectual property practice, even after I graduated and left Boston.

The mining industry decline continued well past my graduation, so I became a registered patent attorney and went to work for several law firms before cofounding my own law firm, Peacock Myers, P. C., which specializes in intellectual property and technology commercialization. Forming my own firm required mortgaging my house, borrowing money from friends, borrowing on credit cards, and taking out a line of credit from a local bank who believed in us. I watched as that line of credit climbed to the max, and then, miraculously, our receivables finally caught up, and we were on our way to profits. I'm a risk taker in general, and it always seems to work out. We have grown from a very small firm to thirty-two employees with clients worldwide in our twenty-one years as a boutique law firm.

As a patent attorney, I'm exposed to a variety of technologies. My favorites, of course, are mining and natural resources projects. I also love aerospace, and I've been a space nut since childhood. I watched Neil Armstrong set foot on the moon in 1969 and Harrison "Jack" Schmitt, a geologist, collect samples on the moon in 1972. I've watched a space shuttle launch and had a tour of the orbiter where I actually got to sit inside. I'm also a science fiction fan—my office is full of astronaut and space photos, my husband and I own a plane that I love to help navigate, and I even own the dilithium crystal from the *Star Trek* television show.

Several years ago, I represented Rocket Racing League, a company that had small rocket planes that raced in virtual tunnels in the sky (visualize NASCAR in the sky). We patented rocket planes, methods of racing, and augmented reality inventions. Two of the inventors were Peter Diamandis (XPRIZE Foundation) and Michael D'Angelo (Aeronautics and Astronautics from MIT).

Peter Diamandis went off to cofound Planetary Resources to figure out how to mine asteroids, and Michael D'Angelo went off to work with Moon Express to develop ways to mine the moon. Michael asked Moon Express to interview me for intellectual property work. The CEO was reluctant since his investor group wanted to use their preferred intellectual property firm, but he agreed to a visit.

I went into the meeting believing, in my heart, that there was no one better suited for this work—a metallurgical engineer with a mining and aerospace background to boot! After the meeting, I got the work, along with a comment from the CEO that I was so very passionate they had to give us the job. Passion is truly part of my mojo. I'm passionate about all my projects, the technology, and my clients. Also, I'm so passionate about ultimately mining in space that I give national speeches about this subject.

When I talk with younger people, I explain that everything you do in life may touch you later on. I worked in mining early in my career, and I have a passion for outer space. Decades later, I'm thrilled to be working with a company to one day mine the moon. I'm also on a mining corporate board and was appointed by the governor of New Mexico to the Mining Safety Board and as chair of the regents of New Mexico Institute of Mining and Technology (my friend Raul Deju's alma mater). I've gone full circle from mining to the moon and back. My life has always been to go for that moon shot, even if it seems very difficult or impossible. With education, a drive to innovate, and passion, how can you lose?

Biographical Comments by the Lead Author

Deborah Peacock is the President and CEO of Peacock Myers, P. C., Intellectual Property Law and Technology Commercialization Services, with its primary office in Albuquerque and satellite offices in New York, Washington, DC, and Oklahoma. She provides legal and business technology advice to an international clientele (one thousand plus clients). Deborah has a BS in metallurgical engineering from Colorado School of Mines (1978) and a JD from Harvard Law School (1985). She is a licensed attorney in New York, New Mexico, and Colorado; a registered patent attorney; and a registered professional engineer (PE) (Colorado and New Mexico). Deborah previously worked in the mining industry in Zeehan, Tasmania (8,642 miles across the big pond from Albuquerque!), and at Kennecott Copper in Salt Lake City, Utah. She was the first woman frontline foreman at Kennecott's Utah Copper Division in the late 1970s. Her technology and practice areas include mining, metallurgy, oil and gas, aerospace, energy, engineering, water treatment, and environmental law. Deborah is a national speaker on "Mining on the Moon and Asteroids." She has received three board appointments from NM Governor Susana Martinez: Environmental Improvement Board (board chair), Regent at the New Mexico Institute of Mining and Technology (board chair), and NM Mining Safety Board (board member). She has received numerous awards and professional recognition, including the Governor's Distinguished Public Service Award, Colorado School of Mines Outstanding Alumni Achievement Award, NM Engineer of the Year, Best Lawyers in America (for each of the last twenty years), Martindale-Hubbell AV (highest rating), SuperLawyers, Ethics in Business, Best of the Bar, and Quality of Life Employer. Deborah is married to Nate Korn, and they love to travel in their private plane. She is a musician (piano, marimba, and percussion) and enjoys rock collecting and anything related to airplanes, rocket ships, space exploration, the future, and the arts. Deborah is the board chair of my alma mater, and in fact, one of my former students had a successful patent processed by her firm. Our interests are aligned, as both of us put New Mexico Tech and education at the forefront. She is a great BFF.

Chapter 10

From Berlin Brat to International Lawyer and Professor

Marcia Wiss

Growing up as a teenager in Berlin during the Cold War, I was pretty accustomed to spies. After all, the fathers of many of my high school classmates were either "official" or clandestine intelligence officers. What is surprising in retrospect is that one of those official spies, General Tobias Philbin, would start me on my career as an international lawyer.

While I was at Georgetown's School of Foreign Service, I had a serious sit-down meeting with our old family friend from our Berlin days, who had a PhD in what was then called Soviet Studies. I asked him if, upon university graduation, I should pursue an advanced degree in international relations like he had or go to law school and focus on international law. His answer propelled me into doing what I have done for forty years. General Philbin said, "Marcia, I wish it were not so, but the reality is, the world does not take working women seriously unless they have a profession. So I recommend you think about law or medicine."

Since my aunt had graduated from Georgetown's Medical School in 1953 and went on to an illustrious career as a surgeon, one would think medicine might be a possibility. Science and math should not have been foreign to me since my grandmother was a college chemistry professor, my mother was an accountant, and my grandfather and father were engineers and inventors. However, I, embarrassedly, told the wise general I had taken an aptitude test in high school that caused my engineer (and West Point graduate) father to say, "Well, Marcia, it looks like you can sell a refrigerator to an Eskimo, but sadly, you are not quite sure how to plug it in." So I went to law school.

Those were the heady days when my law school classmates and I were sure we could and would change the world for the better. The civil rights movement was in full swing—as was the opposition to the war in Vietnam. Lawyers were on the front lines. One of my summer internships was at the Department of Justice's Civil Rights Division, desegregating the elementary schools in Temple, Texas. As a law clerk, I was hardly doing this singlehandedly, but it was empowering for a twenty-year-old budding lawyer nonetheless.

Then, the Mobilization Committee to End the War in Vietnam— the so-called MOBE—organized a peace march in Washington with hundreds of thousands of protesters opposing the Vietnam War. I was a legal marshal, ready to bail marchers out of jail if unjustly thrown there by the police. It did not get any better than this. It went straight to my young brain—I was having an impact—just because I was becoming a lawyer!

Shortly after graduating from law school, a law school friend and I had lunch (I always advise my students looking for jobs to "do lunch"). He said he was leaving the office of the general counsel at the Overseas Private Investment Corporation (OPIC). By now you probably know why I jumped at the chance to take that job. It (1) was international, (2) had a prospect for changing the world since its mission was to improve the economic and social levels of people in developing countries, and (3) did not involve science.

Even after I moved from OPIC to private practice and big law, I like to think I have been helping people make the pie bigger, not just fighting over who gets how much of it. My practice has nearly always centered on project finance. The nature of doing project finance in developing countries is to create infrastructure where there was none. Women would not have to carry water from a distant well, electricity would allow children to study at night, agricultural products could get to city markets on roads and go to distant countries through ports, health services would be available to the poor at clinics, and perhaps most notably, paying jobs would be available for people who were subsistence farmers.

For many years, I provided legal services to the Israel Electric Corporation to finance the construction of electricity generation plants and provide natural gas as a fuel via an offshore pipeline. When my children were little, I sometimes answered their questions about what Mommy did in the office all day by explaining that I kept the lights on in Israel. When I represented Jet Airways (India) in the financing of its Boeing fleet, I felt good about all those people who could now efficiently travel in India domestically and internationally in comfort. Working on a desalination project in Algeria makes me think of people who now have access to clean drinking water. Financing a Caribbean hotel leads me to think of the jobs and increased income previously marginally employed people now have. When I tell clients that their projects have to be done adhering to the anticorruption standards of the Foreign Corrupt Practices Act, I hope those words permeate beyond just that project. I could go on. Call me delusional, but a strong motivation for me representing investors in developing countries over the years has been the positive impact I think it has had on many peoples' lives.

Along the way, I have had great mentors, supporters, and promoters who have told me the real way the world—and law firms—work. In particular, I had to learn what many women of my generation did not. Doing a good job is not sufficient to cause you to receive a reward. My father's colleague at Carnegie Mellon University Linda Babcock wondered why the women professors in her department all earned less than the male professors even though the head of the department was a woman. So she applied her sociology expertise to answer the question and discovered that the women did not ask for raises. They thought their hard work would result in a raise. So Professor Babcock reported the conclusion of her studies in her book *Why Women Don't Ask*. Women of my generation felt it was inappropriate to ask for a promotion, a raise, a better assignment. They expected that those things would be given to them if they kept their nose to the grind stone and just did a good job. I have learned it is not wrong to toot your own horn, to ask for help from your friends and mentors, and to ask for a raise when you deserve one.

It is popular now to talk about double or triple bottom lines, where an investment makes money, is environmentally sustainable, but also has a positive social impact. That has been a goal of mine for years in my international projects.

So why become a university professor too? It is probably in the genes. My grandmother was a university professor of chemistry (so I know you are asking yourself how I can be so bad at science). Her son, my father, has been a professor of mechanical engineering at Carnegie Mellon University for over thirty years. So when a friend asked me to teach project finance and investment with him at Georgetown Law over thirty years ago, I said, "Why not?" I had been doing it in my day job for six years, so I foolishly thought I would not have to prepare much to teach it. I was so wrong! First, I had to learn the difference between doing something and teaching others about it. You need both. Then, after I put some time into it, I realized I did not have to know everything about the subject, just where to find the answer. I relaxed and have immensely enjoyed teaching ever since.

It is tremendously satisfying to see my students launched on successful careers, some even in international project finance. Many others are contributing to the world in other ways as policymakers, lawyers, investors, development specialists, and corporate officers. Mentoring the next generation not only benefits the student; it makes the teacher (me) feel there is a reason God put her on this earth.

So as Raul Deju encouraged me to write this chapter, I tried to reflect on how I got and maintained my mojo all my life. I think it boils down to the following Ten Commandments (but please observe the real Ten Commandments too):

1. **Feel that you are making a difference.**

   This should be true in your family, at your job, and even with people you do not know. Don't just punch in your time. Don't be an Eeyore, Winnie the Pooh's dismally gloomy donkey pal. If your day job bores you and you feel like a cog in the wheel not having a positive impact on the world or your surroundings, look for something else. Do it wisely. Don't quit without a new job if you have to support a family, but don't procrastinate on your decision.

2. **Practice random acts of kindness.**

   Giving is better than receiving, especially when unexpected. Feel the difference between investing ten dollars on the lottery and ten dollars on someone who needs the cash but does not ask for it. Pump up your endorphins. I recently walked into a Buddhist pilgrimage in the island of Shikoku in Japan while I was hiking with friends. As I followed the pilgrimage, it reinforced several religious lessons, including giving and accepting gifts. After visiting a temple, it is customary for people to present gifts of food, beverages, and little mementos to the pilgrims. Those giving the gifts want their gifts to be accepted by the pilgrims and expect the pilgrims to in turn give gifts to others so the cycle of giving continues essentially forever.

3. **Pick yourself up—and let others help you—when you stumble.**

   Everyone makes mistakes and suffers misfortune. Not everyone learns from them. Blaming the other guy, God, or your upbringing does not result in you doing a better job the next time. Hum the Bill Withers song "Lean on Me."

4. **Smile. The world will wonder what you are up to.**

   Don't be a take-no-prisoners stern professional. It is okay to guffaw when a belly-splitting laugh is called for. No one wants to work with a grim person who never sees the sunny side of life. I make it a practice to say hello to people I pass on the street.

5. **Don't step on horny toads.**

   We spent several years in New Mexico at the White Sands Proving Grounds before we moved to Berlin. Living in the desert diversified my view of pets beyond the conventional ones. My favorites were the horned lizards we called horny toads. Being responsible for the care and feeding of the small lizards taught me to respect even God's most insignificant creatures.

6. **Push yourself.**

When marathoners "hit the wall," they know they can finish the race, but it will take everything they have. I have learned that I can too.

7. **Smell the roses.**

This may seem the opposite of commandment 6, but it isn't. If you are going to be a high performer, you need to take a break. If you are going to work 24-7 for a while, when the project is finished, take care of yourself. Watch a movie on Saturday afternoon. Go to yoga. Take a walk. Take a nap. Curl up with a book.

8. **"Do lunch" and have dinner at home.**

As I mentioned earlier, if you might be considering looking for a new job, network and "do lunch." While it may be difficult with a busy schedule to meet with your friends, try to do so— for many reasons, one of which is they might know of a job you would be interested in.

By the same token, one of my regrets having a busy work schedule is to not always have had dinner at home with my husband and children when they were growing up. My husband, who had an incredibly successful career as a diplomat and very senior official at the US Agency for International Development (USAID), was Mr. Mom. He had more than proven himself in the world of international development and diplomacy with three assistant administrator positions requiring the advice and consent of the Senate, having been the USAID Mission Director for four years in Vietnam at the height of the Vietnam War (yes, I know I was on the other side of the tear gas), and having received every important award to which a civil servant could possibly aspire. So he wanted nothing more than to be the perfect father to his children—and he was that. We had a wonderful partnership. I could not have accomplished whatever I have without his support and encouragement. Perhaps I should consider adjusting the old saying "Behind every successful woman is a man."

9. **Just do it.**

As long as you display a reasonable amount of caution and investigation, sometimes you just have to do it. Remember, perfection is the enemy of good. Don't immobilize yourself by thinking of all the risk factors and not being able to choose a course of action. Have confidence in yourself to make a decision. A key to the course I teach on project finance is to identify, analyze, and mitigate all the risk factors in a project before an investment decision is made. Each one of these steps is important: identify, analyze, and mitigate risks; but then you have to decide either to go forward or not. Do not become stuck in constantly reviewing the risks and failing to make a decision.

10. **Support women.**

Years ago, I listened to a speech given by Barber Conable, then President of the World Bank, who said that if the international development community could do just one thing, it should be to assist women. Money spent on women, especially women's health and education, results in more gains for society than any other category of spending. In particular, educated healthy women fight for the health, education, and advancement of their children.

In the years God continues to grant me, I hope to continue helping others, teach the next generation, polish off some of my rough edges, be always a better friend and mom/grandma, and never stop learning myself. Given the longevity in my family, if I watch both ways before crossing streets, I should have at least three decades to do that.

Biographical Comments by the Lead Author

Marcia is the daughter of a US Army officer (a Berlin brat) who spent four formative years in Berlin, Germany, during the Cold War. She is a longtime Professor of Law at Georgetown University and Johns Hopkins School of Advanced International Studies. She recently retired as a Partner with the firm of Hogan Lovells and has started her own boutique law firm. She has been a pioneer in international project finance and global investment, especially in developing countries and countries in transition. Professor Wiss was the 2001 recipient of the Charles Fahy Distinguished Professor Award from the Georgetown University Law Center. Her professional awards include listing as one of the IFLR's World's Leading Project Finance Lawyers; one of the Best Lawyers (2016) Project Finance Law in Washington, DC; and IFLR's Expert Guides' Women in Business Law (banking and finance). She has been the lead counsel on numerous projects financed by the US Export Import Bank, Overseas Private Investment Corporation, and the International Finance Corporation, as well as commercial banks and the capital markets. She has represented clients in international business transactions on the Indian subcontinent, Latin America, the Far East, the Caribbean, Africa, Eastern and Central Europe, and the Middle East. Georgetown University honored her with its highest alumni award, the John Carroll Award, in 2005. Marcia's pro bono activities include working with Dog Tag Bakery to help disabled veterans learn to operate a business—a bakery—and contemporaneously earn a Georgetown University business certificate. She has advised not for profit organizations helping war widows in Bosnia, international development professionals, women's rights advocates globally; the development of television programming for entrepreneurs in Afghanistan and Egypt and increase free trade in agriculture. Marcia and I have been friends for over twenty years. It has been my pleasure to present a lecture at Georgetown Law and to have known Marcia socially as our travels connected us and in business usually in San Francisco and at the nation's capital. Marcia and I assisted a couple of international clients, and who knows where our paths will take us in the future, but certainly we will continue as BFF.

Section 3
Mojo Secrets

Develop a special competency that differentiates you from others. Be creative.

—Marshall Goldsmith, best-selling author

Chapter 11

My Mojo Secret: Charting My Course and Building Blue Oceans

Raul A. Deju

When we left off at the end of chapter 6, I was finishing my PhD and ready to go after my first real full-time job. This job was as a visiting professor at the National University of Mexico in Mexico City, where I led a hydrology research program and taught at the graduate school of engineering. This job provided me teaching experience, allowed me to use my bilingual capabilities, and helped me complete some research I had started during my graduate work at New Mexico Tech.

I also got married, not something that worked beyond a few years. But we had a son, Raul Jr., who now lives and works in the San Diego area. My current wife and I regularly visit him, his wife, and their two kids. As it often happens, a good thing resulted from something that did not fully work out.

From my visiting professorship in Mexico, I returned to the United States, where I worked in Pittsburgh, Pennsylvania, for Gulf Oil Company (now Chevron), doing research as well as running large field projects for their mining subsidiary. I also taught at the University of Pittsburgh and Wright State University. I was happy with my life, but then an interesting call happened that entirely changed the direction of my life.

As I had built a solid reputation in the area of mathematically tracking the flow of contaminants in groundwater, the US Atomic Energy Commission and their management contractor in Richland,

Washington (Atlantic Richfield), asked me to conduct a review of radioactive materials they felt could have leaked from an underground tank called T-106 at the Hanford Nuclear Reservation in the Columbia River Plateau in the eastern region of Washington State. It was supposed to be a part-time consulting project for a month or so. Instead, it became a two-and-a-half year effort that led to mathematically modeling groundwater flow beneath the Hanford Site (about six hundred square miles) to understand the nature of any contaminant movement in the groundwater and to be able to make the right decisions to protect both the environment and the people in surrounding communities. The job wound up involving multiple researchers and included some of the finest people in the world of groundwater modeling. In fact, the environmental studies in the area spawned at that time continue to this date.

I ultimately moved to the Tri-Cities in Washington State (Richland-Pasco-Kennewick) adjacent to the Hanford Site as the project became all-consuming. Well, it was another change that brought me into a different type of work environment. While I understood the technical aspects of groundwater and contaminant flow, this job required new skill sets I had to learn on the job, namely, doing my job in a political fishbowl.

After studying contaminant flow in the groundwater beneath Hanford for a couple of years, I received an offer for a permanent position that intrigued me. The US government was starting to evaluate the development of new facilities at the Hanford Site to potentially store nuclear waste from commercial nuclear reactors at an underground nuclear waste repository. This was a stretch for me, as I had never managed the size of staff required or the multimillion-dollar proposed budget. The project was highly political and had national exposure.

In fact, in late 1977, I was asked to testify before a congressional committee on the plans for this program, and on the date of that hearing, I went boating down the Columbia River with three young ladies and tied the boat to the pier at a hotel across the Federal Building in Richland, Washington, where the testimony was to be presented. One of the three ladies with me on the boat became my wife two years later and has been the love of my life ever since. Unfortunately, one of the congressmen who came in for the presentation on that day was not so lucky. Congressman Leo Ryan was killed in Guyana a year later on November 18, 1978. The happenstances of life provide lots of twists and turns, some totally awful. You never know what is next, so you might as well enjoy the moment.

Mojo kept me going into the early '80s while I headed the work at Hanford to assess the feasibility of developing a deep underground nuclear waste repository at the Hanford Site, but the politics ultimately got to me. I was repeatedly meeting politicians and government executives in Washington, DC, and testifying before congressional committees. As I reflected on what I was doing, it became clear to me that the odds of success on the project were low, not because of any scientific or engineering issues, but because of the mistrust of people about everything nuclear and the prevailing anti-nuclear political climate in the late 1970s and early 1980s. I saw that stage of my career requiring a detour.

As I began to evaluate possible career moves, I was intrigued by the rise in America of the Superfund program, a comprehensive federal effort to clean up thousands of sites deemed to contain unacceptable amounts of hazardous waste. I could see that such a program would be politically acceptable to the public, as in the end it aimed to make our earth a better place to live. It was time for another ninety-degree move, and my wife and I moved to Pittsburgh, Pennsylvania, were I became the vice president of engineering for International Technology Corporation (now Chicago Bridge & Iron Company and based in Holland) and took responsibility for buying smaller engineering companies and melding them into what ultimately became a very large engineering operation covering the entire United States and doing major environmental cleanups throughout the country. I did not know it then, but what we were doing is what MBAs today call "building a Blue Ocean," which is effectively creating a company where there was nothing like it anywhere else, and thus encountered no real competition.

This last ninety-degree turn used my science and engineering expertise, but it required me to learn the role of being the acquirer of other companies and growing them to become a much larger company footprint and to ultimately have the company become a New York Stock Exchange (NYSE) listed company. That used the management skills I learned in my last job, along with my existing technical skills, and gave me the opportunity to learn how to buy companies and successfully integrate them into a bigger enterprise. It was not an easy role, especially when I had to learn on the job, but the success led me to my next job becoming CEO of URS, one of the top ten engineering companies in America (now merged with AECOM into a $26 billion annual revenue footprint), and then becoming president of Chemical Waste Management West, part of the Waste Management group of companies, America's largest garbage and hazardous waste enterprise. I had now finally achieved the goal I told the Mother Superior in my kindergarten I wanted to achieve (see chapter 1). I was indeed a garbage man! Who would have guessed?

Little did I know that while at Chemical Waste Management, my team would lead the waste disposal of the Exxon Valdez spill, one of the most challenging cleanups in the past thirty years and one that taxed our imagination, as it had to be completed in a very short time window given the nature of the Alaskan climate. No project I had ever led prepared me for this task, which required hiring a myriad of people in a matter of days and equally lining up assets needed to execute the job. I used a lot of my mojo in this one, and we built another Blue Ocean.

When the job was finished, I was exhausted. The job taught me one important lesson. You need to take breaks when your body tells you to slow down. The intensity of the Valdez project helped me realize our mortality and gave me a new perspective of the balance between work and rest needed to thrive.

After tens of acquisitions, unbelievable growth, and the establishment of many solid friendships, I left the Waste Management family of companies in 1995 to focus on a less stressful environment and deal with companies as a consultant rather than as CEO. However, the day I opened my private consulting practice together with Mark Langowski, one of my colleague executives in Chemical Waste Management, business began to flow in. One of the opportunities that came through our door was a company called Isadra that was interested in launching and needed capital. Isadra was a search engine company, a topic that was just beginning to be discussed in the mid-1990s but which was hampered by the slowness of data transmission. Well, we raised the capital, developed a search technology that would be miniscule by today standards but was revolutionary by the standards of the mid-nineties. I served as the founding Chairman of the Board of Isadra (another Blue Ocean) and at the same time, in my consulting practice, was handling a myriad of consulting contracts, including one that involved working with two guys who had been my competitors in my days at Chemical Waste Management, Steve Creamer and Chip Everest.

Well, the day came in 1998 when Isadra was sold to VerticalNet, a larger player then in the Business-to Business search effort. The sale involved stock and cash, and the stock was moving wildly. In fact, the stock, over a few months after we completed the transaction, jumped considerably and then followed up by crashing rapidly. Fortunately, while I stopped at the Dallas airport after a trip to look at a potential acquisition in Atlanta with Steve Creamer, I told my broker to sell all my shares. It was while the stock was in the upside leg before the fall, and I learned an important lesson: "Don't be too greedy!"

Just after I sold my VerticalNet stock, I went with my new partners, Steve Creamer and Chip Everest, and we bought a company in Atlanta together with Citigroup Venture Capital. The company was in the field of fly ash management, and I served as president and COO. The offer to buy the company at the price agreed upon was too good to pass. My partners, Steve and Chip, were former competitors but were two of the best guys one could do business with. The company headquarters was in Atlanta, Georgia, and my family and I lived in San Francisco, a long way away. Clearly the slowdown I anticipated in my life in 1995 did not happen; I went on to run a consulting company, serve as chairman of Isadra, saw the completion of the sale of Isadra, and went on to run a new company at the other end of the United States and in a completely different field, all in three years.

The company in Georgia was called JTM Industries and thrived on disposing of fly ash from coal-based power-generating facilities, a simple disposal business but one that we felt had no extensive future. Instead, we wanted to grow the company by recycling the fly ash into a cement substitute that would be ecologically better than cement. We renamed the company ISG Resources and launched forward.

To succeed with ISG, we took a couple of huge risks. One was the risk of selling $100 million in bonds on Wall Street to support some acquisitions across the country, and the second was to convince regulators in various states that fly ash was a better product than cement for making concrete to be used in highway projects and should be a required use in future projects. While risks existed in both counts, we managed them well (not without a few bumps), acquired a few companies on a nationwide scale, and ultimately merged ISG with an existing NASDAQ-listed company called Headwaters. The deal was quite successful, and I stayed on for eighteen months to continue to run the business and then ultimately came back to my consulting company, having perfected the art of consolidating companies and growing enterprises to be multibillion-dollar companies while having great profitability. I felt I had mastered the model of building a Blue Ocean company. The JTM-ISG-Headwaters trip took five and a half years, but it was a great ride.

Back in San Francisco in 2004, I was actively investing in companies and particularly active in the venture capital world. It was one of my "semi-vacation stages," as I call them between major transactions. The word *retirement* has bad connotations in my vocabulary. Well, this period did not last long. Late in 2004, I rejoined Steve and Chip and served as president and COO of Energy*Solutions*, a company we successfully took into the NYSE in 2007 after growing the revenue to around $2 billion per year. I stayed until 2010, a six year period and an equally awesome ride. Curiously, while at Energy*Solutions* my old company URS and my new company won the multi-billion dollar contract to run the waste management activities of the US Department of Energy at the Hanford site for ten years. I had gone full circle and some of my colleagues at Hanford in the 70's enjoyed seeing me come back.

By late 2010, it was time for me to start a different phase of my life. I knew I could not totally retire, but I needed to slow down a bit.

I was sixty-four years old, and I wanted time to develop more fully our charitable arm and spend more time with family. We created an Institute of Entrepreneurial Leadership to foster entrepreneurship, and we developed, together with John F. Kennedy University and AT&T, a program to help service-disabled veterans and minorities who want to become business owners to realize their dreams. I put the same level of energy I had put in my various business endeavors into these programs, and by the end of 2015, over 190 students had graduated out of these entrepreneurship programs. The graduates of this program are now my friends—my wife and I have welcomed them to our home—but most importantly, most of them are realizing their dreams, and in 2015, their companies had a collective annualized revenue exceeding $1.7 billion. Lots of Blue Oceans were built!

In 2015 with the Institute of Entrepreneurial Leadership fully established, under professional management, and fully staffed, it was time to move on and focus on the next leg of my life's endeavors. Currently, I still spend a good amount of my time helping students and mentoring budding entrepreneurs, but I also work as a senior partner in a private equity firm, sit on four corporate boards, and am an elected public official in a local board, a Geologic Hazard Abatement District in Monterey Bay. Nonetheless, my family and I spend a lot of together time and take multiple extended vacations during the year. I now try to greatly balance my life.

What is ahead, I do not know. However, I believe there is always some new ground to plow, and every time I have undertaken some new endeavor, I have learned something. There are yet some Blue Oceans I want to discover.

If you look at my life, you will see that I have lived by clear rules that have given my mojo the support needed to succeed. You will also see that my BFF have pretty much done the same. The mojo secrets in this section all truly are connected to these rules. In the last section of this book, we will cover my "twenty rules to keep my mojo and succeed," and hopefully, you can find them helpful. For now, let me suggest the importance of starting with a good moral compass. Values do matter. Listen to your instincts, as they will tell you when it is time for a change. Build a great portfolio of true friends. Help them, and they will help you.

To me, my biggest treasures are all the friends that I have made in this wonderful ride we call life. I still have my mojo and will continue to nurture it. There is an old saying that still guides my life:

> Good friends are like stars, you don't always see them, but you know they are there.

Now, let's get off my story and my mojo secrets and let's read about those of my BFF.

Chapter 12

Six Mojo Secrets that Sir Richard Branson Learned from Nelson Mandela

Mark C. Thompson

Me, Richard Branson, and Nelson Mandela

I could talk about many experiences in my life that would fill one or more books. But in this chapter, I want to talk about one of my experiences with Sir Richard Branson, the world-class British entrepreneur and adventurer that has been life-changing to me. He has more mojo than anyone I know, and he has been responsible for shaping my life in many ways, including my mojo and my zest for engaging in new enterprises.

As Virgin America announced plans for its long-awaited IPO, Sir Richard Branson confided to me over a late-night beer just how maddening it can be to launch any high-flying business, even with more than 350 other companies under the Virgin brand. Back when the only Silicon Valley–based airline was getting started, Virgin America's competitors viciously contested the newcomer's arrival for what seemed like an eternity. Price wars, lawsuits, and regulatory battles all soaked up precious resources.

"The knee-jerk reaction you feel when you're under attack is to assume a siege mentality," Branson said to me. "But your fight-or-flight instincts are a self-indulgent waste of time and money." Instead, the legendary entrepreneur and his partners focused on reinventing the customer experience for domestic air travel, eventually winning a share in the insanely competitive airline industry.

Branson told me that rather than ever feel threatened or even sorry for himself, he's always been comforted by six principles that guided his longtime mentor, Nelson Mandela, whose circumstances were obviously far more desperate than any of us will ever experience. This is what Mandela shared with Richard and I now offer to you:

1. Let your mission, not your nightmare, define you.

"Resentment is like drinking poison and then hoping it will kill your enemies," Mandela once said. Vengefulness and victimhood would not erase the crimes done to him in the past, nor would they help him build a better future. Mandela could have emerged from decades of jail "still imprisoned by bitterness," Branson said. "Instead he devoted every ounce of creativity to building a lasting legacy—just as each of us should during our lifetimes."

Even on a day-to-day basis, it's easy to be overwhelmed by a blizzard of conflicting priorities and resistance from others at the office or in your company. Who hasn't felt stymied by controversy? I was a founding partner with Sir Richard as he built his Branson Entrepreneurship Centers, and I've been amazed at the billionaire's uncanny talent for juggling 350 companies in the Virgin Group, while also leading a dozen initiatives aimed at saving the planet through his Virgin Unite Foundation. With so many commitments, the only way he can succeed is to focus on recruiting and empowering extraordinary leadership teams to run those 350 companies. Somehow, like my friend Dr. Raul Deju, Richard Branson is also among the most generous mentors anyone has ever had. His example has taught me a very personal lesson about the struggle we face as human beings: our primal need to be creatively engaged and have meaningful impact comes unraveled when distractions and chaos conspire.

When Branson's Caribbean house in Necker Island burst into flames during a hurricane a few years ago, actress Kate Winslet and her family, along with Branson's ninety-year-old mom, Eve, fled to safety. Branson himself had been sleeping down near the beach in a guest cottage when he heard lightning strike his hilltop home. He sprinted out the door *buck naked* and straight into a cactus. "No one felt sorry for me," he joked, "as everyone had more important issues to contend with." Nobody was hurt, but Branson felt a deep moment of loss. He'd raised his family in that house, and the setback gave him insight into how to weigh what's important.

The biggest heartbreak about the blaze for Branson was losing his prized notebooks. He's scribbled ideas and to-do in a set of bound blank books in almost every meeting I've ever attended with him. He's been doing that for decades. "You need to have some way to capture what matters, what you're learning, and what you might find important later, so track your insights in every step of your adventure."

2. Burn the house down.

The disaster also provided Sir Richard with another unique insight about how to harvest failure and innovate at the same time. Here's the key idea: If you lost everything tomorrow,

- would you rebuild your home exactly the same way?
- would you fill it with all the same stuff?

If your business was incinerated and you were given the opportunity to start over,

- would you go about it the exact same way?
- would you create all the same products and services? and
- would you hire all the same people back?

Probably not! So face the brutal truth; this may be a great opportunity to rethink your career or business before a crisis requires that sort of innovation. "I'd not wish it on anyone," Branson told me, "but sometimes the best way to get clear about what matters and the process required is to imagine starting over from scratch!" That's what great private equity people do when they think about reinventing a business. It's time to throw a few things out that don't really work for you, or perhaps you should take more time to be grateful for who and what you'd miss if you lost it. There can be many benefits: Branson's new house is bolder and more beautiful in ways that better reflect who he is today and what he wants to accomplish in the next chapter of his life.

3. Focus on what you're for, *not* what you're against.

Rather than getting sucked into a protracted, bitter feud with competitors or regulators, it's much better to let your adversaries waste their energy fighting each other. Mandela didn't go to war or terrorize his former captors. "He didn't take the bait," Branson said, "and you shouldn't either." Virgin America, for example, didn't get distracted by turf battles and name-calling and instead focused on building a community of customers who loved a fresh, edgy vibe.

Our primal brains are hard-wired by fight-or-flight urges, which means that we're easily seduced by anything that feels remotely like a crisis, rather than those less exciting things that have longer-term strategic impact. "We're too easily driven by instant gratification," Branson told me. It's tempting to behave like Pavlov's dog, leaping at anything that shows immediate threats or rewards. Be wary of urgent things that trump long-term commitments.

4. Pick who and why, not just what and how.

No one builds a great house or business alone. Success depends on the people you recruit to share your vision. Branson was once recognized as one of the world's most remarkable thought leaders by Thinkers50. When I asked him about honors like that, he's always given credit to others "who make each dream possible." He feels "grateful and lucky" to have attracted hundreds of leaders "whose passion is equal" to his own in every single organization that lives under the Virgin brand.

"You have to think about who you will spend your time with based on what you care most about," Sir Richard once said as he stirred the open fire and we sat barefoot on the sandy beach near his home on Necker Island in the British Virgin Islands. Dark clouds suddenly extinguished the brief Caribbean sunset we had been enjoying, as if to signal another storm on its way. "Life is short. Embrace the people who make you a better person," he mentored. Consider someone a friend when he or she helps you become whom you aspire to be, and help them do the same. "You need fewer of those people who zap energy, and you need more of the kind who help you stay on track—true friends who help you find joy and meaning."

5. Being persistent does not mean being inflexible.

"Do not judge me by my successes," Mandela admonished. "Judge me by how many times I fell down and got back up again." When you're suffering a setback in your business or career, imagine how much worse Mandela had it—and just how creative he had to be in a cramped cell every night. From dawn to dusk, he dragged stones in the blinding heat. You can't steer yourself year after year, dreaming that hopeless circumstances will change, he said. You have to change the way you deal with it.

Being flexible in finding a new door every time the last one slams shut is the difference between those who find their way and those who self-destruct. "That's the kind of grit and creativity you need to have mojo and have impact," Branson insists.

6. You don't have to be perfect to make a difference.

Branson once recounted how Mandela had told him that perfection was never a part of his plan and that he "never achieved it." I will never forget the warm embrace Mandela gave me as he almost collapsed in my arms after midnight during his last visit to the World Economic Forum (WEF), the invitation-only summit in the Swiss Alps where CEOs, presidents of nations, Nobel Laureates, artists, educators, and entrepreneur billionaires convene every winter. I was executive producer of Schwab.com, and I was participating in panels at the WEF and interviewing hundreds of leaders in Davos for a reprise to the business classic I had written earlier, *Built to Last*, with legendary Stanford professor Jerry Porras. Our best-selling sequel, *Success Built to Last: Creating a Life That Matters*, feels like Napoleon Hill's epic adventure *Keys to Success: The 17 Principles of Personal Achievement* updated for the new millennium. Surprisingly, almost every thought leader I met at the WEF for face-to-face interviews pointed to Mandela as a role model for leadership. Mandela was clearly the leader to emulate.

In the years before Mandela, an activist lawyer, had been sent to a death camp, he was rarely without zealous overconfidence about his mission to end apartheid. Although he initially advocated a peaceful solution, Mandela eventually took up arms when the path of peace appeared to be a dead end. In 1964, he was convicted of conspiracy and sabotage and sentenced to life in prison. The fact that he didn't start out as a complete saint with perfect grace or humility before his *long walk to freedom* makes his journey even more useful as an example to the rest of us.

"You have enduring impact not because you are perfect or lucky," Sir Richard sighed as he finished a beer, "but because you have the courage to stay focused on building a better future rather than dwelling in the past."

I have now embedded Mandela's six gifts to Sir Richard Branson in my own psyche, and I am proud that they have already led me to some new grounds and taken my mojo to new frontiers in areas I would not have tackled in the past. Five Tony Awards are a testament to these new frontiers.

Biographical Comments by the Lead Author

Mark Thompson is a New York Times *best-selling author and one of the world's top executive coaches, according to the American Management Association. Forbes listed him as a VC with the "Midas" touch. He is a founding member of the World Bank President's Leadership Advisory Council and was a founding patron of Richard Branson's Entrepreneurship Centres and Drucker/Hesselbein Institute. He was a pre-IPO founding board member of Smule.com, Esurance.com (sold to Allstate), Interwoven.com (sold to HP), Rioport.com (pioneered Apple's MP3 player tech), Appurify.com (sold to Google), Trusper.com, Telepathic.com, Digitsz. com, Box.com, Facebook.com, and Pinterest.com and former board member of Best Buy and Korn Ferry. He was chief client experience officer reporting to founder Charles Schwab, who launched Mark as a VC as they co-invested in Integration.com, where Mark served as chairman. He earned his master's degree and was a visiting scholar at Stanford University, where he coauthored with Brian Tracy the book* Now, Build a Great Business: 7 Ways to Profit in Any Market. *Mark and his wife, Bonita Thompson, coauthored the* New York Times *best-seller* Admired: 21 Ways to Double Your Value. *They live in Silicon Valley and Manhattan, where Mark has also coproduced Broadway shows that have earned eleven nominations and five Tony Awards. Mark, one of my BFF, agreed to serve as a founding board member of my Institute for Entrepreneurial Leadership (IEL) at John F. Kennedy University, where he served as adjunct faculty and was awarded the IEL Lifetime Leadership Award. He is also a Trustee of SETI (NASA) Institute. His sixteen-year-old daughter, Vanessa, is also an entrepreneur, as well as a magnificent student. It was my pleasure to name her to receive the Distinguished Membership Award in the National Society for Entrepreneurship (Sigma Nu Tau)—the only high school student in the United States to have ever been so honored. Mark and I break bread routinely, and as two bicoastal humans, we do so on both coasts. I am happy to count Mark as a BFF.*

Chapter 13

Generating Mojo through
Grit and Persistence

Tom Deierlein

If I told you that getting shot by a sniper was the best thing that ever happened to me, you would probably laugh or dismiss my comment. I came awfully close to death. I was given an emergency blood coagulant called factor VII to prevent me from bleeding to death, and a priest gave me the last rites. Seven days later, I went into shock on the flight home from Landstuhl, Germany, to Walter Reed Hospital in Washington, DC. Over the next eight months of hospitalization, I then had ample opportunity to reflect on who I was and who I wanted to be—not that I was an ogre before I faced death, but trust me, Tom 2.0 is a much better version. I am much more patient, less selfish, and more caring, kind, and empathic.

In order to not only survive my injuries but also truly thrive, I was going to need to call on all the mojo I could muster. Luckily, I had been given the skills and attitude that I needed to excel long before that horrible September morning when I was shot. So I would like to share a few of those stories from the first half of my life that prepared me for that battle and helped me to create the blessed life I have built in the ten years since that bullet shattered my pelvis and spine.

Listen to Your Parents

I attribute much of my success to grit. Most of the grit I developed was fostered by my parents. My mom and dad gave my siblings and me a value system, incredible work ethic, pride in our efforts, and a confidence that we could accomplish anything if we put our minds to it. When faced with adversity, my dad would chime in, "You can do it. After all, you're a Deierlein!" They would encourage us and give us the support and resources we needed to do things, but—and this is the key—they didn't help us. We were on our own to plan, organize, and complete the task. Oh, by the way, as I entered eighth grade, the gravy train was over. Any discretionary purchases I made came from my own earnings as a paperboy, golf caddy, and babysitter.

In fifth grade, I tried out for the grammar school basketball team. Keep in mind my older brother Bobby had been the MVP of the county all-star team ten years earlier—the best player in the entire county. This was a time long before the "everyone gets a trophy" world we live in today. Well, I was cut and didn't make the team. The coach told me it was a tough decision, and I was the last to go. He said if he found an extra uniform in the gym basement, he would add me. Today, parents would call the coach and the principal and demand their son be put on the team. Not my dad—he told me to go in the next day, find the coach, and ask if he found that "extra jersey." In fact, I went and found him every day for a week straight until he acquiesced. He sighed and said, "Practice is Tuesday." I like to joke that he stitched the uniform himself. From then on, I was a bench warmer, but I was on the team.

The following summer, I practiced in my backyard for four to five hours a day, and the next season, I was the sixth man—never a starter or a star, but a solid contributor, and I learned my first important lessons in mojo: persistence and practice.

The following year, it was the Boy Scouts' annual Pinewood Derby, where scouts build a little custom car out of a raw block of wood and race them down a wooden track. I asked for my dad's help—he pointed me to the garage and his tool bench. I carved an awkward and pathetic-looking car and even had to buy the fluorescent green paint with my paper route money. Turned out I won the whole derby! Okay, actually I lost. In fact, I came in dead last. But I built my car, and I knew the other dads had built my competitors' cars. I was proud in defeat because the car I entered was totally my own. Plus, along the way, I had found my next critical piece of mojo—ownership.

Set SMART Goals

Mojo is defined as "a magic spell, voodoo, wizardry, or some special power that allows someone to be effective or successful." I personally don't think there is anything magic or special about it. In fact, I end many of my keynotes with a slide that simply says, "I am **NOT** special."

While I agree there comes a time to admit defeat, in my life, the key times where I have set a goal and focused on the achievement of that goal are what have led to my own personal version of mojo. You see, I am not special, unique, or powerful by any stretch of the imagination. My key to success is grit—a resilience and persistence in the face of many failures and setbacks. I have failed many more times than I have succeeded, but I never let it hold me back.

In ninth grade, I failed the algebra midterm. I got a 50 percent, and I think Sister Lucy was being kind, because I don't recall answering half the questions. I was ashamed and embarrassed. I hadn't studied and thought I could get by. I was wrong. The following June, we had to take a statewide standard exam called the Regents. I set a SMART goal to get a 95 or above. So that spring, I put my hands on every single study guide and practice exam I could find. I would study for two to three hours a night, and when May rolled around, I took a practice exam every night leading to the test. I scored 100. The perfect score isn't the moral of the story. It was that I found my next secret formula to mojo: Set goals, focus, put in the time and effort, and the results will come. Period.

At thirteen years old, I decided I wanted to go to West Point. That single goal changed my life and the remainder of my teen years. I was focused. It wasn't just algebra now. It was science, history, English, computers, and Latin. I set the goal to get an A+ in every class. For the next three years, I maintained a 98 percent average and got involved in student government, clubs, Junior Achievement, community, and charity work. Although far from one of the better runners, I was selected captain of the track team. These were all mini-goals and steps I knew I had to take to be competitive for my selection to go to West Point.

In July 1985, at seventeen, within two weeks of entering West Point, I decided I wanted to be an airborne ranger. It is the toughest leadership training course in the Army. It took me five years and three tries, but on July 13, 1990, I pinned on the coveted ranger tab. I failed out the first time on the PT test (failed the push-ups). The second time, I had to recycle the Florida swamp phase (failed my patrols), and finally I graduated. My focus on my ultimate goal allowed me to endure the hunger, the pain, the sleepless nights, the fatigue, and the misery. I could block out the setbacks and failures because I knew my sacrifices would end up in reward.

When I left the military, I knew I wanted to be a CEO one day. It took me fifteen years. But I stayed focused. I earned my MBA over four years at night and on weekends. I took jobs that paid less but gave me broader experiences and larger responsibilities. I made a series of choices so that when the opportunity finally presented itself in 2008, I was ready.

A major part of my mojo is the result of setting SMART goals (Specific, Measurable, Aligned, Realistic, and Timed) and then having the discipline to focus and sacrifice by putting in the hours and making the effort.

Persistence and Determination Alone Are Omnipotent

To be successful, you must be resilient and persistent. A PhD at Wharton, Angela Duckworth has studied uber-achievement and developed a grit scale. It is a bigger determinant than IQ and EQ and all other factors at predicting success. She defines *grit* as "passion and perseverance for very long terms goals. Grit is having stamina. Grit is sticking with your future, day in and day out. Not just for the week, not just for the month, but for years. And working really hard to make that future a reality. Grit is living life like a marathon, not a sprint." Perhaps you have seen her TEDTalk.

Focusing on the original goal itself again becomes the key factor. If you took the time, energy, and effort to set a SMART goal, then you must go in realizing that two things are true. First, there will be roadblocks and obstacles along the way. Second, if it were easy and simple, everyone would do it.

Negative thoughts and self-doubt are a cancer. If you let them start, they will grow exponentially and kill your dreams. They are inevitable, but catch them early and stamp them out quickly. They will creep back in—kill them again. They will keep coming back—kill them over and over. Do not let them win. We all get shots against our self-confidence and ego and belief on our goal. That is natural—just don't let them bring you down or keep you down.

I almost got kicked out of West Point after being arrested plebe (freshman) year. I had to meet with the three-star General Superintendent to convince him to let me stay. I then thought about quitting myself, and a few times I cried myself to sleep. But I didn't quit. At Ranger School, I thought about quitting every day. Every. Single. Day.

On the second day of climbing Mt. Rainier, I literally thought about quitting with every single step. After being shot by a sniper in Baghdad and lying in a hospital bed at Walter Reed for eight months, I certainly had some super dark days. But in each case throughout my life, my focus on the longer-term goals and reading motivational quotes kept me from quitting or giving in to negative thoughts.

Surround Yourself with Positive People and Positive Thoughts

In the end, it turns out I found my mojo not by some secret or magical powers but by being persistent, practicing, taking ownership, setting long- and short-term goals, and having grit.

My parting thought is this: To find your personal mojo, surround yourself with positive people and positive thoughts. I am a lover of motivational quotes and get them in my inbox and my Twitter feed. If

I am having a bad day, I simply read and reflect on one of those quotes. Here is my favorite quote of all time:

Nothing in this world can take the place of persistence.
Talent will not; nothing is more common than unsuccessful
Men with talent.
Genius will not; unrewarded genius is almost a proverb.
Education will not; the world is full of educated derelicts.
Persistence and determination alone are omnipotent. (Calvin Coolidge)

Biographical Comments by the Lead Author

Tom Deierlein, a 1989 graduate of West Point, is a successful serial entrepreneur, Airborne Ranger, and Wounded Warrior. His passion is helping others less fortunate, both locally and globally, through his nonprofit TD Foundation and working with veterans and children impacted by war. Tom was recently named Ernst & Young Entrepreneur of the Year in the greater Washington, DC area and is the cofounder and CEO of ThunderCat Technology, a systems integrator that specializes in data center solutions for the federal government. Started in 2008, ThunderCat is already ranked 60th on the Value Added Resellers 500, has appeared on the Inc. 5000 three times, and was named by Forbes one of America's Most Promising Companies. Tom's call sign in Baghdad was ThunderCat 6, hence the name ThunderCat Technology. He is a Bronze Star and Purple Heart recipient, retired US Army Major, and Operation Iraqi Freedom Veteran. His Civil Affairs A-team helped manage over $290 million in reconstruction and economic development projects in Sadr City, Baghdad, when on September 2006, he was shot by a sniper and critically wounded. Originally told he might never walk again, he has since completed the Army Ten-Miler race and two triathlons. Tom is a Certified Peer Mentor with Wounded Warrior Project and a mentor with the US Special Operations Command Care Coalition. He is a founding board of advisors member of Troops First Foundation and serves on the board of directors of the Joseph Riverso Foundation. He also conducts leadership workshops for Academy Leadership. Tom is an unbelievable fountain of energy, running a company with over $250 million in annual revenue and, at the same time, giving to charity as much time as he does. He has an MS in Systems Management from the University of Southern California and an MBA from NYU Stern School of

Business. He lives with his wife, Mary Beth, and their three sons in Garden City, New York. Tom and I first became acquainted when he was my student and I was his mentor, and we have stayed close ever since. I never cease to be amazed at the energy he possesses and the gratitude he exudes. Certainly overflowing mojo!

Chapter 14

When You Think It's Over, You Have Just Begun!

Harlan P. Kleiman

I have spent my life following my passions and pursuing ventures in areas that appear to be disparate and completely unrelated. One may say my comfort zone is being off-balance. Throughout my varied career, I have created businesses in theater, television, film, investment banking, publishing, and health care. This diversity of interests is the result of my continuing intellectual curiosity.

My pursuits started from cofounding, from my dorm room at Yale, the Long Wharf Theatre in New Haven, Connecticut, now in its fifty-fifth year; to being one of the four people who started HBO for Time Inc.; to leading the team that started MTV for Warner Communications; to creating and exploiting PIPEs (private investments in public equity), the financial instrument that has helped small or struggling companies get another chance; and to developing a company that built and disseminated enabling software to post-acute care hospital patients. My mojo is still active, so why not now tackle how to make the Affordable Care Act financially successful and viable for the working middle class?

What do these endeavors have in common for me? What did I learn from each of them, and what am I still learning today?

Invariably in all cases, I have found that at some point in the endeavor, the process involved is challenged. I find myself in a daunting situation, see no visible path to success, and at that critical point, rather than quitting, I reassess where I was and basically start again my analysis, thus reenergizing myself and finding a new path to ultimately achieve my objective.

Today when I am tackling a new challenge, I almost automatically switch into reassessment mode whenever I think I am stuck on the continuum. But it wasn't always like that.

In fact, I was finishing graduate school, and most of my fellow classmates were either going to work for "corporate America" or were pursuing an academic career. I chose the theater—with no history, no background, and no relationships in that field. Actually, it was with nothing more than a passion to bring classical theater to the heartland of America. It was my personal challenge!

I became intrigued with Repertory Theater. I wrote a business plan, which I was trained to do at Yale, and began trying to interest the people of New Haven, Connecticut, on the need for another theater in their town. I started meeting those who loved and supported theater, and although I met some wonderful people, I could not get anyone interested in my plan. I had been at it for about nine months—sleeping on friends' sofas, sneaking into Yale's duplicating center at night to print copies of my offering, and talking to anyone who would listen.

After that period of abortive attempts and spending the last cash I had, I was about ready to go back to my parents' house on Long Island and see if I could still find a place in corporate America.

Driving back to Long Island on the New England Thruway, I began reflecting on my experience. Did I really exhaust all the avenues open to me? Was I using all the resources and creative skills I could summon? Was I going to let my first entrepreneurial attempt fade into oblivion? Why was I not gaining traction? Was there a need for the product I was attempting to deliver? Was I talking to the right people who could really help me make it happen, or simply to those that I knew were sympathetic to my cause but did not have the power to help me bring my vision to reality?

How much had I broken down the development process into achievable steps that, when each was accomplished, would reinforce my resolve to move to the next one? How well did I know New Haven, even though I went to school there? These and many more questions convinced me that not only was it not time to quit, but that if I wanted to build this theater, I was really just beginning! The more I reflected, the more my resolve stiffened.

At the Rowayton Exit on the Turnpike, I turned my Volkswagen Bug around and headed back to New Haven, but with a new and even more intense sense of purpose. My mojo was back!

I rewrote my business plan, this time emphasizing the benefits a theater like this would have for every element of the community. No longer did names like Brecht, Shakespeare, O'Casey, or Tennessee Williams populate my offering or my pitch. Their impact would be felt when the theater was built.

I made a list of the twenty most important influencers in the area and realized I had only spoken to one of them. I did a reassessment of myself. How could I enhance my profile as a person of the theater to give individuals and institutions the comfort that, if they backed me, I could get the job done? No easy task, as my profile consisted of nothing more than passion and energy.

I then learned of an organization in New York called the American National Theater and Academy, an organization devoted to helping build and grow theater in the United States. I met the executive director and convinced her that my plan was solid and sound, and I was able to get her to endorse my venture and even give me a small grant to get the project moving. Wow, bang! I finally had hit the jackpot!

Armed with this, I began trying to get to the important influencers in New Haven. First, I met the head of the New Haven Redevelopment Organization, then the head of the Yale School of Art and Architecture, and then I visited again with the head of the playwriting program at the Yale Drama School, whose sage advice to me was "Not New Haven . . . Bridgeport!"

That led me to Arthur Miller, Thornton and Isabel Wilder, Louis Untermeyer, major business and legal interests, the editor of the *New Haven Register*, and finally Richard Lee, mayor of New Haven.

The mayor was solicitous but not very encouraging. "We have the Schubert, the Yale Dramatic Association (DRAMAT), and many community theaters. Why do we need more?" I wouldn't let him off the hook. I was going to salvage something from this meeting. In an attempt, I'm sure, to get rid of me, he threw me a bone. "Okay. Go see the fellow who runs the Melebus Club." This was, at that time, the major Republican club in New Haven. "He may be able to help you."

The Republicans hadn't won an election in New Haven in seventy-five years! But I went. The club reminded me of one of those Italian social clubs on the Lower East Side of New York. My reception was actually better than I expected. They appeared to really think the idea of a theater like this was a good thing for the city. They advised me to meet a man named Jimmy Lamberti in the New Haven suburb of Woodbridge. Jimmy was a mountain of a man weighing upwards of three hundred pounds. He greeted me at his gated estate late in the afternoon, and sitting on barstools in his living room, I began my theater pitch. After some two hours of one-way conversation with me exhausting everything I had to say on this subject, Lamberti finally engaged and said, "Are you going to do any Puccini?"

"Help me build the theater, Mr. Lamberti, and we'll do Puccini", I responded.

After many more hours of mostly a soliloquy from me, while finishing a bottle of Strega, the very potent Italian liquor, and the hour reaching almost 2:00 a.m., Mr. Lamberti declared, "I like you, kid. Be in my office at 4:30 a.m. this morning."

His office was in the Food Terminal, which consisted of two buildings of food-processing companies facing each other, separated by a large parking lot loading area. After forcing myself to stay awake, I managed to get to the Food Terminal at the appointed predawn hour, not really knowing what I was going to accomplish when I got there.

I parked my VW and proceeded to Mr. Lamberti's establishment. I climbed a flight of metal plank steps to his loading dock, and then up another flight of steps to his office. In the process, I passed a group of men in long white aprons standing on the stairs. At the top was Jimmy, sitting on what looked to me then almost like a throne.

Lamberti's knotty pine office on the second floor of a bay in the newly constructed New Haven Food Terminal overlooked some twenty-five large Italian women extruding sausage into casings and then boxing them for Jimmy's Lamberti Sausage Company.

Jimmy greeted me, got up, and said "Sit down, kid" as he invited me to take his chair. He then introduced me to the first man on the staircase, who was a purveyor of beef, veal, and lamb. Jimmy turned to me and said, "Tell him about the theater." I didn't get very far when Jimmy said to him, "Give him $1,000" which he did.

He was followed by a grape wholesaler. I barely was able to get the words out about the theater, and I had another $1,000. By eight thirty that morning, after many mini pitches, I had over $65,000 and a commitment to build the theater in four bays of the Food Terminal. Little did I know how good Jimmy was about bringing people together. In fact, Lamberti Sausage Company is now a sixty-five-year old business, and it was Jimmy who brought multiple other businesses to the New Haven Food Terminal.

The Long Wharf Theatre, today one of the most significant regional theaters in the United States, was launched on a glorious day at 4:30 a.m. on the steps to Lamberti's Sausage Company. Assisted by Jimmy Lamberti and then an ever-growing number of community leaders and patrons of the arts, they made that dream a reality in 1965 when Arthur Miller's *The Crucible* opened at the Long Wharf Theatre.

Originally, the main stage used seats borrowed from a retired movie house. The first year's budget was $294,000, and the theater played to more than thirty thousand patrons. Now the Long Wharf Theatre exceeds annual audiences of one hundred thousand.

Had I not renewed my resolve, turned around on the turnpike, dug deeper into what it would take to make my vision a reality, one of the most significant theaters in this country would not have been born.

The serendipitous process that I used to launch the Long Wharf Theatre has served me to launch Shoreline, MTV, Nickelodeon, Pay TV, and other ventures throughout my life. Now, as I try to tackle the Affordable Care Act fixes, I am in the midst of hopefully a repeat performance of an approach I keep perfecting over the best of the past fifty-five years.

Remember, "when you think it's over, you have just begun!" Guess what, the process will keep you young and keep your mind as sharp as ever.

Biographical Comments by the Lead Author

Harlan, truly a Renaissance man, among many other things today, is a speaker and adviser to health-care companies in the patient support and advocacy space, one of many twists and turns in a remarkable career. Harlan currently is advising patient-centric health-care companies, is a sought-after speaker at health-care conferences, and is developing a company to help middle-income consumers deal with some of the unintended consequences of the Affordable Care Act. Also, in 2011 he cofounded Self-Health Network, a company providing post-acute care to patients, acting as its chairman and CEO until mid-2014. His interests span the worlds of finance, entertainment, and health care. Prior to Self-Health Network, he was CEO and Chairman of Shoreline Pacific, a merchant bank in San Francisco that has financed and helped develop over sixty companies. Shoreline financed and developed companies in natural resources, alternative energy technologies, telecommunications, the Internet industries, and health care—raising over $3 billion. Earlier, as head of programming at Home Box Office, he created their made-for-TV programming, including the introduction to pay TV of stars like Bette Midler, Robin Williams, and Steve Martin. He was involved in the first made-for-pay TV movie and the first interactive pay TV series. He also headed the group that created MTV and Nickelodeon, while serving as Senior Vice President of Warner Communications Cable TV Division. Harlan *cofounded the Long Wharf Theatre in New Haven, Connecticut. He produced plays on and off Broadway and produced and packaged touring stage and dance productions worldwide. He holds a master's degree from Yale University, was on the faculty at NYU School of the Arts, and has lectured on theater, film, and TV at Harvard, Yale, the Universities of Virginia and Chicago, and served as special consultant to the Ford Foundation and the National Endowment for the Arts. Harlan has arranged financing for film and television projects with foreign corporations, overseas funds, and commercial and merchant banks. He is also a global giver who has served as a trustee of National Public Radio, a Director of KQED, an adviser to US Strategies Corporation and The Program in Human Values, California Pacific Medical Center, as well as a trustee of the UCLA School of Theater, Film, and Television, and a trustee of the Buck Institute for Age Research. In 2003, he wrote the best-selling business book* PIPES: The CEO's Guide to Successful Private Investments in Public Equities. *Harlan and I live on opposite sides of San Francisco Bay. We first met at the home of a Silicon Valley colleague and found the myriad of things that commonly interested the two of us, which have led to a continuous dialogue and friendship ever since and trips back and forth across the San Francisco Bay while conceptualizing new opportunities. We also love to go on wine tasting and eating adventures enjoying the finer things in life.*

Chapter 15

A Critical Corner Turned Brought Me Purpose and Focus

Bill Hewitt

Just Being Smart Doesn't Cut It

How many times have you seen bright kids squander their intelligence and go nowhere in their lives? My national standard test scores were consistently in the top 1 percent; however, my family's expectations for what I would become were not high. Mensa's membership (the International High IQ Society) is replete with highly intelligent people who have settled for the easy route not consistent with their immense abilities and have just coasted along. I nearly went down that pathway due to an early lack of focus and motivation.

However, I was fortunate to discover three things that allowed me to succeed: the importance of routinely establishing goals and then meeting them, applying innovation wherever prudent, and being able to effectively communicate.

You Have No Excuses—You Can Do It!

A number of my schoolmates had professional parents—lawyers, doctors, engineers, and scientists. Those parents coached their children on good study habits and preparing for college and a professional career. I was not one of those kids. My parents only attended one or two years of high school due to the circumstances they faced as the Great

Depression unfolded. My parents hoped I would attend college but, in truth, would have been content if I found a white-collar job with a company that provided long-term job security. They were haunted by the belief that another Great Depression was lurking around the corner.

In my later high school years, my mother was battling both cancer and a very low blood platelet count. Her hospitalization and medication expenses ultimately exceeded my father's health insurance maximum, and the costs eliminated their savings.

I had applied to the University of Rhode Island because in-state tuition was free for me. I was accepted, and I then elected to major in chemical engineering. My freshman year became a disaster! My mother's cancer worsened, and I witnessed a priest giving her the last rites (fortunately, she somehow beat that instance, as well as two other cancers that followed).

I contracted chicken pox during my freshman year at college. It was severe and kept me in bed for several weeks. Two months later, I contracted pneumonia, which laid me up again. Then I discovered that I had a hiatal hernia, which caused chronic indigestion and kept me awake at night. Too many missed classes, fatigue, and worry took their toll.

Halfway through my sophomore year, things were still not going well. In fact, I came within a few hours of dropping out of school and joining the Air Force (recruiters had promised me the moon and a couple of stars, to boot, if I signed up). However, the night before I was scheduled to enlist, I tripped over the first key element in my mojo.

I'm not certain to this day how it happened, but late at night, I opened my eyes and took stock of myself. I took ownership of the fact that I alone was responsible for the hole I was in. I made a solemn commitment to make something of myself and quit blaming circumstances for my problems. By morning, I had written down tough academic goals and personal objectives for myself, and I vowed to do whatever was required to meet or exceed them.

That evening was the turning point in my life!

Reaching Goals Became My Reward

After my critical evening of discovery, I established a habit of writing down six-month, one-year, and five-year objectives.

I have done this every year. Just the act of committing very specific goals to paper (PCs had not been invented) had a marvelous impact on my outlook. The need to achieve the goals was always present in my subconscious. In retrospect, it affected my day-to-day decisions, even those that had no clear relationship to my objectives.

Successfully meeting objectives that you have established is a great tool to instill confidence. That self-confidence is critical to taking on whatever challenges you will face in your endeavors and accepting new challenges as opportunities. This became the first element of my mojo.

The focus and motivation required to meet and beat my written objectives led to completing my chemical engineering degree a year earlier than I had planned. It allowed me to complete an MS in Mechanical and Nuclear Engineering while I was working full-time for the federal government. It also led me to experience rapid promotions and achieve greater self-esteem. The latter was particularly important, because over and over, I found myself the youngest person (sometimes by ten or more years) to be promoted into middle and senior management positions, and that was a long way from the suffering and the economic turmoil my parents endured.

What was now my ingrained habit (six-month, one-year, and five-year objective setting) also became an integral part of mentoring those whom I had the privilege to manage. My commitment to my employees was simple but effective. If they make the effort to write down their five-year career aspirations and establish objectives for the next six months and one year toward their aspirations, then I would arrange for training and work assignments that would assist them in realizing those goals. It worked well for my employees and also for the organizations that they worked within, because those organizations became more productive and more profitable.

Lessons Learned: Form a Solid Foundation to Foster Innovation—It Will Take Things to the Next Level

The second key element in my mojo has been to realize the importance of innovation. People can do reasonably well by watching and learning from what others have done, whether by reading, through personal observations, or even from anecdotal sources. All provide insights you can build on to create your own successes and avoid serious pitfalls. Applying lessons learned (and taking the time to understand any implicit risks of doing so) can provide you with distinct advantages over your counterparts who chose the far lengthier path of working everything out alone.

But I don't think that simply applying lessons learned is sufficient, because the resulting solutions tend to be just adjustments and not radical departures from the way one previously solved a problem.

What enables a person to more fully open their own gateways to success is both having a firm hold on what has worked before and then innovating to create new and better approaches that elevate the solution to a higher plane. Innovation can indeed create new market opportunities, reduce costs, decrease production schedules, and establish new benchmarks that will inspire others.

Bill Lear used innovation to create devices in his basement (such as the car radio) that more educated men had dismissed as impossible. Steve Jobs used his visions and abilities to drive others to develop innovative products of very high quality. Innovation is the mother of breakthroughs. In chapter 11, Raul Deju talked about using innovation to create a Blue Ocean way of thinking, and in chapter 12, we read how Nelson Mandela transformed himself from prisoner in South Africa to its president. All these reflect a person accepting the possibility that a radical transformation can bring a new way of thinking and revolutionizing the world.

Learning from others' victories and mistakes and searching for ways to innovate has greatly assisted me in every position that I have held. Whether it was convincing my early senior managers that punching rather than drilling holes in solvent extraction column plates would double the plant throughput or convincing a board of directors to exploit new white space in the marketplace, innovation for me was always key to taking things to the next level.

What constitutes innovation? Almost anything that allows you to break out of the mold of "how things are always done" and move things to a higher plane is innovation. I encourage everyone to challenge the status quo with an honest questioning attitude while keeping an open mind. You can just never tell what the genesis will be for that flash of insight that will make a positive difference. It may happen to you in the middle of the night or while you are daydreaming during a business meeting.

An Ability to Communicate Effectively Is Golden

The third element in a road to success is having an ability to speak and write to effectively convey what you are thinking. My background is in engineering, and that became a backbone to my career, whether I was actually working as an engineer or as a manager approaching an array of business issues and opportunities. Being a good engineer by itself, however, can be limiting. While most engineers are skilled at working problems in their fields of practice, they have, in many cases, difficulty putting ideas into words that others can easily understand and find compelling. We as engineers live in the world of technical jargon.

Both at the university and later on at the workplace, the ability to put my thoughts into writing made a positive difference. It worked synergistically with the other two elements in my mojo to open doors and progress in my career.

I believe that you will find that nurturing whatever writing and speaking talents you possess will substantially aid your career. There are many ways to be a good communicator, but they generally involve clarity of thought, believability, and honesty. Most importantly, in communicating about any topic, you have to convince the listener how strongly your heart is in the subject matter you are proposing.

Being able to solve difficult equations is a good skill. Describing a new innovation with the right amount of detail, background, and foresight to obtain backing can be world changing. Writing is critical to developing the winning pitch that gets the attention of your bosses, clients, and investors.

Goal setting, innovation, and writing are the three legs of the stool I have used throughout my life. They have helped me through peaks and valleys and have turned my goals into a history and a legacy. I encourage everyone to try this approach. Clearly identify what your goals are, work to achieve them, break new ground, innovate, and realize your dreams. If we all follow this path, I think we will leave this planet much better than when we were born.

Biographical Comments by the Lead Author

Bill is a both a businessman and an engineer. He found his mojo and turned a critical corner when, after several illnesses and aimlessly coasting during his early university years, he realized that the key to his success required setting some short-, mid-, and long-term goals, frequently involving innovation, and relentlessly pursuing successful completion. At the age of twenty-three, he convinced his senior management to revamp a highly enriched uranium recovery facility using a novel punched-plate solvent extraction concept. Although this required a month-long outage of the plant, it resulted in the plant achieving nearly 100 percent theoretical throughput and becoming profitable for the first time in its fifteen-year operating history. He rose rapidly in both government and commercial organizations through innovation and by establishing and meeting success goals, an unusual thing in the government side of the nuclear industry. He has served as president and board member for several corporations, developed successful strategic plans for Fortune 500 companies, led or played significant roles in several public offerings on the NYSE and NASDAQ, designed and led several corporate turnarounds, and started several businesses. Much of his career has focused on environmental protection and nuclear and hazardous waste treatment and disposal. Bill holds a BS in chemical engineering and an MS in Mechanical and Nuclear Engineering. For the past fifteen years, he has jointly managed a business with his spouse, Kathy, conducting technical research and providing senior consulting services to the US Department of Energy and its prime contractors. Our careers have both converged, as we have both been in the nuclear and environmental services industries for the past forty years, and we have crossed paths in business activities, always as friends and colleagues. Bill is a superb nuclear expert, a great businessman, and most importantly, a true BFF.

Chapter 16

Using Mojo, Not Feasibility Studies, to Create Dynamic Success Stories!

David Borlaug

Mojo didn't exist in my lexicon in the 1960s when, as a youngster, I began working in our family weekly newspaper business in Washburn, North Dakota, but it was there that an entrepreneurial spirit invaded my personality at an early age.

My earliest memories include "catching pages" off the back end of a letterpress rolling out eight pages at a time, a task I took over from my mother when I was six, as she had delivered into our family a sister, following four boys, all of whom were enlisted into the newspaper business. The tedium of the task (our antique press produced a thousand sheets an hour on a good day, which was not often) inspired daydreaming, and while my short-term goal was to move from the back end of the press to being the "feeder" at the top, as the years progressed and I moved through virtually every facet of the business, I learned to quit dreaming and start planning.

North Dakota in the '70s—by that time, I was in high school and selling advertising, writing stories, and capturing images on a Nikon F camera strung around my neck—was much the drab "blank rectangle in America's consciousness," as described by native son and news commentator Eric Sevareid in his book *So Wild a Dream*. But change was looming, and we could feel it along the Missouri River, with talk of an explosion of coal-fueled power plants close to that source of power and, more importantly, vast amounts of water.

Perhaps it was this new sense of optimism, borne out by the mid-'70s with construction of the Coal Creek Power Plant underway, that helped me decide to forgo my thoughts of becoming a rock-and-roll journalist (I actually wrote a weekly music column for our papers) and instead take over the family business, becoming president of Borlaug Publishing Company at the age of nineteen. I gave college a shot, taking English and journalism classes at Bismarck Junior College, wearing a sport jacket to classes so that I could go downtown and sell advertising after class. But the lure of doing big things in a small state with our newspapers was too compelling.

With my brother James adding two more titles to our group of papers, before becoming a more distant partner and moving on to other ventures, we had a critical mass of readership to sell to advertisers in a growing market. Serving as advertising director and de facto publisher (a title that remained with my father, Oliver, among the most brilliant small-town publishers who languished, serving mostly unappreciative readers who struggled with his editorial wit), I moved our newspapers into concepts quite novel for our size and location.

We became the first weekly newspaper subscribers to the *New York Times* service, helping fill our growing page count. We maintained a full editorial page, featuring cartoons by the talented Pat Oliphant, as well as Dad's conservative, well-reasoned commentary. And we created a page of farm news and advertising, which led to the unheard-of notion of producing tabloid special editions with farm and ranch news and advertising, directly mailing them to rural box holders in a multicounty area.

This proved so successful that with a neighboring newspaper family that owned its own press (we were modern offset printing by now), we launched *Farm and Ranch Guide*, which, in just a few years, grew into a statewide agricultural phenomenon, earning the distinction of "America's best-read farm publication" (Starch INRA Hooper, Mamaroneck, New York, readership survey).

By 1985, we moved the farm paper operations to Bismarck and began to print at the *Bismarck Tribune*'s larger and faster press, allowing for more full-color national advertising. All this proved entirely successful, catching the attention of the Tribune's parent company, Lee Enterprises of Davenport, Iowa, and we sold the paper to them.

I spent the next eleven years publishing the *Farm and Ranch Guide* while at the same time making several acquisitions of similar family-owned farm newspapers throughout the Midwest. Today Lee Agri Media, which I created, is among the largest farm publishers in the country.

Turning Mojo to Altruism

While corporate publishing was a fascinating and lucrative venture for me, my entire life changed when I helped create a nonprofit foundation dedicated to the story of the Lewis and Clark Expedition. Our county historical society had built a replica of the expedition's Fort Mandan just outside of Washburn, North Dakota, and with the bicentennial of the journey looming in 2003, I began to direct my passion and energy to the development of an interpretive center and taking over Fort Mandan, creating two world-class visitor attractions.

I left Lee Enterprises in 1999, which proved to be a very advantageous timing to cash out stock options in a newspaper company, and within three days, I agreed to become the volunteer president of the National Lewis and Clark Bicentennial Council, leading the nationwide plans to commemorate the anniversary of their expedition.

I spent the next several years traveling the entire Lewis and Clark Trail, from Jefferson's Monticello in Charlottesville, Virginia, to Fort Clatsop in Oregon; I also served as chief lobbyist for the venture in Congress. It was a heady time, when *earmarks* was not yet a dirty word in Congress, and we formed a Lewis and Clark caucus in the House and Senate, with notable leaders as chairmen.

A year later, after my wife remarked "You need to get a full-time job so you'll get some free time," I took on the role as president of the Lewis & Clark Foundation I had helped form earlier. Mojo kicked in all over again, and through the ensuing years, our center grew from 5,500 square feet to over 20,000, showcasing world-class exhibits and nationally recognized art collections.

A hallmark addition was the Headwaters Fort Mandan Visitor Center, built entirely of coal combustion products from fly ash and bottom ash produced through coal combustion at the nearby power plants. This is when I met Raul Deju, who was then the president of ISG, which was being sold to Headwaters Inc., the company that managed a business using fly ash from the Great River Energy (GRE) coal-fired power plants in the state as a cement substitute in concrete and for a myriad of other beneficial uses. As a result of that meeting, we worked out a cooperative agreement that supported our work from the very beginning, and Headwaters Inc. joined GRE as a major benefactor. The facility actually earned a special award from the Environmental Protection Agency for showcasing the use of in-state recycled materials.

All this was accomplished through a myriad of public-private partnerships, including the state of North Dakota, the federal government through appropriations from Congress to the National Park Service, and linkages with our burgeoning energy industry partners, as well as working with a highly motivated staff, a volunteer board of directors (led for years by Great River Energy's Al Christianson, a man with amazing mojo and caring for the state of North Dakota all of his own), and inspired members and benefactors.

In fact, $30 million was raised through 2015, most of it from the private sector, before we decided to turn daily operations of the facilities over to the state of North Dakota. This was a logical transition, with the state having owned the interpretive center all along and our foundation being responsible for operating and funding it. It simply became time to ensure the permanent future of these remarkable places that have attracted hundreds of thousands of visitors from across the United States and all around the world.

Today, the foundation I lead, along with two staff members, Nicolette Borlaug and Sarah Rosenquist, is embarking on a new adventure, moving our foundation offices into downtown Bismarck and opening what will become an exquisite art gallery. While we will continue to keep that which we created, the Lewis & Clark Interpretive Center and Fort Mandan, in our funding mission, we will now bring our new mission statement of "celebrating history, art, and culture" into our capital city. We intend to live out the words of Thomas Jefferson to Meriwether Lewis upon his return from the famed expedition: "What you have done has been done, I trust, for posterity, that others may not repeat. You have created the canvas that others may complete."

With faith and determination and lacking any feasibility studies, here is what I have been able to accomplish. We were the first to take small-town weekly newspapers and introduce readers to the *New York Times* news service and local editorial excellence. We also created a farm publication in the midst of one of the greatest droughts in Midwest history, soon followed by the farm crisis, and growing all along the way, catching the attention of a corporate buyer.

Then, I used the foresight of a small county's historical society to commemorate the story of the Lewis and Clark Expedition and parlay it into one of America's great historic attractions. And now, beginning anew, I am focusing on history, art, and culture.

It has taken mojo, a lot of grit, and the help of those who surround us. Nothing good would have happened in my life without the support of family and friends. And foremost in that list is my wife, Ruth. The Bible tells us there are Marys and Marthas, and Ruth is a true Martha, working hard throughout her life for the benefit of her family, work, and church. Without her support, including being an integral part of our publishing business, none of the above would have been accomplished.

I have lived by the notion that "none of us are as smart as all of us," and any accomplishment in my life has come to fruition by listening to smart and passionate people—people with mojo. Surround yourself with smart friends and achieve the benefit of collective wisdom and team mojo.

Biographical Comments by the Lead Author

David Borlaug grew up in a newspaper publishing family in a small town in central North Dakota. Becoming president of Borlaug Publishing Company at the age of nineteen, he decided to forego the formalities of earning a four-year college degree and assumed marketing responsibilities for his family's four weekly newspapers in the Bismarck area. In 1980, in the midst of a drought and the historic farm crisis, he launched a regional farm publication, which quickly became America's best read and largest. He later sold the publication to Lee Enterprises of Davenport, Iowa, and embarked upon building a division of similar farm publications throughout the Midwest through friendly acquisitions. Always interested in history, he helped create a nonprofit foundation dedicated to the story of the Lewis and Clark Expedition and their time at Fort Mandan in North Dakota, becoming its full-time president in 2000. He also served as volunteer president of the National Council of the Lewis and Clark Bicentennial for three years. His accomplishments are enjoyed by hundreds of thousands of visitors to the Lewis & Clark Interpretive Center and Fort Mandan at Washburn, North Dakota. He continues to reside in Washburn with his wife, Ruth. They have two grown daughters, Nicolette and Cassandra. David and I first met when one of my companies was doing a great deal of business in North Dakota, exporting large amounts of fly ash from coal-based power plants to be used as a substitute of cement. In the process, we assisted the Lewis & Clark Interpretive Center to use fly ash–based construction materials and worked with the center's developers to minimize the building costs covering costs with significant corporate donations. We have stayed as friends and in contact over sixteen years since, despite the miles between Washburn and San Francisco.

Chapter 17

The Paddle and the Shield: Lessons of Teamwork from Military Legends

Dave Hornbeck

The true soldier fights not because he hates what is in front of him, but because he loves what is behind him.

—G. K. Chesterton

When I got the request from Raul Deju to write this chapter, it truly made me sit down for a while and think how I got to this point in my life. The question "How did you find your mojo?" took me to a recent conversation I had with the CEO of Dimension Data Americas, Mark Slaga, in Raleigh, North Carolina, where nearly twenty years ago I had given up an Air Force ROTC scholarship my freshman year at North Carolina State and enlisted in the Marine Corps as an infantryman. Our lunch wasn't even five miles from the very recruiting station where I originally enlisted. Mark and I were having lunch to get to know each other and to strategize how to maximize the new mentor-protégé relationship between our companies to both drive revenue to our companies and, at the same time, employ more veterans. He asked me a poignant question after we had talked a bit about my unusual background: "Ten years ago, did you see yourself sitting in this chair now having this meeting?" Did I? Not a chance. Ten years ago, I was more worried about keeping my friends and myself alive, not to mention trying to come home with no bullet holes. It was definitely not a straight path that led me to that meeting. From Raleigh to Guantanamo Bay to California to the Middle East and back, my road has wound down

130

some interesting paths that I wouldn't trade for anything. They have also provided me the platform for my road forward.

I began to think about the makeup of my mojo and how I could use it to help my company, Global Blue, succeed. What has been the secret sauce that has carried us through tough economic times? What is the glue that has held us together? As I tried to rationalize these questions, I kept going back to lessons I learned—both through experience and history—about military success, and I realized that much of that can be applied to my business life.

The Spartans

Sparta was a warrior state in Ancient Greece. Many have seen the movie *300* or may have even read the book *The Gates of Fire*, which depicts their great military feat. At Thermopylae in 480 BC, the alliance of Greek nations deployed a small force of only four thousand heavy Greek infantry against the invading Persian Army of two million soldiers. Embedded within the Greek force was a smaller yet powerful force of three hundred Spartans, who managed to create phalanxes that obliterated over twenty thousand Persians. It was this win, coupled with a big win by the Athenian Navy against the Persian ships that served to convince the Persians to flee from Sparta. These warriors exemplified the most efficient fighting force in the ancient world. How were these Spartans able to achieve such a feared and successful fighting force?

From ages as young as six, the Spartans sent their children to the Agoge. This was a training facility that not only taught them to be warriors but also taught the history of Sparta and why it was so important to protect it. The Agoge focused on teaching the young warriors stealth, cultivating loyalty to the Spartan group, and teaching them to tolerate pain. They also taught the young warriors hunting, dancing, singing, and social skills. In essence, they honed their lifelong commitment to the defense of Sparta. The Spartan warrior's most important possession wasn't his sword, as you may think; it was his shield. In fact, Spartan mothers would send their sons off to battle with their shields and the following message: "Come home carrying this or lying on it." With this level of buying into the ideals of Sparta from a very young age, it is not hard to see how they were so successful in battle. To a Spartan, the shield meant everything. It wasn't because it protected them; it was because it protected the men to their left and right. This selflessness was at their core, and it basically meant every man had everyone else looking out for him, not just himself. This attitude, paired with the common drive to protect what was so dear to them, enabled these strong-willed men to come together as a team and fight much more efficiently than they could have otherwise.

The Marine Raiders

In more recent times, the Marine Raiders were the forefathers of Marine Reconnaissance and Special Operations Brigades. They were a group of specially selected men that were trained in guerilla warfare to strike fear into the Japanese military in World War II. They conducted special amphibious light infantry warfare, particularly landing in rubber boats and operating behind enemy lines. They were the first United States special operations forces to form and see combat in World War II. Last year, in 2015, the Marine Special Operations Regiment, serving under the United States Marine Corps Forces Special Operations Command (MARSOC), was renamed the Marine Raider Regiment. This change stresses the lineage of modern Marine special operations forces back to the WWII Raiders. They were so effective that today the legend of the Marine Raiders lives on.

In the early 1940s, the men that would eventually be selected to be the Raiders had already been through the tough training that the Corps was famous for and were known to stand out from their peers. How do you take the best of the best from an already selective unit and get them to work together as a team? The Raiders actually drew some of their philosophy from what Col. Evans Carlson learned observing some Chinese units while he was stationed in China before World War II. He wanted a much more team-like environment in his units, where rank wasn't as important. He looked to his officers to be leaders and not just officers. Translated, they were to lead by example, not by decree. To a Raider, his prized possession was a paddle. It was issued to him on the first day of training and would spend a good deal of time in the Raiders' hands, as they utilized rubber crafts to raid enemy islands. If you were to lose a paddle, then you became a hindrance to your team and could no longer pitch in on the paddling. So over time, it became a symbol of the team philosophy that was drilled into everyone's brain. At the end of their time in the unit, their best friend would steal the paddle and decorate it, then present it back to the owner at a farewell party. This tradition continues today with the Reconnaissance Marines that mark the Raiders as their forefathers. Just like their forefathers, in small teams these Recon Marines are the men that are still making things go bump in the night for the bad guys.

Lessons Learned

So what can these two legendary military units teach us in terms of business strategy today? Many books are written on military strategy and tactics, but many fail to look deeper into what made these men able to realize such amazing outcomes. Were they stronger or better trained? Were their tactics so great that they had the upper hand? Or was it something deeper and more fully ingrained in their ethos?

It was in Marine Reconnaissance that I had the pleasure of serving with some amazing leaders. They didn't lead through decree; they led through example.

Both of these units—the Spartans and the Marine Raiders—had the luxury or curse of being the most exceptional warriors of the time. How did they get these men, most of whom would be capable of leading much larger units than the ones they were in, to work together? Well, this is the secret of their success. They did it through common purpose and selflessness.

If everyone is rowing in the same direction and looking out for each other, a team is a much more effective tool than a bunch of star performers all out to show each other who is better. When applying this to business, the common purpose doesn't have to be as grandiose as the defense of a nation, and the symbol doesn't have to be an implement of war; they just have to move the team emotionally. In Global Blue, the symbolism is to "take care of a Veteran."

After working in reconnaissance with some of the best men this nation has to offer, it has been an interesting transition from the military to civilian life. After declining my commission for being a little too old to be a pilot, I decided to go into commercial real estate. Funnily enough, it was another small-team environment. We were all professionals that had good training, and we had a common purpose—making money—but something was missing. We didn't have an emotional common purpose to make us selfless. Failure was unlikely, as we were a good team, but it still left me feeling a bit empty and truly missing the comradery that I had in the Marine Corps.

I had heard about the veterans' programs for business entrepreneurs, but they were not my fit. Then, one time I was at a trade show and ran into one of the leaders of the Disabled Veteran Business Alliance (DVBA). They gave me a good idea of their program and let me know they were there to help. After some research, I really liked the idea of starting my own business, and I really loved the idea of doing it as a team, just like a Marine Raider. Through some chance meetings, the current owners of Global Blue came together.

Now you may be saying, "This won't work for me. I can't just recreate the military." However, you can easily ingrain the principles of selflessness and common purpose on a fully civilian team. Global Blue is a great example of how these two attributes can be built in to drive amazing results from a team. In the case of Global Blue, we built a culture of listening to each other and using our individual experience to the advantage of all. Part of our common purpose was to bring in new technology and solve complex problems—and of course, we aimed to make money—but our overriding drive was ultimately to hire more veterans and give back to the veteran community. Your overriding drive could be different.

These common goals got us through some of the rough early times. We said from day 1 that we would give back, and at the end of year one, even having made little money, we hosted a charity golf tournament.

Not really understanding how much work such events really were, it was this effort that helped cement the team early. We are now on our fifth annual tournament, and it has become a tradition that brings us together. Now our organization is focused, and going to work feels more like a mission, not a job.

We also strive to hire veterans and to partner with other veteran companies whenever possible. We have hired three new veteran account managers over the last three months, and I have to say that everyone is very excited when we see them get their first win as if we were the individual winners. We are also partnering with other disabled veteran-owned firms around the country to achieve a broader geographic reach. This is a way that small firms can compete for larger contracts, and the fact that we have the common bond of being veterans is usually a good place to start with the relationship.

Again I am not saying the bond in your company has to be only with veterans. Maybe it is cancer or children's charities or animal rescue or the fact that your company is going to change an industry—or as in the case of SalesForce, change the world.

So truly, the simple answer to how I found my mojo is through teamwork and a simple shared goal. Putting a team together is the easy part; it's making the team worth more than the sum of the individuals that is the tricky part. To do that, you have to have all members of the team more interested in its success than that of their own self-interest. It hasn't always been easy, and there have been times when we thought the naysayers may have been right. However, in the end, our common purpose is a uniting factor to fall back on in the face of adversity.

At the time of writing this chapter, our company, Global Blue, has multiple projects in the pipeline, and I happily can report that most of these projects have a positive impact to veterans. We have a large services engagement that we are pursuing with a large utility in California that would lead to thirty more high-paying jobs, in which we would hope to hire as many veterans as possible due to the unique skills they have that make them ideal candidates. Our mentor-protégé relationship with Dimension Data is now fully integrated, and we hope to see great success and growth from the veteran account managers involved. In fact, we hope to continue to bring on more veterans as the relationship grows.

We have partnered with a virtual call center solution provider to develop a program for severely wounded veterans to be able to do contact center or call center jobs from their homes. In addition, we are working with three different disabled veteran-owned businesses on technology installs that we would otherwise have had to turn down due to geographic constraints.

One of the most exciting ideas we are pursuing would lead to many small veteran-owned businesses being started around the country. It is a wireless transmission technology that will enable us to help veterans become their own wireless Internet service providers. This will help many of the veterans from rural areas that would otherwise have a hard time finding employment.

I am also extremely excited about the work I get to do now as a board member of the Disabled Veteran Business Alliance. It helps me focus my giving to my veteran community. Our members have served from the Vietnam era through the conflicts in Iraq and Afghanistan. We have started a nationwide push and are getting ready to help veterans all over the country. Our goal is to truly be inclusive and help to usher in the next era of veteran entrepreneurship. In creating programs for this organization, we plan to apply the same lessons that I am applying to my own business of selflessness and common purpose that I learned from the Spartans and the early and current Marine Raiders.

Take a lesson from the warriors of our past. The next time you build a team of highly exceptional people, find that shield or paddle. Find that common goal that the team can emotionally adopt, and put all else out of the way. It will give your team something to focus on besides themselves, and the results will be exceptional.

As I finally reflect on my words here today, I would like to dedicate them to Corporal Seamus McLean Davey, who was killed in action on October 21, 2005. He died in a place that most will never know, protecting his brothers to the very end. I credit him as one of the reasons I am able to sit here and write this today. May his and all others' sacrifices not be forgotten. *Never Above You, Never Below You, Always Beside You.*

Greater love hath no man than this that a man lay down his life for his friend.

—John 15:13

Biographical Comments by the Lead Author

Dave has over eighteen years of experience leading groups of highly motivated professionals to accomplish complex tasks while exceeding expectations, both in the military and in the private sector. Under his leadership, his company, Global Blue, has grown from a start-up in 2011 to a multimillion-dollar corporation that is providing groundbreaking technology solutions to government and commercial clients alike. Global Blue has been recognized as one of the upcoming disabled veteran–owned IT businesses in the state of California. In January 2016, Global Blue was awarded the John K. Lopez Award for business excellence by the California Department of Veterans Affairs. Dave developed his unique leadership philosophy during his service with the United States Marine Corps. From leading react teams on the fence line in Guantanamo Bay, Cuba, to running anti-IED patrols in a force recon team in Iraq, he had the chance to learn valuable lessons in leadership and decisiveness. Mission accomplishment is something that Marines are well-known for, and Dave ingrained this into his company's culture. He holds a BS in Business Administration, summa cum laude, from California State University–Sacramento. He also graduated from the Marine Officer Candidate School with honors. In 2008, he was one of the first California real estate brokers to earn the LEED accreditation. He has a passion to help other veterans find gainful employment or start their own businesses. He currently serves on the board of directors for the Disabled Veteran Business Alliance, where I also serve. Dave studied in my programs at the Institute of Entrepreneurial Leadership at John F. Kennedy University under the Operation Hand Salute umbrella, and I have mentored him in some of his commercial ventures. Dave and I have similar goals in life and are BFF.

Chapter 18

Change Is What Happens on the Way to Somewhere New

Deborah Steinthal

A wise person once asked me a question: "What brought you here? Are you running from something or towards something?" My answer? "Neither. It was time for a change." I had just made the move from Silicon Valley to Napa Valley—away from my Chief Marketing Officer position at a technology dotcom start-up and into the wine industry.

This anecdote is core to what makes me tick: relentless reinvention. I always seem to be on the way to somewhere new. A mentor once suggested that my energy needs to be tuned and channeled, much like "a blow torch—a lot more effective when focused." Far from haphazard, my reinventions have always felt like the next natural step—nothing I could have planned for.

Eighteen months ago, I was chatting about this with my younger sister, an accomplished neurosurgeon in Germany. Much to my surprise, she answered back, "You chose a very different path than I did. You require change like plants need water. I don't." Since high school, Barbara has been living in the same house in a small German town. For over twenty years, she has been driving thirty minutes daily through the Taunus Mountains to another small German town where she established her medical practice and has been married to the same man for over twenty years as well. During the same period, I lived in Germany, New Hampshire, Pennsylvania, New York City, Israel, and Massachusetts, as well as Menlo Park, Atherton, and Napa Valley in

California, and now in Bainbridge Island, Washington. I have had two husbands and have worked for over 150 different companies (ten inside as an executive, 140 as clients of my consulting practice).

For very different reasons, my sis and I are both successful and fulfilled both personally and professionally. Barbara needs a stable foundation to be able to focus deeply as a world-class physician. I need to see the world from many different lenses to advice leaders strategically on how to grow competitive businesses. Somehow, my restless pursuit of change has given me the knowledge and skills to generate close to a billion dollars in incremental revenues for my clients—small-size to midsize business owners—over the last fourteen years.

Only recently did I realize that a majority of folks are like my sister. They do not proactively try to transform their lives unless they are forced to. And a large majority may not need change to be happy and fulfilled. However, those who do seek out change, or who get stuck or burned out on occasion, may want to read this chapter. If you thrive on change or simply need to change, you have to find ways to get outside your comfort zone. Or nothing will change. This means becoming comfortable with taking risks. Taking risks became easier once I began trusting my own problem-solving skills.

Sometimes, I Had to Jump Off a Cliff to Get Somewhere

The first time I learned this lesson, I had an amazing ride. From 1979 through 1982, I sold advertising space for two trade publications. Building on this strong foundation in sales, I began shifting my career to marketing—where my passion was flaring up. While interviewing for marketing positions in New York City, I found that my publishing background translated poorly into the consumer goods world, where all the marketing action was at that time. So I jumped off the cliff at age twenty-six, moved to Tel Aviv with my new Israeli husband, and eventually launched a marketing services agency with a well-seasoned American advertising and publicity expert as partner.

In hindsight, this took a lot of gumption. I had to learn about marketing on the job. In those days, fortunately, the bar was low. There were less than a handful of experienced marketing experts in all of Israel. Part of me was delightfully oblivious of what I didn't know; the other part wasn't afraid to figure it out. Over the next four years, we collaborated with dozens of Israeli technology, food, and beverage clients. We made some big mistakes, but I learned a ton and even won several national awards for our marketing of collateral work and videography.

What I didn't know couldn't stop me, so I went with the flow. I underestimated the male-dominated Middle Eastern culture and didn't know how hard it would be as a young female to earn the respect and trust of a primarily Israeli male client base. I learned quickly to let questions go to my (silent) male partner while I was presenting to clients; it was much like an ancient era, when Far Eastern husbands appeared as the "front men," although their wives were actually pulling the puppeteer strings. Eventually, questions were directed to me.

After launching my own company in Israel, I eventually made another career move into aerospace and defense. I eventually landed my dream job in the heart of the Silicon Valley, where I ran business incubators converting aerospace technology into commercial ventures for Lockheed Martin. Friends ask me often: how did I achieve such major career shifts?

Once I Broke Through Fear, I Launched in Unexpected, New Directions

As I moved through the next phase of my career and into early motherhood, I had to confront many fears. The thing about fear is it paralyzes you and makes you feel incompetent. While reinventing myself, I began building authentic relationships with people who were much wiser than me and who were eager to help make me a success. Once I learned to believe in my own potential, it was easier to get others to believe in me.

I found the one person who "discovered me." For me, this person was Jack. After returning from Israel, I thought I could leverage my extensive marketing agency experience into the New York City advertising agency world. I soon discovered that the agency world wanted me to start at the bottom of the ladder and that I was overqualified. After nine months of frustrating job search, I met Jack, who was a special adviser to the president of Textron Defense Systems.

Jack decided that I fit their new model, as they wanted to shift from a more rigid culture to a more nimble, externally focused one. Textron's new head of marketing hired me to research and implement new export partnerships with Israel, Japan, and Europe. This position stretched my external networking and internal change management capacities to the extreme, as I ventured out into the global business development arena. This new career was far more intellectually satisfying than the agency world! I found creative ways to work the old boy's network, eventually steering the company away from a dependence on United States defense contract work into a new era of international joint development programs.

I then went on to forge close relationships with the most brilliant, disruptive change makers I could find. These folks are not usually naturally born mentors but are great models for success in breaking through cultural norms. They are frequently isolated from core enterprise culture, have no allegiance to the tried and tested way of doing things, and often require someone who can be their liaison with the political side of the system.

When one of Textron's brightest chief scientists, Dr. Joe, first called me into his office, I knew I had to find a way to follow him around. He taught me the use of paraphrase and synopsis. A sign on his office door read, "Until you put something in writing, it ain't real." He also taught me how to circumvent obstacles. We spent many an hour in the back rooms of the Pentagon and in congressional aides' offices, sipping Pabst Blue Ribbon and plotting tactics that would change collaborative development legislation in Congress—appropriating over $500 million per year to dual use technology development, enabling commercial application spinoff. He also taught me to dislike corporate politics so much that I eventually moved on to a decade-long love affair with the more nimble entrepreneurial start-up scene. I left aerospace eventually to join Oracle and then went inside four high-tech start-ups.

I became fearless at problem-solving. The 1990s were excruciatingly difficult for women trying to break through glass ceilings of corporate America. This was especially so in industries as dominated by male culture as I experienced in aerospace and defense and later in high technology. The male approach to building relationships on the golf course or in strip bars was not necessarily effective for us upwardly mobile, female executives. We were exploring new horizons and learning by trial and error how to have impact. Resilience became my motto: I would gnaw away at a problem until I broke through. I trusted there was always a way around a situation, which taught me to look for possibilities, not dead ends.

One of my favorite stories about problem-solving is when I was given the title of Queen Bee by a top South Korean government decision maker. While at Lockheed, I was program director for a large, competitive proposal—to win hundreds of millions of dollars for the development and manufacturing of a GPS satellite system funded by the South Korean government. I realized that women had little to no stature with this customer, which became a big problem to solve, as the division president had gone out on the limb when he appointed me to this position.

I soon realized that I could steal a page from my previous Middle East experience. I appointed properly pedigreed, all-male engineers to the primary customer relationship team and gave my top male engineer the highly visible program director business card—properly scribed in Korean, of course. Although in taking this leap of faith, I was initially fearful of diluting my power base.

When the South Korean team of government decision makers conducted a week-long site visit, my top engineer led the discussions, even sitting in my chair at my desk during our final meeting with the Korean officials. I was sitting quietly in the corner of my office, observing the negotiation, when the top Korean decision maker suddenly turned to me and proudly exclaimed, "So you are the Queen Bee!" Living in the shadows had been unnerving, but I realized at that moment that I had made a good decision for my company and, in doing so, had built a stronger power base. I also learned that being female in a male-dominated culture gave me the freedom to creatively experiment. After all, I had little to lose.

Early in 1998, I decided to leave Silicon Valley. I was increasingly dissatisfied with the Valley's values and was reevaluating the impact of raising my teenage daughter in the middle of such fierce, conspicuous consumption. Stuck, trying to build a path among too many choices, I was acting like a kid at an amusement park—which rides to choose? I was stuck is a highly emotional journey. For many, this is burnout, unless you learn to reframe and bring some fun into the transition process.

Once I Got Clear about What Mattered Most, I Found Myself Unstuck!

Giovanni Boccaccio, the fourteenth-century Italian writer, once said, "You must read, you must persevere, you must sit up nights, and you must inquire, and exert the utmost power of your mind. If one way does not lead to the desired meaning, take another way; if obstacles arise, then try another way; until, if your strength holds out, you will find that clear path which at first looked dark."

Burnout is nothing more than getting stuck without a story about where you are headed next. When this happens to me, I have learned to make time to become more creative. Once I own a new story again, my energy resurfaces, momentum gathers, the right people show up, plans start to formulate almost on their own, and positive change happens.

My good friend and colleague, Brenda, handles change and chaos with healthy detachment and is rarely flustered. Brenda was my business director at Lockheed Martin, where I launched and ran my second technology business incubator. Brenda has always known she would accomplish her life's aspirations, because throughout her life, she followed a simple little process that she revealed to me: "Between the ages of eighteen and twenty-five, I began cutting out pictures of things I liked and inserting them into a diary. Without really giving it much thought, I inserted the picture of a house I liked, an elaborately decorated cake, and a story of how to sail. I eventually forgot the diary existed. Years later, I found my diary filled with pictures. I was amazed to realize that over the years, I had developed an impressive sailor's curriculum vitae. I had become successful at decorating cakes as a professional, and I had bought several homes almost identical to the ones in the pictures. Years after I achieved these objectives, it then dawned on me that I had subconsciously gotten involved in goal setting. By committing to my objectives formally through pictures, somehow I consciously set the stage for figuring out how to reach them."

Here is what I learned from Brenda: I began to keep a diary, which has given me a voice to my future vision. I knew from my corporate change work how emotional-level visualization practices could motivate changes in behavior. As such, Brenda's story inspired me to compose the circumstances that could nurture my soul. This visualization work ultimately led to my future husband, eighteen months before I actually bumped into him. Here is what I wrote in my diary at that time:

> The Silicon Valley has turned stifling and cold. I crave the intellect, culture, and reality of what is art—organic and natural. Picture the village, the small town where neighbors know neighbors. Picture colleagues who are nurturing and understand how kinship promotes greatness. Picture children growing into adulthood, secure they can reach for the stars and fail and succeed equally with the love and support they need. Picture a lifetime of travel and intimacy and growth. Picture the house in the country, the bountiful garden, and a big dinner with friends who have stories to share and much love. Dusk in the trees, gnats in the shrubs, toddlers dozing, exhausted and dirty from games and sports. An eternity of emotions and hopes and dreams—memories, just forming to become stories told later. A loving body slips into bed alongside mine and stays and forever shares the glow of the aftereffects of an evening of friendship. Oh, joy! I can visualize these images—were they

mine to trace and hold close and memorize; were they mine to turn into memories some day?

A few months later, my fourteen-year-old daughter and I moved to the Napa Valley to decompress, rekindle, and continue to build our bonds. Before too long, I launched into the wine business as a strategy consultant, eventually focusing on artisanal food sectors, and I developed an insatiable appetite for and deep expertise at reconfiguring private organizations for growth and success.

Newly moved into our Napa Valley home, here are notes from my diary: "I finally met my mirror image, my partner in life, my love, my happiness, my soul—John." We have now been together seventeen years, married for thirteen. During our time in Napa, my husband and I lovingly restored the Coombs School, a one-hundred-year-old schoolhouse and vineyard property. The property carries with it a cargo ship of memories of our friends dining alfresco with us, telling stories of how they created their California wine, artisanal food businesses, and the families behind them.

My Life's Biggest Achievements Came from Listening Hard to Others

While remodeling our Napa Valley schoolhouse, my husband and I listened to each other a great deal, even though our differences seemed destined to divide us. Not surprisingly, close friends and colleagues shared additional distinctive concepts about our project. But by listening to each other and others, we transformed a classic renovation project into something extraordinary. Our marriage was strengthened by it, and I learned the true power of collaboration. We wanted to get it right for ourselves, the old house, and the beautiful property it occupied!

A decade into our life in the Napa Valley, I was wooed inside an advanced analytics tech start-up company based out of New York City after the big recession gutted my California consulting practice. I began commuting monthly from Napa to New York City. This was my fourth start-up, and it will likely be my last—the founder's funding dried up, and it is unlikely I will have appetite for that level or risk and uncertainty again.

I challenged my heart to drive more decisions while fighting reason with my conscience. I was facing yet another fork in the road professionally and personally. While I dared my heart to speak, I realized that the last twenty years had passed in a blur due to the speed of my professional commitments. I reflected that life had abruptly become fragile. I was ready to make friends and family a pressing priority. John and I had to make a *gut-wrenching* decision: it was time to sell the home we loved so much, to move elsewhere where I could slow down my career and earnings in order to live at a normal pace.

A favorite quote from Steve Goodier kept going through my head: "I have not always chosen the safest path. I've made my mistakes, plenty of them. I sometimes jump too soon and fail to appreciate the consequences. But I've learned something important along the way: I've learned to heed the call of my heart. I've learned that the safest path is not always the best path and I've learned that the voice of fear is not always to be trusted."

In the summer of 2014, we moved to Bainbridge Island, Washington, where we now reside and where I fell in love with the place and the people. For me it was time for change. I had lived in the Napa Valley for almost fifteen years—longer than anywhere else in my life! For my husband, a third-generation Californian who had always resided two hours from his birthplace, this became a stressful journey. I will forever treasure his deep loyalty in accompanying me in this next chapter.

Listening altruistically to others has allowed me to hear new things. During this same period, my mother, recently widowed and diagnosed with Alzheimer's, also moved from California to Bainbridge Island. And I also became a caregiver to my eighty-eight-year-old uncle who was dying of cancer and who had been living alone in Texas. My longstanding, active listening skills were getting the high polish as I tried to understand my husband's tussle with unfamiliar environs, my mother's struggle with losing her memory, and my uncle's heartfelt wishes in the final weeks of his life.

What I know to be the right answer may not always be so. When we first moved to Bainbridge Island, my husband was stridently against buying a new home until I had rebooted my career. While my voice of reason told me this was a nonissue, as we had the money and I had always been an earner, I listened hard. In this case, I chose to listen to my husband with my heart, and I realized that he was highly stressed about this big transition in his life and was mourning his Napa home and life there. We delayed purchasing a new home for over a year.

My conscience told me that waiting was important to him. By signaling, he had been heard, we undoubtedly saved our marriage. My reasoning was also spot-on concerning my ability to earn. My relaunched Pacific Northwest consulting practice has been booming beyond expectation.

I am learning to not always cede to "what you know to be right," because it may not be the answer to your situation at hand. I have discovered how confidence, intellect, and heart can all come together if I understand priority and timing. This approach to facilitating change has allowed all my voices to feel deliciously balanced at times. Some may call this wisdom.

Ninety Percent of a Successful Transition Is about Harnessing Courage

While our move to Washington was exactly what I needed and enabled me to be more available for family and friends, this transition has been the most complex of all, dealing with change *and* evolving to a new life phase for myself—I am finding courage through reliving old stories in a new place. At times I feel much like a trapeze artist operating without a safety net as I cultivate new levels of resilience while steering us through this new life chapter.

Early into this phase, I am surprised by how much I still question, Have I chosen the right direction this time? Who am I to take this responsibility on for others? How many more opportunities will I have to experience? I am discovering that life has abruptly become so fleeting.

Here is what I am learning:

1. Life doesn't come in neat little packages.

Because of my manifold interests, I find it sometimes agonizing to recount my story with ease. When we moved to the Pacific Northwest, this was a key challenge again: should I say I was headed back inside a tech firm as an executive, or branching out into strategy consulting again? I told my husband one day, in extreme frustration when he wondered out loud why I wasn't closing in on my professional next step, "If you keep expecting neat little answers, you miss the real opportunity."

This time, my real opportunity was not the heady, new tech start-up job where my search had been focused almost frantically for a year. My phone simply continued ringing with winery consulting clients looking to hire my firm. While working on fresh projects, I soon reenergized my portfolio with new Northwest clients, applying what I know best. I have been repurposing old tools to solve new problems and applying old lessons to new situations. I finally am able to claim victory with a renewed sense of purpose that goes deeper than the adrenaline produced from start-ups, and I have the flexibility that allows me more time with friends and family.

During the most intense period of this transition, I ran a variety of scenarios, forcing myself outside my box and engaging others in creating new scenarios with me. As I worked at these scenarios that were shaping my new, best future story, I started craving more stability, a page from my sister's book. I have purposely slowed down to rekindle old passions, relearning how to play guitar after thirty-five years, having long lunches with friends, writing, working out, and planning a five-week-long vacation to Australia with my sister, among other things.

2. I do trust my innate abilities! I do! I do!

I gain comfort from this refrain, not unlike Dorothy in *The Wizard of Oz*, rubbing her red ruby shoes together. Ultimately, it is my well-trained instinct that gives me confidence to commit to the really *big* decisions. When my husband and entourage told me we could sell our Napa property for an amount, my gut told me we could sell it for half a million dollars more. And we did. When my instinct told me we should sell with a sense of urgency, I am happy we did. A 6.8-point earthquake hit the Napa Valley sixty days after we closed on the property and reduced our well from over 20 GPM to 3 GPM in drought-torn California. I never thought we would be thankful for selling this beautiful estate when we did.

In Conclusion

I read somewhere that people either are a product of their childhood or are rebelling against the very notion of their childhood. I am definitely the former, and my sister Barbara is the rebel. Dad was a restless soul too, and because of him, we grew up across four continents. My father was born a Jew in World War II Germany. He was extracted to the United States through the underground in 1944 where he joined my grandfather in upstate New York. It is from dad that I learned to relentlessly pursue what was next.

A product of the *Great* Recession and her generation, my twenty-nine-year-old daughter is a restless soul as well. She learned early that survival is about harnessing change to get somewhere exciting. I wish her a lifetime of energizing discovery ahead, on the way to somewhere new!

The question for me has always been about what to aim for, never how to get change to happen. As I approach the young age of sixty, I ask myself how many more life transitions I have to look forward to, or am I finally craving a stable foundation like my sister Barbara?

I love telling stories that help people get out of their comfort zone and achieve more with their lives. One of my favorite anecdotes is, "The golfer asks her coach, 'Why do I always hit that tree?' And the coach answers, 'Because you always aim for it!'"

As such, I am as determined as ever to aim for something other than a dumb tree on my way to somewhere new!

I am driven by Mary Oliver's piece in *The Journey*:

> One day you finally knew what you had to do, and began, though the voices around you keep shouting their bad advice . . . little by little, as you left their voices behind, the stars began to burn through the sheets of clouds, and there was a new voice which you slowly recognized as your own, that kept you company as you strode deeper and deeper into the world.

Biographical Comments by the Lead Author

Deborah is a dynamic and restless soul who can't sit still. Born in Lima, Perú, raised in Belgium and Germany, she has lived, worked, and traveled throughout Europe, Asia, the Middle East, and North America and is now based out of Bainbridge Island, Washington. Deborah's expertise is in the area of family business transformation, rapid growth strategy, and board and leadership development. A former technology executive at Oracle, Lockheed Martin Research Labs, and four tech start-ups, for the last fifteen years she has been the trusted strategy adviser to over 140 owners of midsize companies, many of whom have become world leaders in their respective industries. Deborah's passion is to collaborate with talented business leaders and enable them to realize their core purpose by envisioning new scenarios and transforming their companies from start-up to enormous success. Avid about giving kids the tools to chart ever-changing lives, Deborah was an early education reformer and has served on several boards including New Tech Foundation seeded by the Bill and Melinda Gates Foundation. She is broadly published in the national business press and is an invited speaker and panelist and is widely quoted for research on key topics, such as family business transition. Deborah and I have brainstormed on various projects and maintained our friendship through the years, now across state lines. We share an interest in the opportunities for growing family businesses. She was a member of the Board of my Institute of Entrepreneurial Leadership during its formative years while she lived in the Napa Valley, and we see each other as our travels connect us, most recently in Seattle for dinner, but who knows where next!

Chapter 19

My Secret Sauce: How Can I Help You?

Roger Werne

Growing up, I was a good but not brilliant student, a good but not great athlete, and essentially an all-around good kid. In high school, I discovered what would become one of my lifelong passions: pole-vaulting in the sport of track-and-field. It was the first thing in which I was better than almost everyone else. As a senior, I won the Northern California high school championship, which was the key to winning an athletic scholarship to San Jose State, the best track-and-field college in the United States. In my senior year, in 1965, I was the eighth ranked collegiate pole-vaulter, twenty-ninth in the United States, and sixty-seventh in the world. Pole-vaulting indeed gave me the knowledge and confidence that I could be really good at something if I worked hard enough.

I majored in engineering and was initially a mediocre student until my senior year when I realized that engineering would pay a lot better than pole-vaulting. It was time to start studying, and sure enough, I improved from a C+ to an A student in one year. Having the motivation to learn made all the difference in the world to me.

Later on, I finished a master's degree with a 4.0 GPA, married my college sweetheart of four years, Leilani "Lani" Nolan—also a Los Gatos and San Jose State grad—and it was time to be off to the University of California at Berkeley for my PhD studies.

But before getting on with my PhD, I had the opportunity to work during the summer at EG&G Inc. in San Ramon, California.

The company was one of the most important government contractors for what was then the Atomic Energy Commission (now the US Department of Energy). This job came about in a very happenstance way. I arrived a little late to the first day of a graduate course. There were two seats available, one on each side of the room, and I arbitrarily chose the far one. It happened to be next to an older engineer named Bob Lee, who would later become my first engineering mentor at EG&G and later led to my career at the Lawrence Livermore National Laboratory. Where would I be today if I had chosen the other seat? To use a line from *Indiana Jones and the Last Crusade*, "I chose wisely."

Family life began in earnest in 1969 with the birth of our first daughter, Lisa, and in 1972 when our second daughter, Alison, came along. My wife, Lani, was the "queen" of the family, insisting among other things that we have dinner together every night with no TV. In retrospect, that turned out to be a very wise practice, for over the years, I found that it encouraged communication on all subjects and helped create a family bond that survives to this day. And the practice continues with my two daughters and their families.

In 1970, the family settled into a suburban lifestyle in San Ramon. Kids were in school, Lani managed the house and family life, and I brought home the paychecks. One important family practice that my daughters later brought to my attention was that each evening around the dinner table, I would ask each of them what they learned that day. In so doing, I reinforced to them my belief that if you learn one new thing each day, then your day is a success. Learning one new thing each day became an important part in my daughters' education, and it is now being followed into the next generation. I believe this is a great lifetime goal.

Back on the education and career front, after one-quarter as a student at the University of California, Berkeley, I decided to work full-time, returning to EG&G and attending the university part-time. I worked at EG&G for six years, designing experiments for underground nuclear tests in Nevada. This was an exciting time, as we were deriving a great deal of knowledge from the nuclear weapons testing program and the associated experiments.

In 1974, I joined Lawrence Livermore National Laboratory (LLNL), which was operated by the University of California, as a mechanical engineer, and in 1976, two years later, I did complete my PhD. At LLNL, I continued to grow and learn and was always willing to help others to get the job done. This "How can I help you?" attitude would be the hallmark of my career at Lawrence Livermore and elsewhere.

I discovered this quality about myself in an unusual way. In 1980, I was promoted to supervisor of the Applied Mechanics Group within engineering. Almost all members had MS or PhD degrees. I had gone from peer to boss. No longer was I doing "real engineering" but was now supposed to direct the efforts of others, each of whom was quite skilled in their particular field. I sometimes felt useless. A singular event demonstrated to me what leadership was about, and it became the first lesson about my "secret sauce." A young engineer needed a master's thesis research project and asked for my help. I had an idea about computer modeling of the welding process and some experiments that would confirm the accuracy of the models. I helped design the project and obtained research funding for the effort. The project moved forward to completion, and he got his MS degree. Soon after, he entered his thesis project into a national contest for welding research. A few months later, we got the news that he had won first place, a very exciting result.

The learning experience for me was that leadership is about getting work done through the hands of others. Your job as the leader is to do what's necessary to make them successful. Your job is to help them do their job better!

In the late '80s, during a weak US economy, the federal government decided there was valuable technology inside the laboratories that should be moved to the private sector to create jobs. The lab director at that time, John Nuckolls, gave me the task of developing and leading the program. That was the seed corn for my later entrepreneurial career.

At about the same time in the late '80s, I began my parallel career as a pole vault coach. It must have begun as a midlife crisis, because my desire to take up pole-vaulting at the masters (over age forty) level of competition was rekindled. I needed a place to practice, so I volunteered as the pole vault coach two days a week at San Ramon Valley High School in Danville. Thirty-two years later, I still coach there and compete in masters competitions. Coaching for me is not about pole-vaulting; it's about helping young people grow by focusing on skill development, working hard, persevering, and dealing with failure and success. In pole-vaulting, you either clear the crossbar or you don't. It's an unambiguous measure of success or failure with no one to count on but yourself. It teaches young people an important life lesson, and I get to help. As I said earlier, pole-vaulting is a lifelong passion, but it's the helping that's the secret sauce.

In 1995, people associated with the University of California San Francisco (UCSF) Medical School approached me about starting a company to make surgical instruments for magnetic resonance (MR) image–guided surgery, a promising new surgical paradigm. The idea was that with the medical expertise at UCSF and the material science know-how at Lawrence Livermore, the new company would surely be successful. The company was called ITI Medical Technologies. It was actually successful in producing a line of FDA-approved surgical instruments for MR-guided and conventional surgery. There were sales of the instruments, but the market never grew like originally anticipated. ITI lasted for over four years before it ran out of money and closed its doors. The company's product line was sold and investors received $0.10 back on each invested dollar. However, the instruments are still on the market to this day under a different company name. ITI was ahead of its time. While not a financial success, I learned a great deal about the process for getting a product from a research mode into the hands of users. It isn't easy!

I returned to the Lawrence Livermore National Laboratory in early 2000 and joined the Non-Proliferation, Arms Control and International Security Program as chief engineer. The mission of this program would be amplified significantly after September 11, 2001. I then spent a period of time working in the Department of Energy's National Nuclear Security Administration (NNSA) office in Washington, DC, educating first responders in places like New York City about weapons of mass destruction. It was enlightening to see how government works; it is definitely not as poorly as most people think.

In 2006, I had the opportunity to return to the technology transfer office at LLNL. Now it was the right time. Finding commercial uses for laboratory technology, dealing with private sector companies, and interacting with the business and entrepreneurial communities were again on my plate, and that's where I am today.

In looking back over my career, I find that leadership is about helping other people be successful. Of course, the action of "helping" has many facets. Help can be the development and articulation of a vision so that people have an idea of what the final results of their collective efforts will look like. It can also be the development of projects, tasks, job assignments, and resources and the development of the knowledge and skills in the people executing the project. Indeed all these are absolutely necessary to eventually fulfill the vision.

The fact is that helping others is almost always situational, with development of the people being the most difficult and challenging part. The leader can contribute to the success of others in small ways through a simple statement, like "Learn something new every day," by teaching them a new skill, by helping them develop a project plan, or simply by leading by example and conducting one's self with integrity, honesty, and respecting others in all interactions, truly through "professionalism," as Bill Wiersma will discuss in chapter 23 in the next section. This is where my mojo lies in my professional, coaching, and family lives—helping individuals become more successful at what they do is my life's work! It has been and continues to be great fun. A life well lived with chapters to follow and a bit more pole-vaulting!

Biographical Comments by the Lead Author

Roger Werne has three important aspects to his life: his family, his forty-five-year career as an engineer, and his continuing hobby as a high school track-and-field pole vault coach, currently entering his thirty-second year as a coach. Pole-vaulting took him from high school to college at San Jose State, then the best track-and-field team in the country. His love for engineering then led him to a PhD at UC Berkeley. Currently, he leads the Lawrence Livermore National Laboratory's outreach to the entrepreneurial community to help seed new companies based on Laboratory technology, and he still coaches young pole-vaulters. Roger and I first met years ago at a meeting of the Keiretsu Forum, an organized group of private individuals that invest in budding ventures. We share similar background and interests in the nuclear and energy industry. After all, what is a better toy than the Fusion Research Center at the Livermore Laboratory? Roger and I also share an interest in entrepreneurship and a love for leisurely cruising the oceans of the world in a midsize ship.

Chapter 20

If You Want to Hear God Laugh, Tell Him Your Plans!

Mark Powell

I grew up in Frederick, Maryland. The greatest fortune that ever happened to me was having parents that inspired me with love, confidence, guidance, and understanding. They instilled in me the belief that I could become whatever I wanted with hard work and diligence.

My Father's Story

My parents, Lawrence and Betty Powell, worked hard and were very creative in making ends meet for our family. We did not have much, but we had a foundation of love. For thirty-five years, my mother was a beautician. She had a single-chair salon in our basement and worked many hours per week to provide additional money for us.

Over her desk in her salon, she kept a quote: "If you want to hear God laugh, tell him your plans." As a child, I never understood the significance and power of this statement. Now that I am in my fifties and my parents have both passed, I truly have gained an understanding of this statement. I will provide two examples that will show you that no matter how well you may anticipate the results, life happens, and your outcomes may be extremely different from your intentions.

My father, Lawrence "Bunny" M. Powell, was born in 1923. He was an adequate student. His upbringing was one of tremendous turmoil.

His family was on the "wrong side of town." The family stories were of bootlegging and other questionable behaviors.

In 1941, as a senior in high school, his brother Charles died at an early age. Soon thereafter, his mother passed away in 1942. During the fall, his father grew very ill, and Bunny left high school for a second time and began working. His brother Austin had procured a job as a foreman in the shipyard in Baltimore, Maryland. My father accepted a job as a welder.

Frederick, Maryland, is approximately fifty miles from where my father worked in Baltimore. This was way before interstate highways had been built. The commute was over two hours each way over dilapidated roads in vehicles that had none of the modern conveniences. He and his brother would leave at 4:00 a.m. and arrive home after 7:00 p.m. each day. This was physically grueling, as the work was very difficult.

In early 1943, Bunny's father passed away. World War II was well underway. All able-bodied men were required to register for the draft and serve in the military. Due to the work my father was performing, building Liberty ships for the US Navy, he was exempted from services as his labor was supporting the war effort.

Now that his father was gone, his need to provide financial support for his family had diminished, and my father sought another opportunity, as the commute and the work were extremely difficult. So my father began to think about a major change in his life.

With World War II in full motion, my father decided that it was time to serve. He looked at the Marine Corps, the Army, and the Navy. He knew that he did not want to be a Marine, and the Army was not very appealing. His thought process led him to enlist in the Navy.

Why the Navy? There were several reasons Bunny wanted to serve in the Navy. First of all, he had been working at the shipyard and had an interest in ships. The most compelling reason for his decision was, however, that he viewed the Navy as the safest career choice.

Even though the Navy was actively engaged in war fighting, my father viewed his chances of survival to be the highest in the Navy. He had the skills as a welder and thought that the Navy would utilize these skills and that he would be working in a shipyard or at a dry dock at a location far from the actual fighting. He also thought that if he were to be assigned to a ship, he would be in a far safer position than in the Army or with the Marines. Aboard ship, you have a place to sleep and warm food, he thought. This was greatly preferable to the thought of being a "dogface" or "grunt" and sleeping in the field and eating food from cans slightly warmed up from small fires.

My father enlisted in the Navy during early 1943 and was assigned to attend boot camp in Bainbridge, Maryland. My father was physically gifted. He played many sports and could run and swim extremely well. My father was also very strong-willed. His parents did not provide him with much guidance, and he learned to survive on his own. This was during the Depression, so the times were tough, and he was truly a result of this environment—a bit of a scrapper and a fighter.

During his training in boot camp, my father was taken from his group and separated. He did not know what was going on, but he was assigned to a different training program. In fact, he was sent to a new naval base in Ft. Pierce, Florida. This type of training was extremely different from Bainbridge, where he was originally assigned. The level of intensity was rigorous on both the physical and mental training. My father was in one of the first classes of special warriors that the Navy was developing for special warfare. He was trained in survival, extreme physical intensity, and the deployment of explosives/ordnance.

Ft. Pierce, Florida, in fact, turned out to be the birthplace of the US Navy SEALs (the US Navy SEAL Museum is now located there), and my father was in training there. After the completion of his training, Bunny was assigned to Sixth Naval Beach Battalion and was transferred to the Little Creek Naval Base in Norfolk, Virginia.

In preparation for upcoming missions in World War II, the military understood that many of the future engagements would be centered upon amphibious assaults. These were attacks that would come from the sea to engage land targets. The Sixth Naval Beach Battalion was created, among others, to include self-contained units that would be deployed to expedite and organize large-scale amphibious assaults. The Sixth Naval Beach Battalion contained beach masters to organize all activities on the shore, engineering to clear obstacles and mines, medical teams to assist with the wounded, and Special Forces to arrive early to clear the beach for the subsequent invasion. My father was trained as a member of the latter group. His "safe choice" of the Navy was now looking very differently.

On December of 1943, my father was shipped out to England. While in England, his unit underwent very specialized training for a large assault. On June 5, 1944, the Special Forces group of the Sixth Naval Beach Battalion was loaded on small ships (LCI) from ships in the British Channel. They were heading to Normandy, France.

At approximately 6:30 a.m. (H hour), my father's unit was dropped into the surf at Omaha Beach. This was the beginning of the invasion of France, known as Operation Overlord, or, more commonly, D-day.

I guess almost everyone has seen the D-day attack portion of the movie *Saving Private Ryan*. Almost all experts agree that this scene depicts Omaha Beach on that morning as extremely accurate. My father's position was approximately one hundred yards from this movie reenactment, in an area denoted as Fox Green sector.

My father experienced some of the most dangerous combat of World War II. It was reported that the Special Forces unit of the early invasion had 40 percent of their personnel either killed or wounded.

My father was one of the lucky ones that made it but never spoke with me about D-day until one day in 1994, as we were having lunch. I asked him, "Were you afraid?" He stopped and really thought about his response. He replied, "I was afraid for about fifteen minutes, and then we organized ourselves and executed. We all did our job."

From Europe, my father returned to the United States for a brief leave and then boarded a ship in California and sailed out in the Pacific Ocean. He participated in other multiple invasions in the Pacific theater.

Some were very small, but others are well known, such as the liberation of the Philippines and Okinawa.

My father later told me that he looked at his choices in 1943 and developed a plan. His major goal was to survive World War II. He executed this plan and joined the Navy, thinking that this was the best route for him to achieve this outcome. While he did survive the war and was never wounded, his course was totally unexpected.

I always thought that the nickname Bunny was quite ironic, as he was physically and mentally hardened by his childhood, and I never saw him afraid, even during the end of his life as he battled terminal cancer.

During my last conversation with him, I asked him, "Are you afraid of dying?" His last words to me were, "Why would I be afraid of dying? I lived my life like a man. Now it is time for me to die like a man."

As a young nineteen-year-old, he made a decision that was life changing. The war also changed him in many ways. He lived at a time of tremendous strife; however, he did not see the larger context of World War II on a global or strategic perspective. He only saw it through the lens of a young person with a simple outcome: survival.

Bunny served with distinction in the war and was highly decorated. He won the Croix de Guerre from the French government, and his unit was awarded the highest decoration available to a military unit, the Presidential Unit Citation. After this experience, my father developed an intense love for the United States and our nation's core beliefs. He was a patriot and truly believed that all citizens should perform civic service, be it in the military or working in their local community. His spirit had a tremendous impact on his life, but it also had a profound effect on my aspirations.

My Story

In the state of Maryland, all fourth-grade classes take an annual trip to Annapolis, Maryland. It continues today. In 1971, Mrs. Stine's fourth-grade class from North Frederick Elementary School embarked on this field trip, and it was a moment that forged a major element in my life.

During this field trip to Annapolis, Maryland, one of the stops was at the United States Naval Academy. While I have some pictures from this trip, my major memory was the sense of awe that I had for these young people in their crisp white uniforms. I also remember the majesty of the campus (the Yard) and how beautiful it was on this sunny May morning.

My mother was a chaperone on this trip, and she purchased a small pennant for me. Upon arriving at our home, I placed this small flag on the wall over my dressing mirror. It remained there for nine years. Every morning when I dressed, I would see that bold Naval Academy emblem. There was never a doubt in my mind that I would one day be wearing that wonderful white uniform on a beautiful spring day, walking across that inspiring campus.

The US Naval Academy is one of the most difficult institutions in the country for admittance. Midshipmen come from all over the nation, and the application process is very rigorous. It is extremely competitive, as you must be nominated by a US congressmen or senator, and then selected by the admission board. A candidate must have high grades, strong board scores, excellent references, and usually be successful athletes.

As I grew from this awestruck nine-year-old to an older child, I began learning more about the Naval Academy. I was so proud of my father's service in the Navy during World War II, and this hardened my intention to serve. We would take family trips to the Naval Academy, and I continued to learn more about this school. My father (my hero) was inspired by my wanting to attend the Naval Academy and serve as an officer. My father's commanding officer was Commander Caruso. He was a Naval Academy graduate, and my father considered him to be the greatest leader he ever saw during his lifetime.

As I developed, I had a lot of success in school and athletics, in wrestling and football. During the summers of my junior and senior year, I spent a lot of time training for wrestling. During this time, I was recruited by multiple schools for wrestling, but I was upfront with every coach; if I could gain admittance to the Naval Academy, it was the only choice for me.

On March 11, 1979, I received a telegraph from the Secretary of the Navy that I would be a member of the United States Naval Academy with the class of 1983! This was the moment that I had wanted for the previous eight years. I worked very hard for this event.

Attending the Naval Academy was very difficult. The school is really set up to make you fail in various areas and then motivate yourself to push harder and succeed. The greatest benefit is that you are surrounded by young men and women who are extremely motivated but really work closely. A class at the Naval Academy is truly a fraternity, and all help one another through the process. It was an honor to be a midshipman.

When one graduates from the Naval Academy, a few things happen. First of all, the Navy "hires" all graduates. In exchange for the world-class education, each graduate is required to serve in the Navy or Marine Corps for six years. This is certain. A person can also serve in multiple jobs, such as submarines, air, surface ships, or the US Marine Corps. My personal decision was to become a pilot in the Marines.

The decision to serve six years is not an option; it is a requirement. Therefore, an individual can rely on what their occupation will be for this period of their life. It is set.

Upon graduation, I was selected to remain at the Naval Academy for the summer as a drill officer for the incoming freshmen class (known as plebes). In August of 1983, I reported to Quantico, Virginia, as a member of H Company attending the Basic School (TBS). Every Marine officer must attend this six-month school before heading out to a specialty school. In my case, I was to attend Naval Flight School in Pensacola, Florida. This is a determined course of study that all must follow.

TBS trains a young officer to become a Marine. It has a strong focus on infantry, because every action, even those a pilot takes, is to support ground combat efforts. My future was determined, and I was working hard at TBS to become a Marine before becoming a Marine pilot.

The weather on October 11, 1983, was bad in Quantico, Virginia. It was approximately forty degrees, and rain was pummeling the area. H Company was scheduled to undergo night-time navigational training. This is a training program where members of the class are individually dropped into very thick woods. With only a compass and flashlight, you must navigate over a three-mile course from one position to another. It is a timed course and is graded for accuracy in completion.

As I was traversing my course through the woods, I came over a hill, and my left leg was trapped. I fell down the hill, but my leg would not move. In the process, I had dislocated my left knee. I tried to walk, but with every step I took, I immediately fell. I was lying in a driving rainstorm during the middle of the night, alone. We have whistles on our gear, and I began blowing this whistle. However, the rain was so loud that it took a long time for someone to get close enough to hear me.

I was finally found, and one of my classmates carried me for a long distance. Within a few hours, I was riding in an ambulance to the hospital. Two days later, I had reconstructive surgery on my left knee. It had significant damage with complete tears of the anterior cruciate and medial collateral ligaments and other injuries.

After seventeen months of treatments and additional surgery, I was separated from the US Marine Corps with an honorable discharge for medical reasons. I was out of the service as a service-disabled veteran.

Emotionally, this was very damaging to me. Since that field trip as a nine-year-old, I only had one goal in life: to attend the United States Naval Academy and serve as an officer in the naval service. That dream had now ended, and I needed to reset my life.

A few months after my separation, I began graduate school and met Lynne Kerr. We married a year later. Now, after thirty years together, two remarkable daughters, and two grandchildren, we have built a wonderful life together.

While I was going through my injury and recovery, I had never been so distraught. I could not see any future, much less the life that I have lived. Over the years, as challenges have arisen, I seem to go back to my mother's quote: "If you want to see God laugh, tell him your plans." Life is truly unexpected and will evolve in ways that you can never anticipate. We must all learn to roll with the punches.

My father took the "safe" route during World War II to stay as far away from potential harm as possible but was involved in some of the most dangerous combat the world experienced during the twentieth century. For many years, I had a singular goal to graduate from the US Naval Academy and serve as an officer in the naval service. In a brief moment, that goal was taken away.

None of us knows the future. We can take all the data and information we have on hand and make a logical decision, but the experience can change quickly. I guess this is called life. Live it to the fullest, but take time to do some good as you go on!

Biographical Comments by the Lead Author

Mark is the CEO of ARGO, a business owned by a service-disabled veteran. He has many years of experience in corporate leadership after leaving the service. As a Marine Corps officer and a service-disabled veteran, he was selected by the Maryland Gazette as "One of the Top 25 CEOs you Need to Know in Maryland." He was integral in founding the Chesapeake Innovation Center (CIC). The CIC was the first incubator in the United States focused on the development of new technologies for Homeland Security. He has served on many civic and charitable organizations in a leadership capacity. He is currently serving as the Vice Chairman of the foundation board for the Anne Arundel Medical Center in Annapolis. Mark is a graduate of the United States Naval Academy and was awarded an MBA from the University of Maryland, College Park, where he was selected as the William F. Holin scholar. Mark started as a student in one of my Operation Hand Salute academic programs, became my mentee, and remains as my friend. He is a great example of succeeding in business while expanding his giving reach.

Section 4

Igniting Your Passion

It's easy to make a buck. It's a lot tougher to make a difference.

—Tom Brokaw, broadcaster

Significant reflections on the Impact of Entrepreneurial Passion

Twenty years from now you will be more disappointed by the things that you didn't do than by the ones you did do. So throw off the bowlines. Sail away from the safe harbor. Catch the trade winds in your sails. Explore, Dream, and Discover.

—Mark Twain

There is no passion to be found playing small—in settling for a life that is less than the one you are capable of living.

—Nelson Mandela

Passion is energy. Feel the power that comes from focusing on what excites you.

—Oprah Winfrey

The road to success is not easy to navigate but with hard work, drive, and passion, it's possible to achieve the American dream.

—Tommy Hilfiger

Passion is one great force that unleashes creativity, because if you're passionate about something, then you're more willing to take risks.

—Yo-Yo Ma

Chapter 21

Finding What Ignites My Passion

Raul A. Deju

To me, living a full life means enjoying the moment as well as being able to go to sleep knowing your day went as well as possible. Many of us compartmentalize life. We have periods of sleep, periods of work, and periods with friends, and we justify and tolerate the need to have bad times during the day in order to be able to afford going to the movies or putting kids through school. Even in the days when I literally had not a cent to my name, I looked at life with the "Latin passion" in my blood as an adventure that needed to be lived and enjoyed to the fullest, since we never have any guarantees that our life would be there the next moment. Having seen a firing squad firsthand does something to you for the rest of your life.

In my model of life, I took ownership for charting my path. I recognized that education had something to do with improving my lot in life, and I knew it would take hard work to get there and afford the education. My approach was to look for ways to maximize my income, legally of course, so I could achieve my education. I then recognized early in my life that one of my traits was to quickly become bored, so I treated my work in a very goal-oriented fashion. For example, I would tell myself "In the next four days, I have to get this done," instead of just coming and going to and from work, as many of us do without a clear purpose. I found that this allowed me to focus and get things done. I also focused on finding a unique way that others may not have thought of before, such that my approach would be differentiated from the approach of others. I still find this useful today in building new companies.

I also found that we all have limitations and have to work within our resources and must work to optimize what is possible. For example, when I was in college, I did not have money to spare, nor a family to send me a check all the time, so I figured out that a way to have some neat vacations would be to complete a research paper on the various things I was doing, get it published, get it accepted to be presented at a professional meeting, and get paid by the research center to travel there. Then, I would add a couple of days on my own, and bingo; I had a first-class vacation. This let me go to places, like San Antonio, New York City, and San Francisco, while in school on a very limited budget. My passion became centered on the following equation (after all, I started as a mathematician):

Being passionate about work + leisure time = Happiness = Life well lived!

I still believe in this formula today. Of course, this may not work for everyone, but it does for me.

I try to always find things to do at work and in life that I am passionate about. For example, I am passionate about building successful companies, and my wife is passionate about quilting. We both support each other's passions. In fact, I have gone to a good number of quilt shows in my life, and I have enjoyed them and have learned much about the intricacies and complexities of this beautiful form of artistic self-expression. She has also gone with me to a number of business events and learned more about what I do. The combination brings us closer together.

My passion in general involves people. People should not be used. People who become friends lead to an ever-growing support network at work and at play. Friends should not be compartmentalized. If they are friends, you need to be involved in their life, and they should be involved in yours. Help and mentor each other.

Life is also incomplete if we don't use our passion to help others. We all need help sometime in our life. Maybe it is sickness, maybe it is failure, but if we are lucky, we have had someone who helped us out of it. So help others when they need help. It is not the government's role to be the sole provider of safety nets. We need to be the primary safety net for our friends and family, and guess what. I have received more myself every time I give.

Remember, you don't have to be Italian to be passionate—love your work, your family, your friends. Remember, if there is something you aren't happy about, you can aim to change it, or if you can't change it (as it can be with health issues), you can learn to make them less impactful on your day-to-day life.

There is always a tomorrow to be passionate about. We can't predict our life's journey, but we can look at what is left of it as an opportunity to tackle something new—a new adventure. To recall a quote from the poet Robert Browning nearly 150 years ago "Ah, but a man's reach should exceed his grasp, or what's a heaven for?" By the way, when I was learning English in Miami after arriving from Cuba, this is the first quote I read in the library and have never forgotten it.

Failure is a part of life. While none of us like to fail, take it as a necessary learning experience and focus on how the specific failure can help you succeed in the future. Don't let failure kill your passion.

Finally, my passion is about the little things. In the morning at home, we watch the hummingbirds eat their nectar and the squirrels trying to outdo the birds on their feeders. We love hearing and seeing the little creatures. I talk to my friends, I do my work. I have lots of date nights with my wife. We visit with kids and grandkids and the extended family. We go out with friends. We help others. We enjoy them all. They fill our passion, and they allow us to make a difference.

In covering the topic of passion, I have to come back to one of my images of passion, the actress Sophia Loren. She has a wonderful quote that so well reflects my views on passion: "There is a fountain of youth: it is your mind, your talents, the creativity you bring to your life and the lives of people you love. When you learn to tap this source, you will truly have defeated age."

Now let's read in the following chapters what some of my BFF think of being passionate.

Chapter 22

Passion Drives Me to Serve

Erica Courtney

Many people strive to be first at whatever they do, but that may require luck, timing, and hard work, and it may depend on others who have paved the way before us. Today, sometimes it seems like there are few "firsts" yet to be accomplished or records to be broken. I have a few firsts under my belt, but that was never the goal. Believing in what I was doing and pushing myself beyond what I thought possible gave rise to passion that got me through a number of tough times. My passion provides me an uncontrollable urge, an emotion that still today gives me restlessness and a drive, not involving monetary gain, but involving almost a duty as a citizen of the greatest nation on earth.

My Upbringing

Like many, I had a pretty untraditional upbringing. I was raised by a young mother in Huntington Beach, California, also known as Surf City, USA, from first grade on. Prior to settling in Huntington Beach, we lived in Colombia, South America, for a few years, which I still remember fondly. Adventure was our middle name.

Florida was my second home only to California, as my grandparents migrated there from Boston to help start what is now NASA. I spent my Christmases climbing mountains and camping, giving thanks to nature. At nine, I became the youngest female to climb Mt. Whitney—the tallest mountain in the continental United States. I still hold the record.

I watched my mom work her butt off to pay the bills and further her education while working in a man's world as a heavy equipment operator. She had always said that on my eighteenth birthday she was going to join the Peace Corps to live out her dream inspired by John F. Kennedy. And so she did. She went to the Philippines and later Ecuador. She taught me to live my dreams and provide service to others.

Sports taught me much—teamwork, dedication, and competition. I ran fast. I was on three varsity teams starting my freshman year. I was the bomb until a younger girl came along and beat me! I worked hard to get better and to stay number 1. However, she was just better, and I learned that I could look myself in the mirror and be okay with that and even embrace it, because I knew I worked extremely hard, and there was simply nothing more I could do. It was about the team and how we could best work together. We ended up winning a state championship as a team, not as individuals. So yes, I know that you won't always be first.

It's Not Just a Job—It's an Adventure

My first year of college, I was bored out of my mind. I definitely needed a change. I thought about the military even though I had no clue what that meant. There was always major pondering going on at the beach— that is what we did in Huntington. Sand clinging to my skin, smelling of the ocean, I walked into an Army recruiting office with a friend, and they asked if they could help us. I replied, "Sure, I am interested in becoming a Marine and have some questions." The fact that I asked Army guys about becoming a Marine showed my ignorance. After six hours of questions and multiple tests, I signed my name on the dotted line to join as a military police. That same night, the Gulf War started. *Oh, what have I done,* I mused to myself as I watched tanks shoot over an open desert all night long. Funny thing is that despite my complete lack of military understanding at that time, I later learned that I have a rich family history steeped in military service, from cavalry officers in the Civil War on. So it is in my DNA!

After my basic training, I was Germany-bound. We worked twelve-hour shifts that turned into sixteen-hour days. Field deployments (showers were a luxury) required MPs to keep the peace on various installations. I had to deal with drunks, domestic abuse, scandal, POWs, deadly traffic accidents, foreign nationals, and more.

I was overseas in a male-dominated world as a young woman with all this authority, carrying a gun. I had to grow up quickly.

Next, I was given an assignment in New Jersey where I became the first female on the Special Reaction Team, kind of like a military version of a SWAT team for serious situations. I moved up in rank quickly and was a noncommissioned officer in charge of a patrol. From there, I was offered an investigative position, which I turned down in lieu of taking a scholarship to complete my education and become an officer.

The Army paid for my school, and I graduated number 1 in my cadet class. I was the first female cadet commander to hold the position for the entire year. Now, I had to make a tough decision and choose what I wanted to be. Well, how about becoming an aviator? I felt this would be the coolest, and I charged ahead.

After nine months of training, the time came for me to choose my airframe. They had just opened up the aero-scout mission to females— the last of all airframes in any service to allow women. Combat arms roles were not open to women previously. Prior to finalizing my selection, I researched the mission of a scout. They are like the scouts in the Old West, and wars past that went alone on horseback to confirm, deny, or report information to the commanders so they could make better-informed decisions. I loved it! Wow, who wants to be a flying bus driver? Not me! I wanted to fly at treetop level and support the guys on the ground. So that was it. I was ready to join the first group of women to become part of the cavalry. It was literally in my DNA.

On my first day of training, I walked out to the airframe to meet my instructor, an older gentleman in a green flight suit who took one look at me and walked the other way. He refused to teach a woman. What? Are you serious? Yep, he was serious. He was from a different time—Vietnam—and was not going to support integration. This was one of the first times I realized gender is a discriminator. My mom never raised me this way. I never thought I was limited because I am a woman. It was so weird to me. But eventually, I successfully completed my training, hardened after my first day's experience.

When I completed my flight training and all my basic combat skills training, I received my first assignment as an officer. It was South Korea. Wait, I thought at that time, wasn't there a guy shot out of the sky a year or so ago for flying too close to the DMZ? Yep. Wow, this is getting real. Welcome to a heavy division cavalry unit with aircraft and tanks as a lieutenant. The tanker guys were shocked to see me come in. Frankly, so were the other scout pilots. About one-third of the guys I had to lead did not want me there for the simple fact that I was a woman. I can go on and on about the comments made and their lack of respect, because somehow, a woman being there infringed on their manhood. Bottom line, I worked hard and stayed true to who I am, and by the time I left, those same guys did not want to see me go because they knew I could do the job, and well.

I learned to have thick skin. I was able to take it as well as dish it. My opinion is that men are, in some respects, far less complicated than women. If you can win them over by hanging with them physically (remember, I was an athlete), that goes far. If you can get past that, in a combat arms scenario, they are more open to next steps—like leading! If I had not liked my mission of being a scout, it would have been easy to leave. However, I was passionate about what we did and the people I served with, so it was easier to stay the course.

September 11, 2001

September 11, 2001. Who could forget it? I was with the Eighty-Second Airborne Division as a paratrooper, which, by all accounts, is America's 911 force that has the capability to deploy anywhere in the world within eighteen hours. I was in charge of logistics, budgets, and contracts. My job was about to get *real* quickly. I had to deploy, support, and receive units from multiple locations.

Throughout all the effort requiring my attention, I fought hard to attend the advanced cavalry course led by the armor branch. I loved the mission more than most. Because of this, I kept the fight. I finally got in with other cavalry officers and Special Forces guys, and wouldn't you know it, I was the first female to graduate. Who knew? I am a scout through and through; I just wanted more training to be the best possible leader. Again, I wasn't trying to break any barriers here. I just did it because I was passionate about being a better technical expert and leading my guys more effectively in amazingly difficult situations. Was it easy? Nope!

I had a guy throw me up against the wall, get in my face, and proceeded to try to intimidate me. Well, remember, I used to be military police, so I know how to take a guy down. My 125-pound frame is often deceiving. After that, the word got around, and I had no problems in that class. I learned that discrimination is their problem, not mine. If they get to you, they win. The key is to not be distracted by drama.

Next in my list of assignments came another highly deployable unit, the Tenth Mountain Division. By this time, wars in the Middle East were in full swing, and because my last commanders noted that I had done a great job, I got pigeonholed in the same job again. It was a big task because people's lives were on the line if they did not get what they needed. Every unit I went to got easier, as my reputation preceded me.

Contrary to popular belief, being an officer in the Army is very entrepreneurial. You are given big picture plans, but you need to figure out how to make things happen. You don't have time to pick up the slack of an underperformer. Also, a learning point for women out there trying to act like men is to stop. We are women, and we have skill sets that most men just aren't as equipped with, and vice versa. Own your strengths and maintain some femininity. Men will see through your insincerity when you try to be something you are not. Success is not just about brute strength. You don't have to be a man to fit in; be yourself.

I often wonder what the Afghanistan men had running through their minds as I directed them as to what to do on a daily basis. They were very respectful, but in their culture, women were never in positions of authority, or even seen around for that matter. I treated the Afghan as I did my guys—with respect—and that carried me far. I couldn't help but notice hungry kids outside the "wire" where the landscape was littered with landmines. I can just say that it bothered me, and from time to time, I organized drives to provide them some basic goods.

In Afghanistan, there were many soldiers kicking down doors like you see in the movies, but there were also just as many that were building infrastructure, schools, and basic services, putting their own lives at risks so that others may thrive.

Now What?

My passion ran its course, and I felt fulfilled with eleven years serving my country all over the world. However, now married and with two small boys, I was no longer invincible. My passion for my family took priority. Having children did make me see beyond myself. I had served my country with distinction, and now I had to face the scary outside world by entering the business world. I started by furthering my education with an Executive MBA. I learned a lot from my classmates, as well as from my teachers. They taught me the "language," and I learned that my military skill sets were very valuable.

I thought differently. I produced. I didn't complain without offering a solution. My genetic makeup is to be a problem solver and kick ass in strategic thinking. On top of that, the military had a lot to do with shaping me.

I worked as a corporate executive for a while, but like in the case of most veterans, it was not a good fit. I am a self-starter, so I formed a small business and began to market the services of this business. Paralleling my efforts, I came in contact with other veterans trying to do the same. In the military, we are generally trained not to sell ourselves but sell our team, yet in business, transitioning veterans must understand how to speak the language of business and sell their abilities and experience.

Over a few years, I encountered many veterans who would off-load their stories on me about things they never talked about with their wives, families, or friends. I was a good listener, but after time, it began to irk me. Why do all these vets keep confiding in me? Is it because I am a female and therefore nonthreatening to them? Is it because I was combat arms and have been there alongside many of them? I tried ignoring it, but life kept throwing me signs to pay attention! I couldn't ignore what was going on.

I began to research trends in our veteran community, trying to find their purpose. The government throws money at the problem, but the process is not very effective. Over half of the veterans that get placed in jobs within their first year of discharge quit. By the second year, 74 percent leave. Clearly job placement needs to be improved.

Private corporations are trying to step in, but they often miss the boat. What we are missing is peer-to-peer mentorship from people we trust and understand. Not suits. Ah, bingo! I got it. The best way to reach the largest number of veterans is through entrepreneurship, since 40 percent of us are starting our own businesses, which provides us purpose versus just climbing into a job.

Veteran-owned firms are also proving to be more successful than nonveteran-owned firms and are twice as likely to hire other veterans. We are not wounded, we are capable, and how great an initiative it is to empower a veteran entrepreneur to make up for lost time and give back to the economy versus drawing from it. Guess what, I had just found a passion that allowed me to break new ground and be close to my kids. I could sink my mojo into this effort.

After attending many veteran organization events all over the country, I gravitated toward the Disabled Veteran Business Alliance, as they are the longest-running organization focusing on veterans in business with an amazing history of accomplishments. I got involved and share a sense of comradery among my fellow veterans. I am now the board of directors President, humbled to have been elected by some amazing people to lead us in a new direction, looking out for our new generation of vets, as well as honoring those before us about to retire from the companies they have created in the business sector.

I have now been both a successful small-business owner and a successful military officer, so I understand both languages well. I see beauty in both worlds and am privileged enough to be able to share that with my colleagues. I am grateful to be here living life, as many I have known are not. I am a scout at heart—always headed toward the unknown. I have had some firsts bestowed upon me personally, but that was never the intent.

After a seven-year break in service, I decided to join the Army Reserves. As the services are now opening their doors to many opportunities formerly closed to women, I hope to provide my perspective and my experience.

What have I learned? First, do what you love, and it will carry you through tough times. Feed your passion. Don't let other people's ignorance get you down. Be adventurous and blaze a trail. Be in the driver's seat and pay attention to the signs. These realizations take time, but as you move forward in life, don't forget to give back. It makes life worth living, and it further feeds your passion.

Passion is defined in the *Merriam-Webster Dictionary* as "a strong feeling of enthusiasm or excitement for something or about doing something; a strong liking or desire for or devotion to some activity, object, or concept." Passion is an emotion connected with loving something or someone. Passion can make living your life a phenomenal experience, and I intend to continue to be passionate of things I can do in the future to better myself, my family, my extended military family, my fellow vets, and my newfound friends in business.

Biographical Comments by the Lead Author

Erica Courtney has been a military police, scout helicopter pilot, and paratrooper in the US Army, having also served in senior logistical, contracting, and management positions in charge of some of the most deployable major operating units in peacetime and in war. Erica is now the CEO of 2020vet based in Silicon Valley, California, and in Washington, DC, offering intelligent logistics optimization and engineering solutions through experienced personnel and innovative technologies that reduce risk, disruption, cost, and environmental footprint while increasing oversight, speed, security, flexibility, and quality. In parallel to her private sector work, she is continuing to serve the nation as a Major in the US Army Reserve and is actively involved in nonprofit causes by serving as President of the Disabled Veteran Business Alliance and serving on the Leadership Advisory Council for Women Impacting Public Policy. Erica has received numerous awards and recognitions for leadership, including those of Oprah Winfrey, who named her "a woman with the leadership background and ability to change the world." Erica has a BS in Communications from the University of Hawaii and an Executive MBA from Florida International University. Erica was a student of mine when she participated in one of my extended Operation Hand Salute programs for service-disabled veteran entrepreneurs, and over time, I have continued to serve as her mentor. Erica and I are collaborating in the process of expanding nationwide the Disabled Veteran Business Alliance. Further, we are friends, and distance does not matter.

Chapter 23

Meeting Unrecognized Needs: A Surefire Way to Finding Your Mojo!

Bill Wiersma

In our zeal to make things better, we sometimes happen on to something we think has legs, something we sense has unusual potential, and our instincts push us toward it. That was my situation the year after releasing my book *The Power of Professionalism,* which to this day continues to receive very positive reviews.

My mentor was wonderfully supportive of my efforts to promote the book and develop collateral material in support of the book. *The Power of Professionalism* was indeed the result of five years' work. This was the stuff I felt had legs. I had a lot invested emotionally. My mentor was known around the world as one of the top five people in the field of leadership development. He was revered by his colleagues. I was among them. But on a brisk winter morning, we met over breakfast and compared notes. We shared the usual sorts of things you might imagine. After we were caught up, he asked me what was next. I enthusiastically explained that I wanted to start a movement based on the book's principles. I briefly shared some early thoughts as to how I would accomplish that. He patiently heard me out and then said, "You know, leaders aren't asking for the type of thing you're advancing."

That was the last thing I wanted to hear, especially from him. For someone who loved the book, his comment surprised me, momentarily putting me back on my heels. I resisted debating the matter. His well-intended, candid observation should have sunk me. But I knew he wasn't judging me, rather he was reflecting what he had seen in the marketplace. No doubt he was trying to be helpful. Still, the mere implication by a guru of his stature that I was barking up the wrong tree would normally be demoralizing. But after giving pause, I felt undeterred and ever more committed to charge ahead. "Give me three years," I said to myself, "and they'll be asking for it then." All this was prima facie evidence that my mojo was in full bloom. I was certain, and I was committed.

Dr. Deju points out in the introduction to this book that "Our mojo is that special power or influence that we have, perhaps our unique talent or ability to make things happen, influence others, be effective, successful, and get things done." Mojos seem magical. My experience in applying the principles found in The Power of Professionalism to that point had certainly been magical. The trouble was, few others knew what I knew or had witnessed what I had seen.

As a seasoned hands-on organizational development practitioner, I sensed something very different about my approach: I wasn't just squeezing new behaviors out of a proverbial orange, but rather growing a better orange. Instead of putting the emphasis on doing, I had placed an emphasis on being. And it turned out to be a unique consulting approach, the potential of which most people either hadn't recognized yet, simply overlooked, or didn't know enough about. When I asked a prospect what their professional development needs were, my approach was never mentioned—consistent with my mentor's observation.

I successfully tested the approach in companies large and small, new-economy and old-economy companies, companies that were market leaders, some that were market laggards, companies that were culturally fit as a fiddle, and others that were on life support.

After some evidence-based testing, it was clear to me that the proof of the concept was sufficiently established. This thing had legs. It worked. It was special. In the world of professional services, it was unique, a Blue Ocean strategy (BOS), as described in chapter 11 of this book. It's only through a BOS that one can create an uncontested market space. Cirque du Soleil, Apple's iTunes, and Yellow Tail Wine, just to name a few, each created uncontested market spaces. Through a BOS, demand is created rather than fought over. It's an enviable place to be. *The Power of Professionalism* and its implementation approach was indeed a Blue Ocean, and it was through my mojo and persistence, as well as my listening skills, that I was able to create a successful launch for a business to reshape organizations through a new culture of professionalism.

To be clear, marketplace demand is created because unique value has been created. Because my approach changes people's thinking, it impacts virtually every aspect of a business. Plus people naturally gravitate to it. Leaders love the fact that by adopting professional values as their organization's north arrow, they were finally taking on a strategic approach to managing their human capital.

Professional values were being baked in, not just bolted on. As soon as leaders saw this approach work, they realized their prior attempts at managing human capital were inadequate, clearly only tactical in nature. This returns me to an earlier point: leaders are not always in a position to know what they really need.

All this built my mojo. My mentor's feedback was the first splash of cold water from a player outside my immediate network. It was the first significant test of my resolve. Fortunately, I passed the test, due largely to my newfound mojo. I explained this to my mentor: in spite of leaders not asking for this consulting approach, I was all in.

Marshall Goldsmith, world-renowned executive coach who knows a thing or two about mojo, believes you get mojo "the moment when you do something that's purposeful, powerful, and positive and the rest of the world recognizes it." It's about succeeding at what you do, as well as feeling good about yourself. Mojo transcends confidence. It's not about swagger; it's deeper, more substantive.

Mojo is earned, not bequeathed. It's a by-product of doing something meaningful, motivated more by collective purpose than by individual achievement. Mojo helped me advance an otherwise difficult conversation with my mentor.

Most everyone dreams about succeeding in a big way at what they do. I was fortunate the success I was having with clients and readers ramped up dramatically after my mentor provided me with a much-needed reality check. Well-respected organizations (for example, Sunsweet Growers) adopted enterprise-wide the principles described in *The Power of Professionalism*. Six months later, 78 percent of all their salaried employees (approximately 240 people) agreed that embracing professional values positively impacted the organization and spurred needed change. In that type of change effort, an acceptance rate that high is unheard of. Scores of other successes, many just as dramatic, also began to accumulate.

Since then, this platform has helped clients win new business, coalesce dysfunctional work groups, become an employer of choice, and change ingrained undesired behaviors, to mention a few. Indeed, the experience has been magical, principally because this approach meets several critical but previously unrecognized, unexpressed needs. The process also helped me shape myself to achieve greater success in the Blue Ocean of professionalism.

How people find their mojo is as different as people are. Some disrupt markets or industries, some establish a new status quo, and some become thought leaders. Regardless of the path, finding your mojo typically involves either creating something new or becoming really good at something. Either way, it requires work—lots of it.

I was never obsessed with finding my mojo, but I have been obsessed with doing great work, with building something special, and with helping people become better professionals. As it turned out, when I fed my obsession, my mojo became my dividend. Consider this thought from executive coach Terry Pearce:

> There are many people who think they want to be matadors, only to find themselves in the ring with two thousand pounds of bull bearing down on them, and then discover that what they really wanted was to wear tight pants and hear the crowd roar.

He suggests there are no shortcuts when aspiring to achieve something desirable. You're not going to reap accolades without first doing the hard work required to achieve something special. It's the price we all pay for excellence. And when you've done the work, hearing the crowd roar is the natural outcome of doing something special and being recognized for it. It's natural to want to be appreciated that way.

Plus, Terry offers an equally important implicit lesson. For the wannabe matador (such as those of us who want to find our mojo), hearing the crowd roar shouldn't be our prime objective. First, we have to be clear about our motives. A higher-order purpose, one that transcends self, is a marvelous elixir that helps us keep our ego in check.

For those looking for their mojo, I have only this advice: find and feed your purpose and passion. From firsthand experience, I can attest there will be many obstacles in your path (though probably not two thousand pounds of bull) that can deter you. Passion, however, mitigates that. For me, developing better professionals was my purpose and my passion. I undertook a daunting campaign of reinvigorating professional ideals into the mainstream because I thought it was something the country (and business) desperately needed. For me, it was a cause célèbre.

Passion fueled me through five arduous years and brought a keystone book to publication. Passion helped me get through the lengthy proof-of-concept consulting phase. Passion supported me innumerable times whenever someone said, "This doesn't pertain to me." Passion inspired me through whenever someone cynically criticized my approach as too simple to have these kinds of impacts. Passion helped me survive my difficult conversation with my mentor.

In the end, I have few bad memories, much less regrets, about the hard work and the tough times. What I do remember is the

- delight a CEO felt after an about-face in his more enlightened way of leading;
- exhilaration a visionary educator felt after revolutionizing his approach in teaching vocational students and transforming his students in the process;

- pride the frontline employee felt after going from the worst employee in her organization to the best (according to the organization's leader);
- thrill the millennial engineer took in discovering a better way in a mission-critical process considered sacrosanct, realizing a four-million-dollar annual savings; and the
- delight a company president took in becoming an employer of choice.

Each of these accomplishments was the direct result of individuals and their organizations embracing professional values as their north arrow. These were the types of results that kept me going, the type that enabled my mojo to reveal itself. It didn't happen overnight, but it did happen. Find your passion, work it, earn your mojo, and hopefully, you'll see similar results.

Biographical Comments by the Lead Author

Bill Wiersma, the author of two highly acclaimed books, The Big Aha *and* The Power of Professionalism, *uses professionalism as a platform for transforming people and organizations. Few foresaw that Bill—raised in a lower middle-class household by a single mother—would become a director at a Fortune 200 company and would advise CEOs and four-star generals. In the world of organizational consulting, his approach is disruptive when contrasted with traditional leadership development, principally because the primary objective is to change how people think. Air Force General Robin Rand stated that* The Power of Professionalism *has been an "ignition source" for the US Air Force in changing their culture. In hindsight, Bill sees that the confluence of his life's experiences, passion, and hard work prepared him for this unique moment in our nation's history when the resurgence in professional values is needed most. Bill and his wife, Holly, have four adult children and live in the San Francisco Bay Area. Bill and I have worked together teaching entrepreneurs and have together mentored a good number of entrepreneurs. Bill and I are true BFF. Routinely, we share meals and discuss current and future book ideas.*

Chapter 24

Coming Through the Storm: Inspiration and Priorities after Hurricane Katrina

Dina Finta

In 2005, I had recently relocated to beautiful Washington State and was splitting my time between our new home in Port Angeles and my native home of New Orleans, while running my company that was based in New Orleans and Baton Rouge. I had lived my entire life in Louisiana until marrying a career military man and making my first move away from the South to the very northwestern tip of the country. My company at that time was a focused, young, motivated group of about fifty employees, who worked developing and providing custom training programs to Fortune 500 organizations. We worked hard to be a profitable and sustainable organization that could provide opportunities for smart people to make good money and allow all of us to grow and prosper. I was trying to limit my travel time versus home time to fifty-fifty, but many months, the on-the-road part surpassed 80 percent. We were growing and doing good things. It was challenging and rewarding, and I felt like the temporary sacrifice was worthwhile. Life was running smoothly. Until it no longer wasn't.

On August 29, 2005, New Orleans was devastated by Hurricane Katrina. I did not understand devastation until that time. We could not work—our clients' offices were gone or damaged. Our downtown New Orleans high-rise office building located directly across the street from the Superdome was flooded and had many of its windows smashed by the hurricane winds. The city was locked down by the authorities, and for many days, we couldn't locate or even communicate with our New

Orleans–based employees. In many cases, I did not even know if they were alive. All our lives were changed in an instant.

I was shocked to discover that in America, we could be unable to simply move food and water to people in need. We take rescue and assistance for granted, and its failure was shocking and disorienting. There was no power. Restaurant and grocery store food spoiled. We're used to impending hurricanes in south Louisiana. Many people left their homes, expecting the storm to turn; hurricanes frequently make last-minute directional changes. The storm always turns. It's almost routine: we evacuate, nothing happens, we come home, inconvenienced but safe and dry, and life goes back to normal.

This time was different. The storm not only didn't turn but also strengthened greatly, and New Orleans felt its wrath. People couldn't get back, and when they could, homes, neighborhoods, and businesses were gone. Just gone! Carried away or buried in mud or soaked in contaminated waters or by the Mississippi River that finally breached the battered levees. This time it was very different. Not knowing how bad this storm would be, I was lucky to get on a flight that I had already booked, but I was diverted to the Baton Rouge airport since the New Orleans airport had been shut down. I was in Baton Rouge when the New Orleans levees broke and the city became overrun with floodwaters, so we were stuck, hopelessly unable to help.

Overnight, my focus had to shift from the strategic and operational focus of running a business to plain survival. All my immediate and extended family members, all my employees, all my clients, and most of the people I knew were directly in the path of the storm. It was no longer a question of making money—overnight, revenues stopped. Receivables stopped. Client contracts stopped. I was deeply saddened, frightened, and completely overwhelmed. These people, these friends, worked so hard for me and the company. Now I needed to get this company back together so they could continue to provide for their families.

My immediate goal was to locate and contact every one of my fifty employees. People had been forced to leave their homes very quickly. Most of the area had no power, landlines weren't an option, and cell phone contact was nearly impossible. I worked very closely with my Baton Rouge–based leadership team, and we were able to use our partnership with Microsoft and work through their resources to eventually confirm the locations of our employees. After several very long days, we confirmed that while many of our employees were scattered and homeless, they were all, in fact, alive and safe. I vividly remember crying on the phone to my husband through sheer helplessness and exhaustion. In fact, almost eleven years later, I am crying as I recall these experiences.

As the days unfolded, new issues continued to surface. Employees were largely still unable to work without a home, clothing, or basic day-to-day items. We had a core group of employees who worked out of our Baton Rouge–based office just sixty miles from New Orleans, and they were strong, committed people who were dedicated to helping their coworkers and community. We also wanted to save our company.

Baton Rouge was strongly impacted by the storm, not only through wind and flood damage, but also through a literally overnight doubling of the population due to the many evacuees from New Orleans that at least temporarily moved there. In our Baton Rouge offices, we were busy figuring out how to do some business so that our small company could survive and keep paying people. The struggle here was that businesses just weren't ready to give or receive business services, even months later. The problems were so much bigger than us, and we were all dealing with huge infrastructure problems across our whole region.

Our client companies weren't there, or if they were, in many cases, their systems were destroyed so they couldn't process invoices or even know whom they owed money to. As a small business, when our cash flow and new revenue stopped overnight, it became a fight to survive.

FEMA, private insurance companies, and other agencies were so overwhelmed with the situation that there was no way to get their attention to a small business like ours that needed help. Many of the area small-business owners made the tough decision to shut their doors right away as a way to minimize their financial risk. I realized that as a small business, we needed to work together if we were going to survive. Our friends at Microsoft were very concerned for us and kept reaching out to figure out how they could help us. Through these conversations, I, along with my friend and coworker Jamie, led an effort that focused on helping Louisiana small businesses back into operation with Microsoft-donated resources and support, software, and computers. We were later awarded recognition from Microsoft for our post-Katrina efforts.

As I analyzed whether I could keep the company in business, we were also working with friends and business contacts across the nation to send basic supplies to our Baton Rouge office that I set up as a resource station. There was even a delay in getting this seemingly easy process moving, because for a time, delivery trucks couldn't get into our area. Eventually, the donations of water, nonperishable food, clothing, baby necessities, and anything else you could mail started flowing, and we were able to ease the efforts of hundreds of our personal and business connections in a small way through these contributions. We focused on what we could do. My priorities had completely changed. I was still frightened, still overwhelmed, but no longer helpless.

Within a few months of the storm, I had lost about 50 percent of my employees. Many had evacuated New Orleans and could see no way back to a place where they had no home, no job, and no resources on which to fall back. I remember many times feeling hopeless about the prospect of trying to stay and rebuild. I made the commitment to work to keep my business alive and realized pretty quickly I'd need to find business outside of Louisiana. Six months after the storm, we moved much of our operation and established our headquarters in San Antonio. My New Orleans location did eventually reopen, and we did some good work and made positive progress for a while but eventually had to close that location. It still hurts me to think about it.

At the time of this writing, it's been nearly eleven years since what locals refer to as the Storm. Katrina still marks our timeline. Every person there was impacted; every one of us felt the heartbreak, but also the strength and community and the will of our home to heal itself. When the New Orleans Saints won the Super Bowl in 2010, we took it personally. That was us! Our New Orleans! Though the game was played in Miami, New Orleanians flocked back to the city to be "at home." My family gathered at our New Orleans Warehouse District condominium, and when the game was won, cheers erupted throughout the city. Even from inside you could hear joyous celebrating, bells ringing, and horns honking. A hundred thousand revelers spilled out into the city streets that night, and it wasn't all about a game. We were proud of our city, and we loved one another. That night we were all friends; we cheered, danced, and embraced in the streets. We needed this. We needed something to celebrate.

Hurricane Katrina changed me, it changed what was important to me, and it refocused my mind and goals. I loved what I was doing with my company and the people I was doing it with. But I learned that what I was most passionate about was in positively impacting the lives of others more personally than in the corporate training world that I had been part of. Ultimately, this led me to eventually do a course correction and reinvent myself. Now my husband and I are in the San Francisco Bay Area, and I work with entrepreneurs, helping them apply their passions to build, launch, or grow their businesses, and also work with people in larger organizations, helping them become enthusiastic, engaged employees who make a difference when they go to work every day.

Follow your passion. Balance your life. It can change overnight as there are no guarantees in this world. Keep your priorities up front and the things that are important to you front and center. Surround yourself with caring, passionate people. Don't ever become paralyzed.

Imagine the impact if you move with people who share your passion. You must be the change you wish to see in the world.

Biographical Comments by the Lead Author

Dina Finta's diverse business background has been put to the task to help the personal and professional development of corporate professionals and entrepreneurs. Coming from a family of educators, Dina founded and led a corporate training and development firm based in New Orleans, concentrating on custom content mapped *to specific business goals, and led her team impacting individual performance through technology and business skills education for Fortune 500 organizations, such as Entergy, Chevron, Tesoro, and large government entities, such as the state of Louisiana, the US Navy, and the US Department of Agriculture. Following a move to the San Francisco Bay Area in 2010, Dina pursued her new passion of impacting the lives of others through nonprofit work and leadership in socially impactful organizations. She and I met while she was running the Bay Area programs for an international nonprofit. She joined forces with me on a full-time basis by 2011 when she became an anchor in the creation of the John F. Kennedy University Institute of Entrepreneurial Leadership to guide and mentor entrepreneurs to achieve great success. She has further partnered with me on multiple projects. Currently, Dina leads the academic side of a dynamic team, teaching and mentoring over two hundred entrepreneurs who now lead companies with annual revenues totaling over $1.7 billion. Dina has served on multiple nonprofit and start-up boards and was named as one of the 40 under 40 Business People to Watch in Louisiana. She currently resides in the San Francisco Bay Area with her husband, Jim, and dogs Nola (New Orleans, LA), Deuce, and Nobby. Dina went through the adversity of Katrina while she was in New Orleans but never gave up and still doesn't. She is a great example of someone who has focused on gratitude for the last decade, giving tirelessly to the goal of helping entrepreneurs succeed. I am proud to have her as one of my BFF. In fact, in April 2016, Dina was appointed the Director of the Institute of Entrepreneurial Leadership at John F. Kennedy University, the organization I founded in 2011. We still work together helping others.*

Chapter 25

Living on Purpose

Jill Osur

What lies behind us and what lies before us are small matters compared to what lies within us.

—Ralph Waldo Emerson

Sports defined me in my youth. As an identical twin, I had a built-in playmate, and my sister Jennifer and I excelled at all sports. I played three sports in high school and then decided to pursue softball in college on an athletic scholarship at the University of California at Berkeley. My twin chose basketball in college, and while I think I loved basketball more than softball, I wanted an identity other than being "one of the twins." Taking on leadership roles and speaking my mind always came easy to me. Playing sports helped me foster these talents and allowed me to be a leader on the field and eventually off the field as well.

I played catcher, and I loved being involved in every play, from calling pitches, to making sure my teammates were in the right position, to shouting out words of encouragement so that our team could play well together. I lived for competition and thrived in it. I was so passionate about sports that it made me feel unstoppable. I had some great coaches, and I also had coaches that weren't so hot. At an early age, I was very conscious about how words that coaches said would either positively impact the team or have a negative effect, which certainly wasn't the intention. It was interesting to observe in myself how negative words from coaches could impact my performance in a negative way. We've all heard how sports are a microcosm of society and can bring out the worst in us. The beautiful thing is that they can also teach us how to handle the stresses of life, work, and family. There isn't a day that goes by that I don't find a relevant lesson in life that I learned from playing competitive sports. If you have a bad at bat or if you make a bad decision in your business, the game isn't over. You make the necessary adjustments and continue competing with the faith that you have what it takes to win the game.

During my time at Cal, while I was playing softball, I suffered an injury that would forever change the trajectory of my life. I was blindsided while skiing and broke my neck between the first and second vertebrae. By all accounts, with the break where it was, I should not be here today. I had surgery to fuse my neck together, and after a long recovery, I was back on the field for the next season. I was on the field, competing again, but something just felt different. I did not have that burning desire or passion as I did prior to the injury. I still loved playing softball, but something inside was telling me that there was more out there for me. It's interesting how things happen in life that make you reexamine your path, your goals, and your passion. While all this was happening with my neck, my coach at Cal was dying from hepatitis after being stabbed on the beach in Puerto Rico. She passed away after my sophomore season. This was in 1987, and professional women softball was just beginning in the United States with only a few teams, so I did not see that as an option. With my coach passing away and my passion for continuing with softball not at the level it was before my neck injury, I decided to hang up my cleats and to be a full-time student.

At the end of my junior year, I took a class on the political economy of industrial societies and had a great professor by the name of Dr. Milos Martic. I really didn't know what I wanted to do after college, but knowing my interest in politics, he encouraged me to do an internship with Senator Pete Wilson in San Francisco. I told him that I was a Democrat, and his response was "I don't care. It's not what you know but who you know that will help you in the future." I didn't know it at that time, but this truth would be with me during every phase of my professional career. He hit the nail on the head, as it was that internship that then got me an internship with outgoing Mayor Dianne Feinstein, putting me in a position that when she decided to run for governor, I was one of the first hires for her campaign, and every job I've had since then can be linked in one way or another to that original internship with Senator Pete Wilson.

While I struggled to find my passion and purpose, I spent a few years in politics, including starting my own political fund-raising business and working for several state and national candidates. It did not take long working on the inside to see how dysfunctional politics are in this country and how much is driven by money and political interest. Well, at that point, someone I met at Dianne Feinstein's office was connected to an executive placement firm in the nonprofit space. She got a call asking if she knew anyone they could talk to about starting up a new chapter for the Special Olympics in Northern California. My former coworker knew that I could raise money, but she did not know the athlete side of me and what a great fit this would be. I had always wanted to volunteer for the Special Olympics while I was in college but could never figure out how to do it as their presence in Northern California was so small. This was one of the reasons the state was being split into two, so that they could now create a leadership position to do a better job in the north with volunteers and community outreach. I was so passionate about the job that I went into the interview believing I was the only one they were talking to. You could say that this approach was naive, but in hindsight, going in with that kind of passion and purpose absolutely differentiated me from the pack and got me the job offer.

I spent fifteen years at the Special Olympics and raised over $150 million for the organization. During my time there, I became an expert at cause-related marketing, a cooperative effort between for-profit businesses and a nonprofit organization such as the Special Olympics. This excited me and brought out my entrepreneurial juices; however, the complacency of the Special Olympics with the status quo ultimately drove me to a change of direction.

Toward the end of my tenure with the Special Olympics, I was able to attend a conference at the Center for Creative Leadership in La Jolla. While talking to one of the counselors at the center, she convinced me that I was much better suited for an entrepreneurial environment than for a structured corporate environment such as the Special Olympics.

Then, by happenstance, on March 20, 2008, I was approached by a restaurant owner, Jeff, whom I had done some fund-raisers with while at Special Olympics. He then proceeded to offer me the job of being the CEO of a new sports-centered tech enterprise he was launching, and guess what. I jumped.

I loved my new gig. We were building a platform that would allow young athletes to learn to think, act, train, compete, and even give back like a pro. We had professional athletes that would be featured on our site that could provide great advice to young athletes. We had a fabulous tech team that was building our disruptive technology platform, and people were writing checks to be involved as investors like there was no tomorrow. I had a great team that developed content, worked in the community, and was executing a launch and marketing plan. Other similar companies around the country were getting phenomenal valuations, and the future for us looked incredibly bright. That is, until the tech market crashed, and everything wasn't so bright anymore. It's amazing how tough situations can teach you so many valuable lessons in life. I certainly wasn't looking for more valuable life lessons at that time, but things were happening at a fast and furious pace all around us, and the crash had an impact on everyone.

The first real lesson out of this experience was that not everyone is wired to be an entrepreneur, and many of our employees were not entrepreneurs and were devastated by our shutdown. The second real lesson was learning whom you are working for, who your investors were. In my case, Jeff and his partners ran away from the business. However, as it happens from time to time, I met Paul, who was Jeff's CFO, and he and I have since worked together on a number of ventures.

Paul and I have been involved in a number of ventures in the intervening years since the sports venture and shared office space in the same building. One day we were talking about business in general, and as we are brainstorming, he brings to my attention an opportunity in the wine distribution space. From this platform, we have now started a new company to produce our own wines and recently purchased Myka Cellars, an award-winning winery, and brought the winemaker on as our director of winemaking. We have now deployed our own production facility in El Dorado County, and we are opening up to three new wineries and six new tasting rooms this year and shopping for vineyards as we speak. We've begun exporting to other countries and have many of our brands in national chains. Each of our brands also will set aside cases of their best wines for us to put the Veterans Spirit logo on them and have 100 percent of the profits donated to GallantFew, a veterans' nonprofit.

This time around, we own the companies, we control the decisions that are made, and we can stay true to our mission of building a great company while making a difference in the world. It hasn't been a cakewalk, as all businesses have challenges as they grow, but when things get tough, I know we will do the right thing, and that allows me to sleep at night.

My journey to find my mojo has taken me in many different directions, but I have no regrets as the journey has allowed me to harness the fire within combining passion and purpose.

My key moments and takeaways from my life that helped me find my passion and purpose and tap into my mojo can be summarized in seven points:

1. If your life was going to end tomorrow, would you be able to say you were doing your dream job? Know what drives you and what you're passionate about. For me, it was finding the right environment that allowed me to be passionate, to be competitive, and to be around like-minded driven people that wanted to make a difference in the world.
2. It's not what you know, but whom you know. Networking is the key as I found out through every step of my journey.
3. Know yourself. Is money your driver, or is it making a difference? This will help you ensure that you are around like-minded people and that your actions are aligned with your intentions.
4. Whom you do business with is as important as the business you are doing. Life is about the journey, so having great people with you on your journey can ensure you stay true to your core values. It's easy to be your true self and to stay in your

mojo when your environment is a healthy one. People are a key element to a healthy environment. Follow your intuition!

5. Control your own destiny. If you are in control of your business, you can build it to earn great profits and to also make a difference in the world. Take my advice on this one and do it much sooner than I did. You'll sleep much better at night.

6. Follow your intuition. Analytics reports can tell you a lot of valuable information, but there is nothing more valuable than following your gut and intuition.

7. Faith. I didn't talk much about faith in this chapter, but through every experience I've had, I have always had faith that things happen for a reason. I have faith that good things happen to good people. I have faith that I will be able to make a big difference in this world. I also have faith that we can lead by example for the next generation. And lastly, I have faith that the energy we put out in the world is what we get back.

A wise friend of mine once told me to do what I love and the money will come. Follow your passion, find your purpose, surround yourself with great people, and the rest will fall in place.

I have had quite the journey, but I can comfortably say that I have no regrets. I know I'm fortunate to be alive, and I wake up every morning with gratitude and the intention to make a difference. I have been able to share these gifts with my three children and let them know that yes, there will be ups and downs and plenty of challenges and even some failures (or learning steps, if you prefer), but if you find the silver lining in all your experiences and you use these experiences to define who you truly are on the inside, then you will be able to align your passion with your purpose and lead an ignited life full of energy and adventure. Live on purpose and do it with passion, and your journey will be extraordinary.

Biographical Comments by the Lead Author

Jill is a former collegiate scholarship softball player at the University of California at Berkeley that has been able to combine her passion for sports and competition into a successful and prosperous career as a consummate entrepreneur. Jill has helped over ten start-ups launch, is a seasoned sales and marketing executive, and holds board seats on a number of regional university career development programs. Jill was the recipient of a 2012 Bronze Stevie Award for Female Executive of the Year in Consumer Products for companies with up to 2,500 employees, as well as a finalist for the 2009 Stevie Award for Best Entrepreneur. Jill is the current founder of Veterans Spirit, a socially conscious wine and spirits company that donates 100 percent to charities the profit from every bottle sold. These charities are supporting our nation's veterans. Jill is also president of GoldLine Brands, a winery group in Northern California, and Zeal Wine Group, a wine distribution and import company. Jill spent her early career in political fund-raising and brought that aggressive style of fund-raising to the nonprofit sector, which proved a potent tool for the Special Olympics Northern California and Nevada for more than fourteen years. Jill has a black belt in karate and is married and has three children. I have known Jill in many capacities, she and I are both mentors to entrepreneurs, both of us believe in supporting our veterans, and both of us are wine and food enthusiasts. While I have enjoyed attending business meetings and nonprofit events with Jill, I consider her a friend and, most importantly, enjoy visiting with her and her husband and enjoying some wine and a good dinner.

Section 5

Leadership and Tenacity: Dealing with Adversity

All the adversity I've had in my life, all my troubles
and obstacles have strengthened me . . .
You may not realize it when it happens,
but a kick in the teeth may be the best thing in the world for you.

—Walt Disney

Significant Reflections on the Impact of Tenacity and Leadership on Entrepreneurs

I can't imagine a person becoming a success who doesn't give this game of life everything he's got.

—Walter Cronkite

Obstacles cannot crush me. Every obstacle yields to stern resolve.

—Leonardo da Vinci

Fearless is getting back up and fighting for what you want over and over again . . . even though every time you've tried before you've lost.

—Taylor Swift

The most difficult thing is the decision to act, the rest is merely tenacity. The fears are paper tigers. You can do anything you decide to do. You can act to change and control your life; and the procedure, the process is its own reward.

—Amelia Earhart

The greatest leader is not necessarily the one who does the greatest things. He is the one that gets the people to do the greatest things.

—President Ronald Reagan

Chapter 26

Never Accept Defeat and Stay on the Moral High Ground

Lt. Gen. Ricardo S. Sánchez

Growing up in the deep southern part of Texas during the 1950s and 1960s, I never imagined being blessed with the levels of responsibility and success that I have enjoyed during my lifetime. My hometown of Rio Grande City is still a poverty-stricken town that lies along the banks of the Rio Grande River on the US–Mexico border. Rio Grande City is the county seat for Starr County, which remains to this day one of the poorest counties in the United States. Most families there lived in poverty and relied on government subsidies to survive. It was known as welfare back then. My siblings and I walked with my mother to the local government warehouse to pick up our food rations every two weeks. This usually consisted of rice, beans, powdered milk, some type of canned meat, and blocks of cheese. Dreams were limited to getting a new pair of shoes or maybe being able to afford a meal at Caro's restaurant, which was one of the "fancy" restaurants in the city.

Even though we were poor with little of material value, my family was blessed with an extremely tight-knit network of extended relatives that were steeped in faith, tradition, and most importantly, the strong values of honesty, integrity, and respect. This was a blessing that I would not appreciate until many years later. It was this foundation of values that I built upon over the years as I encountered professional challenges and increased responsibilities.

My parents and grandparents were third or fourth generation Texans with limited education. My father completed the eleventh grade, and my mother, the fourth grade, but both clearly understood the value of education, and they instilled that in all of us. No one in the Sánchez or Sauceda families had ever even considered going to college.

The vision for my future was clear. I had to finish high school and go to work as a laborer in South Texas or enlist in the military. Military service was one of the few well-known paths of escape from the poverty of Starr County, but eventually, just about everyone came back from the military and settled back laboring somewhere in the county.

The impact of my Hispanic heritage value system goes back to my earliest memories. I clearly remember the constant pounding that we were subjected to as my brothers and I faced challenges. *No te rajes* (don't quit) and *siempre diga la verdad* (always tell the truth) were the mantras that came from every quarter—older brothers, parents, grandparents, and the extended family. We learned quickly that quitting was not an option.

If I got in trouble, the parental interrogations inevitably started with "Vale más que me digas la verdad"—you better tell me the truth. This was immediately followed by "I am going to find out the truth anyway, so if you lie, then things will be much worse!" I tested my parents a few times, and things did in fact get worse. As time went on, I became an absolute believer in this lesson.

Defeat: The Early Lessons

Two incidents from my school days in Rio Grande City stand out in my mind as the source of my knowledge that there was a special power that existed within me to control my own destiny. The first one occurred in my fifth-grade math class when my teacher embarrassed me in front of the whole class by declaring as she returned my daily quiz, "Ricardo, tu eres un burro." Ricardo, you are a dummy! I had worked late the night before helping my uncle in his tailor shop and had not done my homework.

It was no surprise when I did not do well on the quiz. This ignited a ferocious desire to prove this lady wrong. I knew I was not a dummy! I had failed the quiz, but that didn't define who I was or what I could do! It would never happen again. Never again would I allow someone to define me as a failure, especially when I was confident that I could master the task.

As a nine- or ten-year-old, I embraced a work ethic that would drive me to extremes, especially in challenging situations. Knowing myself would become a natural result of this constant search for excellence. Whether out of a fear of getting embarrassed or a deep desire to win, the end result was the same—work as hard as necessary to meet or, preferably, exceed the standard. Initially this was focused on my personal achievements, but later it would become the driving force behind my leadership style in the military.

The second incident occurred when I was a junior in high school. As a sophomore, the Junior Reserve Officers Training Corps (JROTC) program came to Rio Grande City, and I immediately signed up. I thrived in the discipline, rigor, teamwork, and patriotism of the program. As a seventh grader, I had started talking to my parents about going into the Army but knew hardly anything about what that meant. As a JROTC cadet, I was sure I had found my calling—I was going to be a soldier. Our instructors talked to us about West Point and college ROTC opportunities, and the first four-year scholarship was awarded to a young man who was two years ahead of me.

I began to consider the option of going to college. The possibility of going to college was no longer something that only the well-to-do children did. If the military paid for my tuition and actually gave me a stipend, then it would be possible. During my junior year, I decided to apply to West Point. I went to see the guidance counselor to get the application forms. After waiting for a short period of time, she called me to her office and asked me what I wanted. After explaining to her what I wanted to do, she firmly and bluntly stated, "Ricardo, what you need to do is go become a welder like your father!" and she dismissed me. I was stunned.

For a couple of days, I considered her comments and thought that she might be right. I had already been helping my father as a welder's apprentice, so it would be a path of least resistance. But a couple of weeks later, I realized that being a welder was not what I wanted to do with my life. I had to escape the poverty conditions of Starr County.

Again I was faced with a situation where someone was defining who I should be, and if I accepted the counselor's guidance, then it would be a catastrophic defeat. I had to fight! I decided that if she would not help me, then I would do it myself. With the help of my professors of military science, I applied for the military academy and for college ROTC scholarships. Upon graduation, I had four-year ROTC scholarships from the Army and the Air Force and a first alternate nomination to the US Naval Academy.

An Immediate Wakeup Call

I was commissioned as a Second Lieutenant in the US Army in July 1973 and reported for duty to the armor battalion of the Eighty-Second Airborne Division at Fort Bragg, North Carolina. This initial assignment would set the pattern for the rest of my military career. There was one other Hispanic officer in the unit when I arrived. He was fired within six months of my arrival, and I would not serve in a unit with another Hispanic officer until approximately twenty years later.

I had grown up in a closely-knit family very isolated from the discrimination that existed within America in the 1960s. I quickly learned that as a Hispanic, I was seen as the stereotypical slow learner and as the equal-opportunity quota product that would never quite be able to perform at the level of my peers, especially the West Pointers. Hispanics were underestimated and treated accordingly across the board. Discrimination manifested itself in two ways—individually and institutionally—but very quickly the individual discrimination went underground. The institutional discrimination was more insidious and harder to identify. As Hispanics, we would not be afforded the opportunity to take on the challenging jobs that were prerequisites for promotion and for selection as a commander. If you did not command, then you were definitely not competitive for promotion to colonel.

This became clear when I received my first efficiency report from my battalion commander. The Lieutenant Colonel (LTC) was from South Carolina with a military heritage that stretched back to the Confederacy. An officer's initial efficiency report was completed after 120 days in the unit, and the senior rater had to personally counsel each officer. When I was called to the battalion commander's office for my initial efficiency report counseling, I was told to knock on the door, wait until I was told to enter, march to a position two steps in front of the Lieutenant Colonel's desk, salute, and report.

I had put on my best-fitting uniform that day and did a last-minute check as I nervously knocked on the door. I heard the loud "Enter!" so I marched into the office, stopped, did a left face, and with a brisk salute, said, "Sir, Lieutenant Sánchez reporting as ordered." The LTC gave me the order to be "At Ease" and proceeded to tell me that I was doing a good job; however, he was giving me a rating that was 20 points lower than those of the rest of the lieutenants in the battalion because of who I was and where I had come from. He went on to say that if I was lucky, I might be able to catch up to the other lieutenants' level of performance in seven to eight years. He must have talked for about fifteen minutes, but that is all I remember!

Here was another opportunity to use what I had learned in the streets of Rio Grande City—no te rajes. I was being underestimated, treated as the stereotypical Hispanic, and being channeled toward mediocrity. There was no attempt made to mentor me. From that day on, I would take on every task with the same purpose—accept nothing less than excellence. To do this, I knew that I had to work harder than every other lieutenant, and I had to master all aspects of my profession. It was critical for me to find a balance of knowing what the Lord had blessed me with and where my shortcomings were in order to become a better leader.

Becoming tactically and technically proficient was the price of entry into the business of being a leader, and I had to learn how to train my subordinates in order for my unit to succeed. In the business of war fighting, there is no way to achieve individual success unless your unit succeeds. My soldiers had to be competent and well trained.

Success depended on the entire team's ability to perform, which in turn inextricably linked my success to the success of my subordinates. This lesson drives my leadership approach to this day—it is just as applicable in my current role as a CEO as it was while I was a soldier.

Staying on the Moral High Ground

In the quest for excellence and victory, I sometimes faced seemingly insurmountable challenges. In the heat of battle, one can begin to question whether our approach will lead to victory or, at a minimum, prevent defeat. This inevitably led me to ask an extremely important question: Am I willing to compromise my integrity and the ethics of my profession to achieve this particular objective? I never encountered a situation where the answer to this question was positive. I was willing to do everything possible to win, but straying off the moral high ground was never an option.

From my experiences in Rio Grande City, I had learned that I must never compromise my integrity. If I didn't tell the truth as a young boy, I knew that I was guaranteed to get a spanking. When I had not told the truth, it was extremely difficult to keep my story straight. I had considered this value as an absolute all of my career, but my toughest test came as a General Officer.

Moral Courage Can Be an Uncommon Virtue

Toward the end of my professional military career, I was blessed with the responsibility to lead Combined Joint Task Force 7. This task force had responsibility for all coalition military operations in Iraq during the occupation period from June 2003 to July 2004. During this very difficult period in America's Iraq War history, the forces under my command performed magnificently. We achieved the heights of glory with the capture of Saddam Hussein in December of 2003.

Those of us that have led combat operations for extended periods of time know that bad things can happen in the blink of an eye. This is exactly what happened in November 2003 at Abu Ghraib prison. The abuse and torture of prisoners at Abu Ghraib was a strategic failure for America, and it happened while I was the Commanding General. The story broke in April of 2004, about three months after I had already initiated an extensive investigation.

The ensuing scrutiny, media coverage, pundit speculation, and general hysteria linked to a presidential campaign were all key ingredients for a perfect storm. The intensity of the political rhetoric put me in an untenable position. I was faced with a critical choice as the unending investigations began to unfold. The truth was harder than anything the nation's leadership was willing to accept in a public forum. I personally experienced the depths of despair as I endured the relentless speculation, unfounded allegations, and the endless number of pundits who thought they understood the situation on the ground better than those of us that had been living it for months. This was a looming personal defeat that seemed to have no means of escape.

My rationale for how I was going to endure was simple. I decided that I would never compromise my integrity and that I would stay on the moral high ground. I would tell the truth regardless of personal consequences—this is what my parents had taught me, and it had been reinforced by my religious beliefs.

Luke 8:17 states, "For nothing is hidden that will not be made manifest, nor is anything secret that will not be known and come to light." I was prepared to fight to the bitter end. There was nothing that could be uncovered that would even come close to an unethical, unprofessional, or illegal action on my part. I would rely heavily upon my faith, my family, and my long record of excellence.

At the end of the day, after years of investigation, what I had known as a senior leader in April 2004 was repeatedly validated. I faced criticism from pundits and some of the investigators, but I never lost the support of the entire military chain of command. I had never left the moral high ground, and I had never accepted defeat.

E Tan, E Epi Tan (Bring Your Shield Back or Die on It)

It is said that in Ancient Greece, at the time of the Spartans (see the story on chapter 17 of this book), the mother of a Spartan would hand her son his shield before his first battle and tell him, "With your shield or on it!" This is the kind of commitment I pray to my Lord that I exemplified as a warrior. I repeatedly learned that the power, or the mojo, that allowed me to be extremely effective as a soldier came from the lessons that I had learned as a child in the streets of Rio Grande City. Those lessons gave me a passion to excel that permeated my being and became the core of my leadership style. From this foundation came a passion that has never been extinguished and will continue to guide me the rest of my life: "Never give up if the cause is worth fighting for."

Biographical Comments by the Lead Author

United States Lieutenant General Ricardo S. Sánchez retired from the US Army in November 2006 after thirty-three years of service. His assignments included tours in the United States, Korea, Panama, Germany, Kosovo, and the Middle East. He served as a tank battalion commander during Operation Desert Shield/ Storm. As a general officer, he was the Director of Operations and the Director for Strategy, Policy, and Plans for US Southern Command, which was responsible for all US military operations in the Western Hemisphere. Later he was the director of operations for US Army Europe. He led all US and Coalition military and interagency operations in the US sector in Kosovo from December 1999 to June 2000. In June 2001, he assumed command of the First Armored Division in Germany, and in March 2003, he deployed the division to Iraq for Operation Iraqi Freedom with an initial responsibility to secure the city of Baghdad. In June 2003, he assumed command of V Corps and Combined Joint Task Force 7 and was responsible for all international coalition operations in Iraq after the fall of the Saddam Hussein regime. He commanded the US-led occupation of Iraq until July 2004. At retirement, he was the highest-ranking Hispanic officer and only the third Hispanic to achieve the rank of Lieutenant General in the Army. After retirement, he has provided independent consulting services to international entities in Africa, Central America, Mexico, Europe, and the United States. In May 2011, he became the CEO for Operational Technologies

Corporation, and in June 2014, he assumed the role of CEO for OpTech Enterprise Solutions (OES), a Disabled Veteran Business Enterprise providing supply chain management, logistics, and business process outsourcing solutions for government and commercial clients. Sánchez graduated from Texas A&I University (B.S.Ed. math and history) and the Naval Postgraduate School (MS-Operations Research Systems Analysis Engineering), Monterey, California. He is married to Maria Elena Garza Sánchez. They have four children: Lara Marissa S. Leija, Rebekah Karina, Daniel Ricardo, and Michael Xavier. Adam Leija, son-in-law, and three grandchildren, Isabella Hope, Victoria Grace, and Christian Alexander, complete the family. It is my pleasure to know General Sánchez. He is my friend, and in 2014, it was my pleasure to nominate him to be inducted as a John F. Kennedy Laureate for his lifetime of accomplishments. I am happy to count Ricardo as a BFF and a shining example to others. We both serve proudly on the Advisory Board of the Disabled Veterans Business Alliance.

Chapter 27

Team Mojo

Larry Rockwell

I am a trial lawyer, an adviser to start-up businesses, a father of six children, a husband of thirty-eight years, and a baseball fan of nearly sixty years. Those decidedly are not listed in the order of importance. As I stand on one side of a prism, they are the refractions emanating on the other side. In that sense, they are connected and overlap.

I was fortunate to manage youth baseball and softball teams to succeed over the course of twenty-two years and to have been advising start-up businesses on strategies to thrive and grow for at least that long. From time to time, we may hear how our experience in one endeavor provides lessons for success in another and how our struggles and stress along one journey give us skills to succeed in another. At other times, it seems that the skills, exhausting effort, smarts, and luck that all contribute to small and large successes in one field do not let us achieve success in business, whether in a start-up or in a mature company. While common elements may be found in every successful team, I suggest that it is how the elements are fused together that brings one group success and leaves another disappointed. The secret sauce that makes the fusion take hold is "team mojo."

I am a witness to the power of team mojo—the supercharged effect when every team member's perspiration and inspiration come together at once and produce a wonder. It is an accelerant that elevates a team's good performance to great. But like many good things, for me, the lesson powerfully arrived in an unexpected way: the closing game of my twenty-two-year softball-managing journey. Perhaps more importantly, for a team of bright-eyed, energized, and dedicated twelve- and thirteen-year-old girls, the lesson of team mojo arrived near the start of their life's journey as a gem to carry, teach, and inspire them forever.

As I noted, I am a baseball fan. Actually, the simple word *fan* understates it, since I was *raised* a Boston Red Sox fan. It seems that as one ages, the passion for the game among us Sox fans grows exponentially, rather than along some linear path. That, combined with six children, led to twenty-two years of managing youth teams. That means twenty-two years of assessing talent (think employees) at tryouts on cold days in January (think cramped quarters when short of funding), racing through traffic and then coaching in a race against the oncoming dusk (think meeting deadlines for beta testing or product releases), dealing with the parents who all have their own views of how you should manage (think investors), setting the lineups (think the business plan and projections), blending the "talent," managing the games, and then seeing losses and wins. We tell ourselves—the team, the investors, and the customers—that a goal in this situation is "to have a good time." What remains unstated but drives us is to get what each team member and investor will admit that he or she really does want: to win the "trophy" of a championship and have a successful investment.

It begins with the nervous movement, the slight rustling of papers in hand, and the effort to appear calm while making small talk with friends along for support and the others in line, trying not to betray nervousness. Ah yes, you think, maybe this is the entrepreneur in line to register to present a ten-minute pitch for funding, while not betraying just how desperate the funding need is. Actually, no, this person is that entrepreneur fifteen years ago as the thirteen-year-old lining up to sign up for softball tryouts.

She next sees the stage, the softball diamond, the person on it, the people in front of her in line, the judges—she sees everything except how she will be more impressive than those before her.

Her number is called, she steps forward, and at a quickening pace, she takes her place in front of the audience of strangers—investors, coaches, judges. These are the people she wants and needs to impress with her energy and her talent. Will she make the grade? Will they like her? Will they recognize how much she wants to succeed as a team player, a leader, a winner? Most importantly, at least she thinks, will they choose her for their team? But this is a softball tryout and not a test of a business plan . . . or is it? How little they differ—as she may realize when she makes that funding pitch years later and gathers her team.

She gets the phone call—someone in the audience chose her. She succeeded. She is on a team. She has a team, and she hopes they all share her ambition, her desire, her goals, and her dream to succeed and win against her competition. Then the team members meet—the players/workers, the leaders, the coaches, the investor parents, all of whom are on what they profess to each other is a common mission: have a good time and succeed.

Practice begins, and each team player takes a position where it is hoped she will best help the team perform its best. Some will excel and others will not, but all along, the goal remains for the team to succeed, bringing the product or service to market or bringing the team a win. That thirteen-year-old girl on this team is about to learn in her last game that an individual's mojo is important, but it's team mojo that best assures delivering achievement of her goal now as a young woman and later to her start-up business. Only time will tell if she holds on to the lesson of this season.

So I reached a weekend in June, seeing twenty-two years of managing in the rearview mirror, along with the ambition, adventure, losses, and wins each season brought, like a leader of start-up businesses looking back on the near and real successes. Twenty-two years doing anything seems like a long time as we measure time, but not too long to still bring into sharp focus some otherwise fuzzy life lessons. What came into focus that day on the softball diamond is that in business and in life, stories of someone succeeding where they kept hold of mojo may be interesting, but the stories of people collectively regaining team mojo provide even greater inspiration, hope, and powerful lessons to take with us to the next adventure.

This girls softball team's final push—the entrepreneurs launching their product—came on a very hot day. I was determined to soak it all in—every minute, every swing, hit, catch, or miss—everything. For when other seasons ended, there lingered the hope for the next game, but there might be no next game after this weekend, no new start-up to lead. So all the attention was laser-focused on this one game, these two hours, these twelve girls on the team, and the memory they were creating.

They took the pregame hitting and fielding warm-ups, and then it was time to start the countdown to the end. And with that realization that this really was the final, the "how it would end" story unfolding, this game began to matter in some very core way much more than I had thought it would just an hour earlier. I gave the pregame pep talk that I had come to know well and had found worked. I was lucky that the players every year were talented, and so the teams I managed never had a losing season. To win more than you lose, I would always tell the players at the start of each year, was something to strive for in softball and baseball, and in that way, this sport was like life. More successes than losses should make for a pretty good life. This year, we had already accomplished that. But these kids knew, like all kids know without me telling them long before they enter into their work life, that the last game of a season was not like every other game, and ending with a win was a whole lot more desirable than winning any other game.

Then the train wreck that would be this game started. In the first inning, the first ball was a pop-up between the first and second baseman that dropped between them. The second hit was dropped by the second-base fielder.

Then the catcher made a great throw to the third baseman to pick off the runner stealing from second, but rather than tagging the runner out, the third baseman decided to give us some excitement by making it a rundown that ended with the third baseman throwing the ball over the head of the shortstop, allowing the runner to reach third and run home.

Our batters seemed to carry the bag of the unlucky with each of them, and one could see their mojo evaporating in the hot June day. My daughter came to bat and made an out, and over her next three at bats, she struck out twice and hit into a groundout. This performance came from a year-long hitting hero. Our power hitters struck out. Balls bounced off our fielders' legs, went over their heads, and found seams to get to the outfield. By the third inning, I found an uncommon calm coming over me—more like a resignation to the fact long ago learned that some games just do not work out as hoped or planned.

After all, I figured, wasn't it just a game? Yes, it was supposed to be. So I paced the third-base coach's box, mindful of the good times and of my daughter's admonishment a game earlier to say only positive things.

But in that third inning, with the players in steam heat, we caught a break of sorts delivered by our fourth-string pitcher—a girl I put in to pitch since we were losing by a lot. Her dream was to be a pitcher, and she might as well be at least one player taking a positive memory away from this mess. She delivered five pitches and three outs and no runs. There you go, I figured. Maybe this was to be the game highlight, a break from the game we had been playing.

But the game continued like a train wreck, and we got to the last inning trailing 15–5. So now comes the last inning to bat, the last chance, the last hope, the chance for prayers to be answered. It was about to become very clear that these girls were going to grab hold of mojo and use it, shake it, squeeze it beyond any common measure, mix in great sweat, and provide a story of great inspiration for themselves.

It started with our team getting a couple of hits. Then their pitcher couldn't find the strike zone, and we got some walks. We then got a couple more hits—or errors depending on how tight you score the book—and some more walks and some runs. Then our team got a gift of a shade tent being put over the dugout, courtesy of the team scheduled to take the dugout for the next game. Go figure—a chance to take advantage of luck. How often it is said that success often comes when one is prepared to take advantage of a bit of luck. These girls were ready.

The players for the next game arrived along with their parents, and we now had what, by any measure, was a crowd. We also had scored five runs. Then it was six and then seven, and now it was getting very interesting, and I now was living very much only in this moment and nothing else. The other team had brought in three pitchers this inning and we had but one out. They gathered as a team at the mound, and I could hear the coach reminding them they had a lead, so they should just concentrate for a little longer and the season would end with a win.

Our girls, like a great start-up team, could feel something taking hold, bubbling up, and looking to bubble over—team mojo, the collective confidence and enthusiasm that pulls defeat from a cliff's edge and drives a team to succeed when failure seemed so certain moments ago. Now the sun didn't matter, and this game might be like a knife turned in the wound or something rivaling a miracle. Our team had by now scored seven runs, the score was 15–12, and the bases were loaded. If you'd have told me the story to here, I could have told you that the batter in this scenario was almost always the last batter in the order (who missed most practices but wanted to be there for the last game, like a start-up's enthusiastic weakest link) or the coach's daughter (yes, the start-up leader's go-to person). And the story more often than not ends with a strikeout or the other team's defensive gem. We are then left to face each other in defeat and say "It's okay" when it sure does not feel anything like "okay."

And yep, it was my daughter up to bat; it was going to be the story ending with the manager's kid, I figured. As she walked to the plate, I called time. We met and I put my arm on her shoulder, and I knew the one thing I wanted from her was to let that mojo take over. I did not know how to put that in words, so I went to plan B: say what I knew from saying the same thing for twenty-two years in hundreds of games and to my own children in the car, on the field, and anytime they picked up a bat: *swing fast*. Think only one thing: swing fast. Think nothing else—nothing else at all. Let what you know to do, what you have trained to do, what you want to do, take over. It's what she will hear years from now when pressed against deadlines to deliver. Whatever then happened was out of her control. She would have her last at bat, knowing she did it right, did it well, and did herself proud.

I walked back to the third-base coach's box with a little smile, thinking for just a moment that "who'd have thought" and maybe this once. I turned, clapped my hands to cheer her on, and bang—a line drove off her bat that stayed as close to the third-base line as it could and still be fair. People who know baseball will tell you that when a right-handed hitter hits a ball on the third-base/left-field line, it means she swung fast—very fast. She cleared the bases of runners, and the game was tied. My daughter, a heretofore star, who had two throwing errors, two strikeouts, and no hits on that hot morning, had just knocked in three runs to clear the bases and tie the game—she had her mojo back big time, and it was looking contagious. The team stood and cheered, and now they all had their mojo back big time.

We are talking now about watching a tsunami come in to change how this game would be viewed in the rearview mirror of time and by those judging it. There was one out, game tied, and the second position batter at the plate. A smile, a nod, and then a strikeout swinging fast at a high pitch when hoping for an outfield hit.

There was no music and no announcer, but I will tell you in that next moment, the team sensed it, the investors sensed it, the spectators sensed it, I sensed it, and the good news was the next batter, our Ms. Slugger, sensed it—we had grabbed and now were shaking that mojo. Our Ms. Slugger was the team's strongest hitter and regularly was the cleanup hitter. But the night before the game, I got to thinking, why did Barry Bonds always hit third? Maybe those other teams—those other businesses—have something to teach, and I could take a page from their best practices. Maybe it was time to move up the big hitter to the third spot so perhaps she'd get an extra chance to hit, and I would not be seeing her in the on-deck circle when the game ended. Well, well, well, here we were—Ms. Slugger was up to bat. Maybe those pros knew something about whom to put in the third batter spot. Maybe those other successful businesses that had thrived on mojo had something important to teach.

I called time, I walked up to her, and it then became a brief moment burned in a memory as I grabbed hold of the bill of her batting helmet and looked her in the eyes: "This is all good—if you make an out, we still do not lose. If you get a hit, maybe we win. Either way, there is nothing bad that will come with this at bat. This will be the best at bat you will have for a long time, because anything you do is good, and you don't often get to say that." Was that the start of a get-your-mojo speech? After all, if you let yourself rely on fundamentals and your instincts, you let the mojo flow. I paused, not long, but just long enough for her to let it all sink in and catch a breath, and then I added, "Okay, let's keep it simple, huh? So just wait for a pitch you think you can crush—in or out of the strike zone doesn't matter—and do it." She looked at me, she smiled—and I mean a big smile—and those eyes spoke before she did: "I got it. I really do."

First pitch, she got it. She got all of it into centerfield like a missile, whistling past my daughter running from second base. I was making windmills with my arms as she passed me by on third, and I followed her all the way to home as she jumped on the plate—16–15 for those keeping score. For the daughter and her dad, game over, season over, maybe baseball careers over—with eleven runs scored in the last at bat and the daughter getting the double to tie it and scoring the sixteenth run to win it. We are talking here about serious buckets full of mojo.

With this, my twenty-two-year baseball coaching career ends. Ah yes, the summer game of softball, teaching the power of team mojo while serving up joy, redemption, and memories. So as you take a pause from the stress, the worry, and the grind—whether over coffee, in traffic, or at a beach—remember those times on the softball or baseball diamond and you may see you really have done it before, and the seeds of the skills you need were long ago planted and are now ready to thrive. And yes, about endings, if I get to meet up with the old Sox nemesis Yogi, I will tell him he was right about when things are over.

Everything said here clearly applies to entrepreneurs in business as well—the power of leadership and tenacity, never giving up, but most importantly, the infectious nature of team mojo that gets all the wheels in a team humming in unison to deliver results. As Will Martinez told us in chapter 4, you can't solo Mt. Everest—so when your entire team is humming, this infectious team mojo is the only way to go places you have never been.

Biographical Comments by the Lead Author

Larry is a fortunate father of six successful children, grateful husband of thirty-eight years, a successful twenty-five-year CEO/CFO of a midsize law firm (now Donahue Fitzgerald LLP), an accomplished trial lawyer, a business adviser to numerous start-ups, an advisory board member of public and private incubators and accelerators since their advent in the 1990s, and a youth baseball/softball manager for thirty teams over twenty-two seasons. It was from this last effort that he learned that tryouts can be as stressful as any funding pitch, that like many important meetings, tryouts seem to land on lousy weather days and that refining the skill of talent assessment pays dividends far beyond the business world, and in the end, it is where one truly can, on full display, learn many of the skills needed to get one's mojo back. He received from UC Berkeley both a BA in economics with distinction and a BS in business (Haas School) with honors and graduated Phi Beta Kappa. He graduated with a law degree from the University of California Hastings College of the Law. He initially practiced business law before becoming a trial lawyer for over thirty years (while serving as the law firm's CEO/CFO). He now focuses his time on his family, clients, and the challenge of golf—the latter being another opportunity to get his mojo back through at least perspiration. His story brings to life a summer day a few years back where the experiences of many past seasons of perspiration, vignettes of inspiration, and pains of education came together to inspire a collective success and provide the reminder that getting back one's mojo really can come about from infusing education with perspiration, inspiration, patience, and a bit of luck. Larry and I have served on a board together, jointly mentored entrepreneurs, counseled business associates, and more importantly, adhered to a pizza and beer night once a month where we get back to the business of living and being friends.

Chapter 28

Know Your Reason Why

Phyllis Newhouse

I have strived all my life to make the American dream a reality for me and my family. I was born in North Carolina, one of eleven children, with very modest means, and was taught by my parents that you must have hard-work ethics, determination, and self-drive to achieve anything in life. Truth be told, my mother, Mary Frances Winchester, was the first entrepreneur I ever knew. It would not be until I began my own journey that I realized that a lot of who I became as a CEO was what I witnessed as a child.

I watched my mother work with a tight budget, resolve conflicts, build teams, and definitely build each one of her eleven children up to be the best they could be. She always said to us, "Make the best better." My mother told me at a very young age that I was born to lead. That seed she sowed in me has stayed with me all my life. What a blessing she has been to me.

When I think back on my early life, my thoughts of success began many years ago when I was in high school. I remember my English teacher had a quote by Mark Twain on the blackboard that said, "*The two most important days of your life are the day you were born and the day you discover why.*"

That quote has stayed with me until this very day.

I spent twenty-two years in the military where I learned leadership, logistics, finance, sales, talent development, mission planning, and strategic road mapping. I helped build organizations within the military and mentored many while serving in the military. Before retiring as a senior leader, I knew that I wanted to be an entrepreneur. With my military experience, I thought, why not launch my own company—an Atlanta-based technology company? It almost seemed like a plain vanilla no-brainer. But who am I to know?

But here's the thing I knew: the military gives you the manual on leadership, and all you have to do is execute. As an entrepreneur, I was aware it was definitely not going to be an easy road to success. Although, yes, I had tremendous experience that I could apply, there was no manual for guaranteed success. That was the challenge, and I was going to have to figure it out from scratch. I also knew I had the right mind-set, and I knew the reason that I wanted to take this journey.

When I was a kid, I remember that I was always asking adults why. As I think back to when I have spent time around kids, I have also probably been subjected to a barrage of the most classic of childhood queries: "Why?" From a very young age, we somehow know intuitively that the real motive behind an action is the most important piece of any story.

I knew that in order to take on this journey, it was very important for me to know my reason why. Why did I want to launch my company? Why was my legacy so important? I wanted to show others—whether that meant family members, women, African Americans like me, veterans—hey, you can start from scratch, and you can build something big. I wanted them to know that if you have a plan and work very hard, success can happen. Because my why was so strong, I knew that failure was not an option for me. Knowing why you're in a business is crucial to success. I have seen multiple businesses fail because entrepreneurs never stopped and asked themselves what motivated them. When it comes to your business, regardless of whether you've already launched or if you're still in the brainstorming phase, knowing your why will help you stay committed to your dream, determine your level of success, and help others get on board too. When you're passionate about the why, success is almost a given. My partner, Hervia Ingram, and I reestablish our company's why every three years. We recheck our clocks!

Put your dreams on paper! Once you have done that, pray over your dreams! Think about them. I've always been a three-years-out person. I think, "What do I want to be in three years?" Then I write that plan out. I knew that I was going to be an entrepreneur. I felt so strong about this decision in the last three years of my military career, and I started to do all the things to prep myself. I began thinking and planning to be in business prior to leaving the military. I took business courses. I researched businesses. I began to talk to business owners. I listened to all the challenges they had faced, the hard work, and also the rewards it brought them when the business was successful. I knew that with hard work and determination, I could be well on my way to owning my own business. I remember the first day, sitting at home and saying, "Wow, I don't have any customers. I don't have a plan. I don't have any revenue. I have to do something today that makes a difference tomorrow. Every day I must have this attitude."

In 2002, my journey as an entrepreneur began. My company, Xtreme Solutions, was born. I always get asked about how I got my start. I have to admit, that day changed my attitude for life. Truth be told, I started with a blank vision board that very same day. I thought I could build anything I wanted in business on this board, so I started mapping it out. I put the day I was going to launch the business—June 2, 2002—on the board. Where do I want to be in two years? I checked on the Internet regarding downtown buildings for office space, looking for where my future offices might be. I pulled a picture of a building that I liked the looks of, printed it out, and put it on the board. I wrote a personal check for $1,000,000 and put it on the board. My list of future clients and number of employees—they went on the board. I literally built my company on that vision board.

On my first day as CEO, I was sitting at home, thinking, "I still don't have any clients, so I've got to figure out what I can do today to get one client. What can I do to earn revenue today so I could meet those long-term goals I've set?"

It was a very scary feeling, but I will tell you this: everything on that vision board was achieved in record time. Two years later, we moved into our new space, and it wasn't until five years later when I pulled out the vision board and realized that our new offices were in that building I had put on the board.

This process has reaffirmed for me the importance of vision. What sort of vision do you have for your company? If you see it, you can build it. That's how I got my team to buy into 42 percent revenue growth for four straight years—because every day when I would go back to speak to them, I would say, "Let's talk about the 42 percent." We didn't have 42 percent growth; we had 60 percent and even went to 98 percent growth in one year. And now in 2016, I have won a contract worth over $250 million.

I live by the idea that we speak concepts into existence. We believe them into being.

I truly believe the core characteristics of my success have come from the discipline I learned in the military. It transferred to everything I did, from writing a business plan to focusing on a sales strategy.

When Xtreme Solutions first approached AT&T as a client, the mobile telecommunications provider had a rigorous checklist of what they needed before any company could be a supplier for them. I had no employees at that time, but I was "very diligent" about getting certifications that normally take between six to eight months to get. I got some of these in two or three weeks. It was a tremendous amount of work, but I just didn't believe in procrastination.

I often get asked the question, what do you fear the most? To be successful as an entrepreneur, you have to be fearless, and before I started my business, I was afraid of heights. In my spirit, to rid myself of fears, I went to the Piton Mountains in the island of St. Lucia in the Caribbean. The peak was 2,458 feet, or a half mile up from the nearby waters. It was a straight-up Caribbean volcano. I challenged myself to climb the Piton Mountains, and it took me seven hours. Along the way, I never thought about quitting. I kept saying, "I know this will be worth the aches and pain I am going through when I get to the top." I kept thinking, *God has given me all I need to be who I need to be. That's today, tomorrow, and forever.*

When I got to the top, something changed in me that day. I knew that with a strong mind and will, I could achieve almost anything. I kept that thought in my mind the entire time I was climbing to the top. While sitting at the top of the mountain, it reminded me of everything I've done in life so far that just wasn't easy. The results are not easy, and there's pain along the way, but sometimes the view is worth it. I still think of that moment sitting at the top of the Piton Mountains when I encounter business challenges. In that moment, I rid myself of any fear, forever.

I really believe that mojo can be the difference between winning and losing, between your happiness and sadness, between your success and your failure. It may very well be the secret ingredient that is missing from your business today. As I reflect on my lack of fear, my vision for my business, and what has worked for me, I offer the reader the following tips to keep your mojo on the up and up:

1. *You must stay away from any negative influences.* We all have heard the adage "Misery loves company." Well, this is truer today than ever. The best example of negative influences can be found in social media. Thankfully, we all have a choice. You can participate or not. You can watch the news, read the newspaper, or not. Many who want to get their mojo back are boycotting these negative social media outlets and other similar formats. This is also true with the coffee machine talk or watercooler conversations. Choose not to participate with the negative ones, and you will be happier and may even see your mojo level improve.
2. *Seek the little wins.* The little wins will create bigger wins, and bigger wins will definitely help you and your team to get the mojo back. When we lower the bar to the little wins, we increase the likelihood of winning. These wins can be selling a business line or a small project. It can be something as simple as helping a team member be more successful. If you try this and believe in this dynamic, then you just need to get a few little wins under your belt to get started. I know that a few little wins will make a difference and help you refill your mojo tanks.
3. *Take inventory of what is happening in your journey. Write it down.* I can tell you how important this has been for me. I have

been very consistent in writing in a gratitude journal for the last ten years. This has allowed me to develop a spirit of gratitude and to see many more positives in life than negatives. A simple exercise is to create two columns. In one column, list all the things you are grateful for today. That includes things in your professional and personal life. On the other side of the page, list all the things you want to happen but have not happened yet. This is your intentional gratitude page. This is where you can give thanks in advance for something that through your faith you believe will happen. These can include your health or your financial well-being. I like to do this every day for myself. I find that the list of positives is always much longer than the negatives. Within just a few minutes of reflection with this graphic in front of me, my positive attitude moves up a notch. I then begin to feel so grateful.

In closing, I think that mojo is not something you can see or feel; it is something we must know and understand. In order to get your mojo going, you must get clear on your motivation.

Know the reason you want to lead. It cannot be for the money. It cannot be because you just want to be a CEO. When I first started the business, my reason was my son Ezekiel. Your reasons have to be so compelling that failure is simply not an option. Trust me, your mojo will be 100 percent ready, and you should have the tenacity to persevere. As Larry Rockwell mentioned in the preceding chapter, your mojo may even inspire others and create team mojo. Wow!

Biographical Comments by the Lead Author

Phyllis always strives to make the American dream a reality. Her personal story is as uplifting and inspiring as the things she has accomplished. Born in North Carolina, one of eleven children, with very modest means, her hard-work ethics, determination, self-drive, love for enhanced technology, and desire to make a difference to others have all led to her recognition as one of the top leaders in the technology industry and one of the most influential women in technology today.

Phyllis is a retired Army noncommissioned officer and a service-disabled veteran with more than twenty-two years of military service. She has vast experience in information technology planning, strategic growth planning, and professional services. Since founding Xtreme Solutions Inc. in 2002, Phyllis has grown the business into a profitable multimillion-dollar company with highly skilled professionals in more than twenty states, supporting several prime contracts with civilian and defense agencies of the federal government and providing IT end-to-end solutions in information assurance, cybersecurity, and network support to numerous Fortune 500 companies around the globe. Phyllis was honored in Atlanta by 100 Black Men of America with the Marilyn Johnson Women of Color Achievement Award in 2012 sponsored by IBM and PNC. The inaugural event was hosted in Baltimore in 2010 through a partnership between the Women Presidents' Organization and 100 Black Men of America. She was also acknowledged for her commitment to economic empowerment within her community, and in 2015, it was my pleasure to present her the Chuck Smith Entrepreneurship Award from John F. Kennedy University for a lifetime of entrepreneurial accomplishments. Most importantly, I consider Phyllis a true friend one of my BFF.

Chapter 29

Making Use of Life's Hardships to Be of Service: A Story of Grace and Perseverance

Tom Gorham

A Turning Point for Me

In September of 1998, I made a decision that would shift the course of my life completely and for the better. I sat in the Santa Rita County jail again for the forty-seventh time. I was caught in a perpetual cycle of drinking, living on the street, and inevitable incarceration. I had been court-ordered to Options Recovery Services for almost six months but had been sent back to jail four times because I was both unwilling and unable to stop drinking. On this particular trip, I had a thought. It was more like an epiphany for me because I had never considered a life beyond my decade of homelessness. I was hopelessly mired in a belief that I would die on the street. I had no need or motivation to turn my life around.

As I sat there on September 8, 1998, I felt very uncomfortable with the thought that others cared more about me than I did about myself. It was the staff at Options Recovery Services, particularly Dr. Davida Coady and the Drug Court judge, Carol Brosnahan, who believed in me before I could believe in myself. On that date, I decided to stop drinking cold and start a new chapter of my life.

I actually went on to complete the Options Program and stayed around to volunteer for the next couple of years. My health had deteriorated to the point that I was collecting Social Security disability insurance. I knew that I needed more challenges in life if I was going to remain sober, and I decided to return to school at the age of fifty.

I entered an addiction certificate program at John F. Kennedy University. By that time, Options had found a little money and gave me a stipend to work there, but the real payoff for me was that I was given the chance to take the science that I learned in school and combine it with my life experience and build a program that would serve as a blueprint for others. It felt like a miracle that those ten-plus years of homelessness and alcoholism were suddenly a resource! Also, I was excited that someone believed and trusted me.

Options in the Early Years

When I initially entered the Options program, there were ten to twenty participants. Every year for the first ten years, that number increased by about 50 percent, until it got as high as 235 at one time. The reason for that was that we were free and immediately available to those with a need and a desire to change.

Davida Coady, the founder, realized that in the Bay Area of San Francisco, there were no treatment slots for addicts that did not require getting on a waiting list. She also noticed that there were few treatment opportunities for those, like myself, who had no way to pay. Her belief that you look for the need and fill it and the money will soon follow was not a concept that I shared but was apparently working as the program continued to prosper in spite of little financial resources.

The Options approach also had one huge advantage in that our priorities could be pure in the sense that we could allow clients to show us their needs, and we could do our best to meet them. In other words, we were unrestricted by government funding obligations to concentrate on building a unique model of addiction recovery.

We were the poorest program in town, but we filled the need in the community. Others were beginning to rally around and form important partnerships that we still have today twenty years later. Counter-intuitive thinking has been part of our secret sauce all along.

It is interesting that while government agencies in our area were desperately seeking solutions to societal problems like homelessness, drug use, and crime, they were seeing our consistent success with some of the most challenging populations and with very limited financial resources.

We had many naysayers in the beginning, but one by one they came to see that we were solving many of those needs with little help from government money. The city of Berkeley quickly gave us free space in the downtown Veteran's Hall, which was largely unused because of structural damage. It would have been extremely challenging to pay rent and do what we have done since the beginning.

Options started in the Drug Courts, and when laws were passed in California (Proposition 36) that supported our type of program, our years of volunteering in those courts positioned us to start getting paid for our services.

Housing individuals while in an outpatient treatment program was a need that we quickly realized would improve their chances significantly. Running a residential treatment program provides safety for clients but is costly. So our solution was to provide cutting-edge, evidence-based services at low cost and add clean, sober, and tobacco-free housing for our clients. This kept clients in treatment and, to our amazement, actually turned a small profit. Bingo! Another example of filling a need that turns into a sound business model. Counter-intuitive thinking at its best!

We leased our first house and put a lot of effort into rehabilitating it. The home was in East Oakland and had been abandoned for some time. The homeless had been using it as a safe haven to crash and use drugs. It was a mess! We fixed it up and filled it up and were in for a surprise. The owner paid us a visit and put the house up for sale. We learned a tough lesson but scrounged enough money to buy our first house.

The need for housing led us to buy another and another. By 2005, we had six recovery residences. Most of our clients had no way to pay rent, so we partnered with Alameda County Social Services, who allowed their general assistance to be used to pay their rent. The houses also provided an opportunity for our clients to learn to live a life without drugs, alcohol, and crime in a safe, supportive environment.

Tom Gorham 2.0 Better Than the Earlier Model

Looking at my own development, I stayed in school and earned a bachelor's degree in liberal arts with an emphasis on psychology. I didn't stop there because the clients showed me that we needed to be able to understand and treat other mental health disorders. Our mission statement said that we would accept all individuals that came to the program and shut the door on no one. We were doing that but failing to make a difference in some of the folks that we were trying to help.

I signed up at John F. Kennedy University for a linked degree in counseling psychology. It is here that I learned what I call the parallel process. In other words, as we learn how to help others to develop themselves, we work on developing ourselves. In addition to pursuing my education, I got involved professionally by getting on professional boards and meeting the leaders in the field of addiction and recovery. I learned from them, and they became fascinated with our emerging model.

Many of my colleagues got involved and helped out in many ways. Options became known on a state and national level. I made it my business to see what the Betty Ford Clinic and other leaders of the alcohol-and-drug-treatment world were doing. I was surprised to find out that the quality of our services were as good as any out there, and amazingly, in most cases, we were providing them at no cost to all our clients who had no money to pay. I also stayed tuned into foundation monies that would support nonprofit programs such as ours.

Our first big break came when the California Endowment decided to support our idea to start our own mental health clinic. They gave us enough support to hire a couple of case managers and therapists to see clients who needed additional support and possibly medication referrals.

We again learned from clients that if trauma issues were not addressed while they were in treatment, they would soon relapse. We also were seeing a steady need for medications for mental health disorders and, on occasion, needed to make appropriate referrals. We also saw immediate success and found ways to keep the clinic going after the funding ran out. I knew from my own experience that some issues were too delicate to be discussed at the group level and that individual therapy would provide a safe container to work on them. Another concern was that, amazingly, most psychotherapists have little understanding of addiction, and we would be better off training our own.

By 2008, Tom Gorham version 2.0 had evolved well enough, and the model was definitely much better than version 1.0. My life had a purpose, and I was succeeding, albeit with many immense challenges. Options itself had well over two hundred clients that we were seeing from one to five days per week. I again knew, from my own experience, that we would become the only community that many of our clients would have.

In my evolution, you must understand that my whole family had died from substance abuse. My father and brother died from lung cancer because of many years of tobacco use. My sister died of cirrhosis from years of alcohol abuse, and my mother died from an overdose of prescription painkillers and alcohol. Options Recovery Services was really the only community that I had that supported my continuing efforts to stay clean and sober. It also provided me with the meaning and purpose to give my life the new energy that was missing before.

I also knew that there would be many more like me who, for a variety of reasons, would need the same opportunity. So to serve these two-hundred-plus clients, we used the parallel process to train staff from graduates of the program. Like me, many clients felt that they were beyond help and needed to have role models who were living proof that they could turn their lives around. They also needed someone to believe in them so that they might see hope for themselves. I like to call it spiritual CPR.

As a result, over the years, the Options staff has evolved into a blend of volunteers, state-certified addiction professionals, and others that were drawn to our cause. Our graduates, like me, were deeply indebted to the program that basically saved their lives. This loyalty to the mission transcends any amount of money we could offer, and this has manifested itself on many occasions when we had financial shortfalls and everyone on the staff sacrificed as a team. We always survived and became a stronger program as a result.

At San Quentin

In the fall of 2005, I received a call from the president of the state certification board for addiction treatment programs, of which I was a member. He told me that a couple of life-term inmates had sent him a letter asking if we could help them learn how to become counselors at San Quentin State Prison. They stated in the letter that they had long ago stopped using drugs and alcohol, which are readily available in prison. They themselves had stopped using through the help of various twelve-step programs. They now wanted to help other inmates that were there for shorter terms and, in particular, those that were younger. They hoped we would visit them in San Quentin and find a way to train them to a professional level. How novel, lifers wanting to help newbies!

I went to the prison and met with them and was thoroughly impressed not only with their idea but more so with their appreciation that we showed up at all. I decided to get involved and help them. I put together a training that included all the requirements for state certification. We trained a group of thirty-five men who were mostly at San Quentin for life sentences. Eighty-seven percent of them passed the state exam. The national average is around 70 percent. The dedication and gratitude of these men were incredible.

Options then received a grant from the California Department of Corrections Community Partnership Program for over a million dollars to start a pilot program at San Quentin to lower recidivism. We created a model that lowered recidivism by over two-thirds of the rate at that time. We have been supporting that program at San Quentin ever since with Options funding. Again, I was amazed to get a great opportunity that I did not expect because we were just filling a need.

At Solano State Prison

In 2008, I received a call from California corrections officials. They asked me if Options would train fifty men at Solano State Prison to become state-certified counselors like we were doing at San Quentin. That was the beginning of the Offender Mentor Certification Program, which now will be in place in all thirty-four California prison facilities. This is one of the things of which I am most proud to have been a part of. As a result, thousands of inmates are receiving the treatment they so desperately have needed to stay out of prison! I believe this will help lessen recidivism and will give all these men the opportunity I had.

On January 1, 2014, the Affordable Care Act went into effect. This was a complete game changer, not only for the country, but also for Options Recovery Services. For years, we had accepted and treated clients who had no way to pay. Suddenly almost all our clients had some ability to pay. We applied and were contracted to provide treatment for individuals who had Medi-Cal insurance since 2003. This only covered a small fraction of our clients, who were mostly women with children. Men rarely had this insurance, and if they did, it was because they suffered from a severe physical or psychiatric disability.

I remember that the day after the Affordable Care Act was in effect, we had to do intakes for about 125 clients. The paperwork was enormous, but talk about a reverse marketing strategy; we had the market cornered for clients to whom treatment was not available before the Affordable Care Act. What this meant to Options Recovery Services was that we had to up our game. By this, I mean that we had to start documenting all the work for which we wanted to get paid for. We also had to look at the clinical practices that we were using to make sure that they were in compliance with what the Medi-Cal coverage would pay for.

Needless to say, we again were well positioned to capitalize and adapt. Most agencies don't like to accept Medi-Cal because it does not pay as high of a rate as private insurance. But to us at Options, who had been seeing the majority of our clients for free; it has been a blessing. The Affordable Care Act has had a domino effect on our housing as well. Three quarters of our 185 current clients take advantage of our clean, sober, and tobacco-free housing while in treatment and beyond. As a result of universal insurance for substance use disorders, the government suddenly can invest the money that used to pay for treatment into recovery residences.

This means that Options has been contracting with several agencies that want to place clients into our housing at market rates. Options Recovery Services is the only provider that can currently meet this need in Alameda County. This truly has been a Blue Ocean strategy (see chapter 11). But we will take no credit for that because we were only trying to fill a need, and it paid off.

Tom Gorham 3.0

Just as in tech products, I continued to adapt and evolve. In September 2014, I enrolled in an entrepreneur certificate program at John F. Kennedy University because I planned to apply for the executive director job that was about to open at Options Recovery Services. I had not been involved in the business side of Options Recovery Services up to that point.

It was there that I met Dr. Raul Deju (the lead author) and Mrs. Dina Finta (see chapter 26). I had known Ann Marie Taylor (chapter 31) for many years during my involvement with the university, both as a student and an alumni member. Anne Marie introduced me to the team of Deju and Finta. All three of these individuals helped give me the skills that I would need to lead the Options organization and take it to the next level. I completed the business planning needed to take Options to the next level, and together we raised money to over double the current physical building capacity of the program.

I had never hesitated to reach out and get the credentials that would give me and the program the best chance for success. I started the journey at forty-nine years old, and I took all the steps that were necessary for my own personal and professional development. That is the perspiration part of my life.

The passion or mojo piece is fueled by my gratitude for the grace that I have received. Most of the people that I lived with on the street already died there. I was given a second chance in life and decided to run with it. I decided to spend my energy to help others in a similar position in life and to leapfrog into the next chapter of their lives by working at Options. In the 18 years that I have worked there, almost 10,000 clients have walked through our doors. Nothing short of a miracle in my estimation, and to be part of that is a dream come true.

I took the steps that I did because I knew that people had to take me seriously, and if that were to happen, I had to do the work and get the degrees and the letters behind my name. As a result, I have a feeling of accomplishment in that I have made my life meaningful and, as a result, given the opportunity and hope to others as someone else did for me. Today, I have gone from a homeless, hopeless alcoholic to an executive director of Options Recovery Services, president of the Addiction Professional Association, licensed marriage and family therapist, and certified addiction professional.

I offer you a challenge to push yourself to the next level and get to work. You never have to look too far for a need to fill, and it's always time for personal growth, because if we are not busy growing, we are busy dying. Options Recovery Services has gone from one woman's idea of how to help poor addicts recover to a premier treatment organization with a three-million-dollar annual budget! Maybe in the next ten years, we will not have ten thousand but twenty thousand graduates and will have contributed to reducing recidivism in our prisons as economically as we can. Wow!

Biographical Comments by the Lead Author

Tom Gorham was homeless on the streets of Berkeley and Oakland for over a decade. He was despondent and hopeless and saw no future. After hundreds of incarcerations, he ended up in a Berkeley Drug Court where he received help for his alcoholism at Options Recovery Services in Berkeley, California. At the age of fifty, Tom returned to school at John F. Kennedy University, where he earned two degrees and two certificates. He became certified as an alcohol and drug counselor and licensed as a marriage and family therapist. He helped develop a dynamic treatment program for individuals like himself, and in eighteen years, he has worked with thousands of individuals struggling to maintain sobriety. He is the president of the Addiction Professional Association for California. He is also now the executive director of Options Recovery Services, the institution that literally saved his life. Tom works in California prisons to train inmates to become certified alcohol and drug counselors. He teaches courses at universities such as John F. Kennedy and UC Berkeley Extension, and he trains other mental health professionals in addiction studies. Tom's rise from alcoholism, homelessness, and incarceration to a licensed and certified professional, board president, and executive director challenges other individuals to redefine their lives. It has been my pleasure over the last few years to be a mentor to Tom, who graduated from the Institute of Entrepreneurial Leadership. It is also my family's pleasure to be a donor to such a good cause as Options Recovery Services.

Chapter 30

Walking the Mojo Path with Sisters at My Side: Discovering That You "CancerVive" Against the Odds

Anne Marie Taylor

Ten years ago, I learned to bear the unbearable while traveling through the frightening path of stage IV breast cancer. Many times, I questioned my mojo and my ability to take another step beyond the hideous tolerance of poisonous chemotherapy, disfiguring surgeries, and arduous radiation. But in those lowest moments when I could no longer journey alone, many others stood within my sisterhood ranks and gave me their strength to fight the battle.

Friendships and connections with other women have long been part of my life's scaffolding, holding me up in benevolent support as I've worked on building and growing myself into a whole person. The construction of "me" has been complicated with stops and starts, failures and room redecorations, upgrades and tear-outs, but one constant in this laborious process has always been my female compatriots: two sisters by birth and many others by alliance.

During youthful times, when dealing with strict parents and pimples and first boyfriends, my juvenile girlfriends gave me an outlet for tears and laughter and swapping adolescent horror stories. High school years as a teenager meant that my closest girlfriends became *the absolute experts* in everything; I deemed most adult ideas to be ridiculously outdated, while my female peers always knew the latest and greatest.

I attended Scripps College and loved this vibrant academic environment with all the women on my campus surrounded by a plethora of potential male companions at the other Claremont Colleges when we wanted to venture forth. For me, college was a bastion of female camaraderie with late-night conversations and intellectual debates on all topics worthy of opinion. Three of us became inseparable, and together, we created intricate designs for our lives through the classes we took, the causes we supported, the sports we played, and the romances we enjoyed or endured. What I learned from being part of this collegiate trio of deep and authentic female friendship was that if it happened to one of us, it mattered to all of us.

Before starting my first master's degree, my mother and I set off from California, driving across the country to set up my next life as a graduate student in Columbia, Missouri. Mom has always been the strongest female influence in my life, except for those few teen years when I thought she had lost her mind and she thought I had lost mine! Making our way across nearly two thousand miles and seven states, I remember clinging to each familiar story she recounted about her life, upbringing, hometown, parents, boyfriends, marriage, volunteer work, career, and her own chronicles of enduring female friendships.

We talked . . . and talked . . . and talked about how much we both talked! I most loved the account of her neurosurgical nursing days and the friendships she forged with several other newly minted Mayo Clinic buddies. They all shared one particular yellow dress that got passed around the dorm to whoever was going out on a fancy date. My mother giggled about what the dress would say if only it could talk and tell how many men's arms had been wrapped around its delicate yellow pinstripe!

And in the same way, my mother had experienced the deep influence of girlfriends, women have befriended and blessed me with their presence and their wisdom. As I've developed all kinds of rooms in the structure of my life—marriage, motherhood, toddlers, teenagers, career transitions, philanthropic endeavors, caring for elderly relatives, and even death—I was always surrounded by my "sisters" in life and in love. People and jobs and locations change and shift, but the stalwart framework of my life has been those female legionnaires, living and loving alongside me, intertwined in my life by sharing the battles, the victories, and the defeats.

My female friends were present to gather and celebrate that first day my baby stood up and took her first step, to applaud that day when I walked across the stage earning another advanced degree, and to hold me and to cherish me through every day sandwiched in between. They have teased me about the tenacity of my personal "aim high" mojo, and they are often comforted by me when together we share in the joy and irony of life.

One day, however, one decade ago, with one phone call and one diagnosis, my carefully constructed building of life as a wife and mother of six children, and as a working professional and community advocate, came crashing down. I had breast cancer, the bad kind. Invasive, the kind that finishes you. Ten years ago, I needed my sisters to pick me up and to care for my wounds when the weight of life felt larger than my mojo could handle. I relied on them to bear arms and fight with me and even to fight for me when my spirit wearied.

I tried desperately to keep my balance through drastic surgeries that left me an amputee, vile chemotherapy poisons, indescribable nausea, high-dose radiation, failed reconstruction with broken ribs and a collapsed lung, and prolonged excruciating pain. Cancer is a road no one should ever walk alone, but I was most fortunate to not only have my faith and my family, I had my female friends to lean on during each hesitant, uncertain step.

God, family, friends were all there, but none felt truer and more encouraging than my cancer ladies, my band of sisters, my circle of support. They filled my doorstep with flowers the morning of each surgery. Seven of them crafted and sewed a queen-size patchwork quilt of my favorite designs. Five of them created a comedic papier-mâché tabletop display of little red infantry soldiers (the red Adriamycin chemo) attacking the cancerous tumor, bringing lighthearted humor to the gravity of my debilitating treatment. They gathered in prayer and laid hands on my weakened body before every chemo treatment and every transfusion.

Two of them routinely took away my family's dirty laundry and returned with folded clothes and ironed shirts. Hundreds sent beautiful cards with notes of comfort and encouragement. They forwarded e-mail messages to women in other countries, praying for this one wounded in their flock, tending to me as a shepherd cares for her disabled lamb. They carried me across their backs and shouldered my illness as if it were their own disease. Three coordinated my family's meals for an entire year and brought my family nearly continuous home-cooked dinners.

They sat with me as the crimson poison dripped into my veins, and they talked of things beyond the sterile oncology environment. We sucked on frozen popsicles and chuckled as I would shuffle to the bathroom with IV tubes tangled around my legs. We mourned my body when it was deprived of health and the breasts that had once defined my feminine shape, but my scars became signs of victory in battle and tenacity.

The ladies in my gourmet group held back laughter in public when one of my cotton breast forms slipped out of my shirt and landed in our salad, and they didn't stop caring when my body resembled a twelve-year-old's hairless, amorphous form. They didn't make fun when my polyester wig frizzed and singed and smoked while I stood too close underneath a heat lamp at my first social outing in six months.

My kindhearted oldest daughter, whose personal friendship is a visceral bond beating between our two hearts, helped her younger siblings write words of strength and beauty across my bedroom mirror using bars of Ivory soap. I was able to look beyond the reflection of my emaciated body and bald head by reading those words, "Be anxious for nothing, but in everything with prayer and supplication, with thanksgiving, let your requests be made known to God, and the peace of Christ which surpasses all understanding will comfort you." And she must have stood tippy-toe on a chair to reach up and tape a message of resilience and fortitude onto the ceiling above my pillow so that I awoke to her words: "You are loved and beautiful."

Piece by piece, the bricks and mortar began to take shape again, and the silhouette of a new life building arose out of the wreckage. A new shape to this edifice, one with increased purpose and intentional design, had replaced the naive innocence of my past. When I turned fifty, my family arranged for a full year of "Lunch with the Ladies," and I enjoyed meeting one on one with my fifty closest friends at the same wonderful restaurant. No better present, no bling or bauble, could have been more meaningful or precious as compared to those incredible weekly luncheons with diverse women who've all been players on my team and had a significant influence on my ability to maintain my mojo.

I've been able to share my cancer story with others and to minister in ways that only my own personal experience has allowed. Once, I was called to the bedside of a woman I barely knew but whose need for companionship beckoned me, giving me the chance to support her and pray with her as a sister during those final few months of life. I've communicated via phone and e-mail or text messages to women across the globe who needed to borrow my strength as they fought against disease. I am pleased to rent my mojo.

One of my more recent friends, Debi Hemmeter, cofounded the Lean In Foundation with Sheryl Sandberg; she and I share the same passion for interconnections and joining female forces during the ups and downs of life. Debi articulates what I've experienced from my sisterhood—that the more women help one another, the more we help ourselves. Both of us have discovered the myriad of ways that women will sacrifice and negotiate for others, and we are both quick to encourage women who need to more openly advocate for themselves.

It's important to have confidence in yourself and to negotiate for what you deserve. Debi, for example, is now impacting women through twenty-five thousand transformative Lean In circles, driven by the awareness that when women act like a coalition, true and lasting results are produced.

I write this message now to all those incredible CancerVive sisters of mine who ministered to and cared for me and to all of you who are in need of caring or who have served as soldiers in caring for others. My mojo message to you ten years beyond a terrible diagnosis now echoes what I have learned and what I read every morning taped to the ceiling of my bedroom: You are all loved and beautiful.

Whether one is fighting a disease or the seemingly impossible tasks involved with creating and growing a business or caring for one's family, friends are the extended family that helps us through one vicissitude after another. The worst thing for anyone is being alone without anyone with whom to share feelings and fears. Just as was the case for Dr. Deju, who was overwhelmed by leaving his family in another country but was supported by his own brotherhood in America, or by Jackie Baghavan, who trekked through the back roads of Cambodia to escape a genocidal regime, winding up in a refugee camp, it was my sister friends who helped me escape and succumb to the forces of a miserable breast cancer.

You are all God's truest gift to one another. Surround one another in trials, in exultations, in the mundane, and the sublime of every day. Stand strong as the scaffolding of one another's lives. Build each other up with the gentle, loyal hands of connection and friendship. My journey has been your journey as well, because no one should ever walk these roads alone.

Once you take a journey like I have, you can also appreciate the value of every living moment, and it reinforces the importance of friends as part of the daily routine, and you appreciate times with your husband, kids, grandkids, and of course, my sister friends, as we are all BFF.

Biographical Comments by the Lead Author

Anne Marie Taylor serves as Vice President of Advancement at John F. Kennedy University, a private nonprofit predominantly graduate college in the San Francisco Bay Area of Northern California. As the chief fund-raiser and development guru at the university, she has significantly increased and developed strategic relationships with education advocates, this year opening the Sanford Institute of Philanthropy aimed to build nonprofit capacity and promote leadership. Particular areas of her social focus include investing in veterans transitioning from the military into classrooms, and support for behavioral health interns working with at-risk youth and disadvantaged families. Anne Marie is actively involved on the Summit Bank Foundation Board, East Bay Leadership Council, California Shakespeare Theater, John Muir Health Foundation, and Tesoro Corporation and PG&E's Community Councils. She is a lifetime sustainer with the Junior League of Oakland East Bay, president of Tuesday Forum professional women's group, and a certified Covey 7 Habits trainer. She actually started her career with the Wall Street Journal's San Francisco bureau. She earned a history/literature BA from Scripps College, an MA in journalism from the University of Missouri, Columbia, and is completing her MBA at John F. Kennedy University, specializing in nonprofit leadership. With her husband, Thomas, Anne Marie raised six ambitious children who are Stanford, West Point, law school, medical school, and engineering graduates, with the caboose now at Dartmouth College in a combination of premed and biophysical chemistry. She and I have known each other since I began teaching in the evenings as an MBA professor at John F. Kennedy University nearly eighteen years ago, and she assisted me in launching the Institute of Entrepreneurial Leadership in 2010. Both she and Tom, her husband, are former students of mine in the MBA program, and both are true friends. I have always admired Anne Marie's power of persuasion when it comes to obtaining assistance for those less fortunate. As you read in this chapter, she never gives up!

Chapter 31

Authentic Leadership:
The World Is Your Apple

John Sánchez

My Authentic Leadership Journey: Never Give Up!

As I peel back the layers of serial entrepreneurship, I have to go back to the time when I was a twelve-year-old boy growing up in California. My first introduction to entrepreneurship and authentic leadership came from my baseball coach, Vern Miller. Coach Miller was an entrepreneur by day, as owner-operator of a successful plumbing business, and a volunteer little league coach in his off time. He was an Army captain who earned a Silver Star during his service in the European theater of World War II, and like many others who lived through that period, he had many life lessons to share with his players. He had his own rulebook, and at every practice, he went out of his way to impart honest feedback (whether we liked it or not) about life on and off the field.

From him, I learned about many topics: adversity, anticipation, discipline, grit, integrity, shared values, responsibilities, and work ethic. Having no children who played the sport he loved, he went out of his way to show his players how to recognize and overcome personal impulses that can lead to problematic leadership behavior on and off the field. His simple phrases have stayed with me to this day. I can still hear him telling his players to never give up.

Personal and business life never came easy for me. I was born in Vietnam and, with my family, moved to Southern California after the fall of Saigon in April 1975. As the second of three children, I ended up growing up in a small home with fourteen family members. Here is the backstory: My parents took full guardianship over nine of my mother's younger brothers and sisters who were refugees from Vietnam. I learned invaluable life skills at a very early age, including multiculturalism, integration, and simply surviving on very limited financial resources.

Perspective is a fascinating concept—though we were poor by American standards, we were rich by Vietnamese standards. My first supermarket experience with my immigrant family members illustrates this point. Fully stocked shelves and produce counters are what most Americans take for granted, but witnessing my family react to what a supermarket offered, you'd think we won the lottery. They could not believe the quality and accessibility of basic-need products. We didn't have much growing up, but I never gave up.

I started working at the age of twelve, where I would sit in the back of a supply truck at 5:00 a.m. to get to a local parade where I would pull a cart, selling cotton candy, popcorn, soft drinks, and toys. Selling came easy to me, and I would often be a top earner of the mostly migrant laborers who worked the parades with me. My perspective: I had the *opportunity* to make cash money in the greatest country in the world. Listening to the stories at home, I realized how lucky I was compared to the kids that were left behind in Vietnam.

I continued to work throughout my teen years, always taking sales job after sales job. Little did I know that surviving led to foundational skills and life lessons that were to become my building blocks, my *mojo*, for future entrepreneurial pursuits.

Discovering Authentic Leadership Requires That You Stay True to Your Values

We are all dealt a hand, and it is up to each of us how to play it. Having good mentors and advisers, if you are lucky enough to get them, helps tremendously. Listening more and talking less, as well as doing more and thinking less, are fundamental when launching a new business.

Quickly determining the viability of a product or service will save you time and money. Family and friends that give you honest feedback are your best friends.

Putting myself through college and professional school, while contributing to family needs, I carried a lot of responsibility early in life. I am the businessman that I am because I am driven by experiences that have shaped my ability to build and grow businesses from the ground up. Starting a business takes unique skill sets and personality traits. Being resilient, having perspective, and not giving up are requisite soft skills. Having the ability to sell, execute, plan, and execute some more, diligently and with integrity, is a requisite hard skill. Managing cash flow and treating start-up capital like lifeblood is essential. A little luck can't hurt. Anticipating the next steps, staying ahead of the game, and actually executing on those instincts empower the entrepreneurial path and optimize the leadership style I have adopted over the years.

When I started my first company, I made sure a core value ingrained in our corporate culture was to keep clients first. By staying true and authentic to this value, our clients understood the unspoken—the trust, integrity, and ethical boundaries that followed were inevitable. The point where these aligned helped this company take off, which led to a successful private equity exit. I have stayed true to this model, and it continues to work for me.

Because I have learned that so much of the growth and success of our companies are dependent on sales, the CEO and its dedicated employees must be great at sales. As we started to grow, mentoring our first sales employees who were facing headwinds in the market in the aftermath of the bursting of the dotcom bubble, I never had to veer from my core values to succeed. In my coaching and mentoring, I always kept hearing Coach Miller's voice: "Never give up. When one door closes, another will open." In the sales and client-driven businesses I have started and built, this always held true. The building of the founding team was critical, as the values of the company flowed through them.

Years later, as a junior sales associate, I worked closely with Rose to become a senior sales professional recognized as a top producer in our industry. She had now become a mentor to new sales associates. I heard the words of Coach Miller in her coaching and mentoring of new hires and colleagues as I passed by her office and as I attended one of her meetings.

Coach Miller never hesitated to give authentic feedback. Honest feedback is at the backbone of the companies I have built. Many employees have come back to me several years later to inform me that while it was difficult at that time, the honest feedback they received enhanced their success as their careers progressed.

Executing Authentic Leadership:
The World Is Your Apple

Another mentor I was lucky to have, Roy Spiers, a World War II veteran who flew a B-17 Flying Fortress in the European theater for the Army Air Corps, sold bobby pins door-to-door as his first job after the war. Realizing he was a great salesman, he went on to start several successful companies. He actually served as a founding volunteer member of the Entrepreneurial Department of the Marriott School of Business at Brigham Young University. Early on in my career, I was fortunate to have had several conversations with him, and I credit Mr. Spiers with planting the entrepreneurial spirit in me when he told me, "John, the world is your apple. You can do anything you want."

I will never forget his advice to me. This advice relates to purpose, which is essential to achieving satisfaction and is timelessly applicable to me and current and future entrepreneurs. When you work on what you are passionate about, more likely than not, it plays to your strengths, leading to where you will have the most success because you are intrinsically motivated.

But be warned, being an entrepreneur is never easy. Adversity, setbacks, and struggles are all part of the journey. Those are the times that I dig deep and draw on the words of those two war heroes I was lucky to have known: "Never give up" and "The world is your apple. You can do anything you want." Those are the times when you dust yourself off, get up, and keep going. Surround yourself with family, friends, and great people. Find *your* mojo. Success in the face of adversity is testament that you are on the path to authentic accomplishments.

Have no fear. You will succeed.

Biographical Comments by the Lead Author

John Sánchez is a serial entrepreneur passionate about the business of law, legal process outsourcing, and emerging technologies for the legal industry. Some companies he has founded and led in the legal industry include Black Letter Discovery and BarGraders.com. He is an early student of mine and is a founding member of the board of leaders for the Institute of Entrepreneurial Leadership at John F. Kennedy University, where he also served as a volunteer mentor for AT&T's Operation Hand Salute, a supplier diversity program to mentor and develop business enterprises owned by service-disabled veterans. John and I have schemed and continue to scheme new business ventures, and I am certain he will continue with much success. He has worked and lived in Asia and North America and is currently based in the San Francisco Bay Area, where he lives with his wife and two children. I am proud to have John as a BFF who is close by.

Chapter 32

Man Your Battle Stations!

Kaney O'Neill

Lying in a hospital bed in Newport News, Virginia, I did not want to go on with my life. I had a life-threatening injury. My future was dark. At twenty-one years old, I thought all hope was lost. I wanted to close my eyes and go to sleep forever. But I heard my grandfather's voice in my head: "Man your battle stations!"

Lt. Eugene O'Neill was my beloved Popsie. He was a fine storyteller. I must have been about twelve years old when I first heard this tale. When he relayed it (which he did many times over the years), I could almost hear the ship's bell ringing and the sea waves crashing about. The year was 1945. WWII was going full blast. Popsie was stationed off a tiny island in the South Pacific. It was just past midnight, and along with many of his crewmates, he was sleeping on his Navy vessel when the booming voice called out over the speaker, "All hands on deck! Man your battle stations!" A Japanese Zero had been spotted and was headed for his US Navy ship on a kamikaze crash death dive.

Every sailor on board ran to their stations, but none on board could believe what happened next. The kamikaze pilot mistakenly thought the airstrip he was aiming for was an aircraft carrier's flight deck, when it actually was only a makeshift airfield on the tiny atoll next to Popsie's ship. The pilot crashed like a giant fireball that lit the night sky as it exploded. Whew! That was a close one. Popsie made it through that midnight and many more and came back home, married his girl, and lived a happily-ever-after kind of life.

Popsie always wore his WWII veterans cap everywhere he went, as if it was a badge of honor. Many of the vanishing unsung heroes from WWII often do. Popsie was not only a naval officer and a gentleman; he was the finest man I've ever known. He was my grandfather. He was especially proud of me when I told him his service inspired me to join the US Navy.

By 1997, I was nineteen years old. I had my own cap now. All sailors are issued one in boot camp at the Great Lakes Naval Station. Boot camp isn't easy, and it's not supposed to be. It's a sailor-forming school preparing young people for whatever challenges one may face in the service of our country. There were other benefits I later discovered, ones that I came away with that have served me ever since.

All throughout boot camp, you practice various exercises that are in actuality preparing you for the final boot camp evaluation—passing battle stations. This grueling twelve-hour ordeal assesses both physical and mental strength. Recruits race from battle station to battle station at double time. Your performance is evaluated both individually and as a team. Some of the exercises take place on a mock battleship, the USS *Thayer*. Sleep-deprived recruits are kept in constant motion—an intentional tactic to push you beyond what you think is your physical exhaustion point.

On board the ship, you are exposed to a variety of dangers or battle stations (based on past historical events, such as the attack on Pearl Harbor). At one station, you are exposed to a simulated missile attack where mock mass casualties occur. There are fires on board that must be fought, a man-overboard exercise, even exposure to actual tear gas. When you are facing the heat of real flames, when you jump into cold water to retrieve a one-hundred-pound-plus dummy, when your eyes are burning in the gas chamber (or as the Navy calls it, the Confidence Chamber), you completely forget that it is a mere exercise. You are there in the moment, with adrenaline pumping, giving it all you've got and then some. Making it past each of the challenges is the goal. Never even thinking of giving up was drilled into me from my very first day at boot camp. Not everyone makes it. Not everyone should.

I successfully completed Navy boot camp and moved from recruit to sailor, and Popsie was there in the audience at my graduation ceremony, beaming proudly.

Prior to joining the Navy, I worked as a waitress and struggled to pay my way through community college. I was in the best physical shape of my life. Growing up, one of my natural talents was swimming. During high school, I competed internationally and became a champion swimmer. At the time of my enlistment, I was still growing into the person I wanted to become and dreaming of adventure. My love of the water made the Navy a logical choice, and I decided to utilize my swimming ability and enlisted, hoping to "strike" for the job of search-and-rescue swimmer. I was convinced that serving my country was the right thing to do. I was full of hopes and dreams of traveling the world, jumping out of airplanes to save lives, and falling in love. As I held my hand upon my heart, reciting the Airman's Creed, I never imagined that the very last line, "I will never falter, and I will not fail," would one day become my personal mantra.

I was ready to let the journey begin and sail whichever one of the seven seas the Navy assigned me to. But oddly enough, I never sailed on any ships. In fact, I never even made it out of the shipyard or into the water! The ship I was assigned to, the USS *Nimitz*, was in dry dock for a complete overhaul. Was I swimming on search and rescue missions? No, I wasn't. Instead, I was armed with a respirator and needle gun, chipping paint off a ship. I wasn't swimming—but I was learning in the Navy some lifelong lessons about perseverance and how to deal with setbacks. I was taught the vital importance of paying attention to details, to do my best work, the value of what it means to be a dedicated team member, and most importantly, I learned from those around me what it takes to be a leader. I worked my butt off and became the best paint-chipping sailor I could be.

Eighteen months into my naval career, a fateful storm landed where I was stationed. Like Popsie, I too had a run-in with a kamikaze, albeit a different variety. One translation of *kamikaze* is "divine wind," and I faced my own version that September day of 1999 when my physical world changed forever. Hurricane Floyd blew into Newport News and hurled me off a second-story balcony, severing my spinal cord and ending my military career. The doctors saved my life using backup generators, but the diagnosis was devastating: quadriplegia—complete paralysis from the chest down.

There are no words to describe how traumatic it was to wake up from an injury completely paralyzed. From that fateful day forward, I have never walked, stood up, dressed myself, or even opened my hands. I lost movement, sensation, and control over my own body. My hands are permanently closed. I have no feeling from the chest down. My life didn't only have battle simulations waiting; now I faced the realest of the real deal kind. My plans, goals, and seven-sea dreams were overboard.

Hearing my grandfather's voice in my head was my lifesaver. "Man your battle stations!" My mojo returned. I decided to take action.

The first few weeks of rehabilitation were especially tough, realizing that everything in my immediate physical reality had changed. I learned that I would forever be dependent on other people to have my basic needs met. I didn't have to starch those creases in my uniform—someone was dressing me and lifting me out of bed into my motorized wheelchair.

Boot camp was nothing compared to the grueling task of rehabilitation. I fought against my own body to regain as much movement and strength as possible. The memories of my Navy boot camp helped get me through those dark times. Back then, I didn't think I could run miles under without stopping, but I did. I ran all day in boot camp, even to the mess hall. I didn't think I could willingly expose myself to tear gas or fight fires, but I did. After my injury, I became my own drill sergeant. "If I could do that, I can do this." I reminded myself on a daily basis all throughout my rehab to improvise, adapt, and overcome!

I learned how to breathe on my own without a ventilator and how to cope with my changed circumstances. I spent many hours staring up at the ceiling, trying to figure out what to do with my life with such a devastating disability. I finally came to realize that the storm did not take all my strength. I still had my mind, and I had to figure out how to best use it so I could have a productive life and a reason to live. I hadn't been much of a student before, but I couldn't use this as an excuse. New obstacles were before me. I needed to redefine my dreams, reinvent my goals, and prepare myself to become the best new self I could be.

At this point in my life, I realized I needed to go back to work. Start a career. But what could I do? I remembered the line from Popsie's story, "Man your battle stations," and so I did.

I went back to school to complete my education. Six years later, I graduated from Northwestern University with two degrees, a master's degree in learning science and a bachelor's degree in learning and organizational change. Now, I thought, I was ready to sail the seas of business. Full of hope and fresh ideas, I was eager to find just the right organization to work for where I could make a difference. Unfortunately, the workplace reality is that opportunities for persons with disabilities are things companies *say* they want to provide but rarely do. My job hunt was a lot of hunting but no game. I had hit a dead end, a blind alley, a complete stop. Now what? On to the next battle station!

In retrospect, I'm glad I wasn't offered a position out of school, because it gave me that push I needed to start my own business. I had faced enough challenges to know now that there's a way to roll around them, over them, or through them. If I couldn't find a company willing to take a chance on my success, I would start my own. But what business? I looked no further than my own backyard.

Commercial roofing is in my DNA. My father, my brother, my cousins, my uncles were roofers. They all encouraged me that I could do this. I took business classes and started learning everything I could about managing a company, as well as mastering the intricacies of the roofing trade, studying the products and systems, and learning to navigate the requirements of submitting a successful bid. I loved it.

In 2007, ONeill Contractors, my own company specializing in commercial roofing, hoisted its sail and left for the open seas of business. I was at the helm. Like the swimmer I once was, I dove into the entrepreneurial waters. In the beginning, it was mostly treading water; it took a full year before I finally landed my first commercial job—putting a roof on a maintenance building for the Army Corp of Engineers. Like in all the battle stations I encountered in boot camp, this job presented me with unexpected challenges that had to be overcome—unseasonable weather conditions, the wrong flashing to be taken down and reinstalled, personality clashes within the roofing crew, and more. But I understood from my military service that you just have to put your shoulder to it and push through the problems. I've since learned that problems are present on every job. Some small, some big, and some costly!

Not too surprisingly, given the level of my disability, I've had numerous physical setbacks. Sometimes it has meant forcing myself to take time out of my chair to heal my body from a breakdown from sitting too long. Sometimes a hospitalization has meant canceling an important meeting or missing out on an upcoming bid. I just had to get over those bumps in the road and keep on going. From my boot camp drill routine, I now look at obstacles as one more hurdle that I have to get over.

In the eight years I've been in business, I've lost many more bids than I have won, but as Michael Jordan once said, "You will never miss the shot you don't try." Losing out on hard-fought bids with many hours of work put into them didn't deter me from going for my goals. I began to hit a few shots and next a bunch of game winners. Today, I've roofed buildings where 747s are built, and I'm contracted to do the hangar where Air Force One is parked. I have even put a roof on at the very hospital where I recovered from my injury, a kind of rehabbing the place that rehabbed me! I opened up a new office last year and keep on working hard, setting new goals for myself.

I'm not a nineteen-year-old Navy recruit anymore. I'm a thirty-eight-year-old woman with a five-year-old son. He's my joy. My physical limitations present ongoing challenges on a daily basis. I know it's going to call out for me to man my battle stations again and again. I will fight that next battle too and do my best to whoop its butt like I have the ones before. My mojo was gifted to me by Uncle Sam. I'm grateful for the grit I learned and the never-give-up motto I came away with from the Navy.

Life is a series of battle stations for all of us. We all have to get up and get into action no matter what befalls us. Like my grandfather in his WWII hat, I wear my Navy veteran shirt with pride. We vets stick together. Now when I roll through the gates at Great Lakes Naval Station, it's as a federal contractor, proud that I can still be of service to my Navy. Thanks, Popsie, for helping me get my mojo back.

Biographical Comments by the Lead Author

Kaney comes from a long history of military service. Inspired by her grandfather, Eugene O'Neill, a World War II veteran, Kaney joined the US Navy at the age of nineteen. Her dreams of serving her country and traveling the world were cut short on September 15, 1999, when a hurricane struck the East Coast and changed her physical world forever. A fall from a second-story balcony left her paralyzed with a spinal cord injury. Although this accident ended her military career, it marked the beginning of a whole new journey. After her rehabilitation at Hines Veterans Hospital, Kaney realized that she had to reinvent her future and her dreams. With determination, she poured herself into her education. Four years later, she graduated cum laude from Northwestern University with a BS in learning and organization change and then went on to obtain a master's degree in learning science also from Northwestern. Despite these credentials, after graduation, job offers never materialized. At this point, she didn't know where to turn. Pushing past this new roadblock in her life seemed impossible. It was then that she realized she would have to create her own opportunity. She shifted gears again to create a family roofing business that would reflect her personal values and the leadership skills she gained in the military and in college. In 2007, ONeill Contractors became a reality, offering a broad range of roofing services designed to meet the diverse needs of building owners within the government, commercial, industrial, and institutional sectors based out of the greater Chicago area. Eight years later, ONeill Contractors has successfully completed contracts for multiple large corporations, the US Army Corps of Engineers, the US Air Force, the US Navy, the Department of Veterans Affairs, and others. Kaney applied the principles she learned at Northwestern about successful organizations and what motivates employees to become lifelong learners. In 2015, Kaney was named NVOBA Magazine's Women Vetrepreneur of the Year. Kaney and her family started a relationship with me when she studied at the Institute of Entrepreneurial

Leadership, where I served as Director. It was my pleasure to mentor her there and continue to do so to this date. The friendship bonds are strong, and the character of Kaney is such that I am convinced her future is very bright. She is a true example of perseverance to the rest of the world.

Chapter 33

The Perfect Club

Cecelia Lakatos Sullivan

For almost twenty years of my career, I jumped from one opportunity to another. I was very fortunate. Strong performance led to promotions and new areas to explore. I wish I could say it all stemmed from a well-planned personal three-, five-, or ten-year plan. Some planning, some luck, some wonderful mentors. At work, I drank the Kool-Aid—great company, loyalty, work hard, show no weakness, make the money, and benefit from collective success. I have the battle scars of the glass ceiling. I chose not to be "one of the guys."

My husband, Pat, a surgeon, literally spent his days saving lives. At home, we enjoyed our chaotic life. Our lives centered on managing logistics: logistics of his call schedule and my global travel schedule, kids' projects, sports, pets, some sleep, maybe exercise, and even a date night here and there. When our third child came along, we moved from man-to-man coverage to zone coverage. I organized our lives with one of those old-school day planners complete with yellow stickies and color coding by family member and activity.

My thirty-ninth year was a turning point for me. My mother had been diagnosed with a terminal autoimmune disease. She chose palliative care for the last year of her life. When Mom entered hospice, my parents did not have the financial means to hire full-time help. Out of four siblings, I lived the closest to my parents. Pat and I took a step back. We had three little kids and two demanding careers. Helping out with my mom was a full-time job, not something we could add to our lives without a major adjustment. We decided I would take a leave of absence, a pause from my career with the intent to return. Financially, we could make it work as well. However, we had a little hiccup in our plan when I requested a leave of absence from work and it was denied. It brought me back to choices—help or hinder. And much to the company's surprise, I chose to resign immediately from my executive-level job at a large corporation to care for my mom during the day while my father cared for her at night. Even though Mom and I had always been very close, I didn't realize at that time that my mom's last year of her life was her final gift to me.

The first six months were so unpredictable. Mom went from this energetic little Scottish lady to a wheelchair-bound prisoner. Her body was becoming more deformed from the meds and lack of oxygen. Despite the physical changes, she never lost her sense of joy. My mom found joy in the smallest of things: sunshine on her face, my youngest child rubbing lotion into her hands, or watching *Dirty Dancing* for the thirtieth time with my two sisters and me.

We made every effort to get out of the house for a bit every day. She loved turkey club sandwiches, so that became our thing, setting out in search of the perfect club. It became our living metaphor for fighting complacency and never giving up!

One day during lunch, my mom stopped and looked at me with her piercing crystal-blue eyes and said, "I can't believe it took me getting sick to stop you from dying of a heart attack. At least, I get to save your life." I guess for some time, she was concerned with my level of stress. I regularly made it through the day on four hours of sleep and lots of coffee. Mom was right though. When I resigned from work, I was wound tight. I had let go of choosing what happened in my day and instead allowed autopilot to take over in my life. My mom helped me carve out time to enjoy life a bit more and rediscover joy. I loved being with my children and having time to play. That year I started running regularly and began my yoga practice. Yoga also reignited my spiritual awareness. The combination helped me get through that year.

The last six months, Mom was confined to the hospital bed in her home. This ugly autoimmune disease slowly stripped away her lung's capacity to process oxygen. Any activity challenged her remaining energy. For me, I now fully understood the care my mom, at sixty-seven, needed for her last days. Simple things like brushing and flossing, bathing, and combing out her hair were taxing. At that point, my mom needed diapers, and I had to change them or make her bed without juggling her too much. I was struck by the utter humility of our lives and the love and tenderness required to care for not just my mom but also everyone around me—spouse, children, and friends. Humility and compassion are a practice. I'm very grateful for the visiting hospice nurses who helped my mom and me get through those last few months. My mom lost consciousness two weeks before she died. I was with her when she took her last labored breaths, and later that evening, I felt her spirit pass through me. Ironically, my mom died a year from the day I resigned to care for her.

Fast Forward

At forty, I decided I did not want to return to full-time work. In the year that followed my mom's death, I didn't work outside of the home. I chose not to return to the big corporate environment. Happily, family quickly consumed my time. When I enrolled my youngest in prekindergarten a couple of years later, I knew I wanted to work in some capacity outside of the home. My entrepreneurial spirit kicked in, and I started my consulting practice. My mojo was returning.

After assessing strengths and interests, I started CLS Consultants, my own company. Fortunately, I built my practice through word of mouth and personal references. My career experiences, ranging from finance to supply chain to systems development, fit well with my focus on becoming an interim CEO for small- to medium-size businesses. Consulting was a good gig for me; it gave me the flexibility I desired for my family and my mental health, and it was intellectually rewarding. The plug-and-play aspect was fascinating for me. And I loved comparing and contrasting organization cultures, leadership, customer bases, and employee teams.

My clients ranged from franchise owners to software development companies to architectural firms. No matter what environment, I found that the key to a company's success was their people, not only at the leadership level, but also throughout the organization. I had learned and practiced to create a leadership style with the guiding principle of transparency and compassion, and it worked for a number of companies during my consultancy practice.

Then, a couple of years into my consulting life, an attorney approached me to consider a turnaround service contract. This contract proved challenging in many areas—forensic accounting, litigation, customer relationships, employee engagement, and of course, negative cash flow. On paper, I could make the argument either way—shut the company down or make it financially viable for future growth. The company had an added complexity, the need to handle nonfunctional family dynamics—the founder and her son were key leaders of the company, along with other relatives sprinkled throughout the company. I accepted the challenge and the client.

I entrenched myself that first month to understand the financials, contracts, and the key areas of additional risk. I mapped areas of success and built trust with the owner and founder of the company. Many of our discussions centered on my evaluation of her team and the lack of professionalism and transparency up and down the management chain. I spent time in the field and the corporate office, observing workflow and employee interactions.

The owners hadn't communicated my role or what I was doing there. I found it weird and surprising to me that folks were hiding information all over the company. I had never been in an environment where hiding news was so prevalent at every level. A wall had been built up against the establishment.

The founder's top leaders, the senior vice president and the chief financial officer, were incompetent and out of sync with one another. They didn't even like one another. They hid in their offices with closed doors and blinds. More importantly, they were not forthcoming in providing information to the founder. After month one, I prepared and presented my interpretation of the factors that were destroying the company. The owner was shocked at how much she didn't know. At that point, she gave me 100 percent control of the situation.

And so it began; my new voyage took sail. We built a strong bond or friendship for that matter, and she allowed me to align my values with the organization. I then moved to rebuild the place and move the company to focus on providing a terrific customer experience with employee engagement and consistent profitability.

I wanted to build an organization that highly valued employee contributions, and I wanted to lead with the humility and compassion I learned from the experience with my mom. Even though it was a relatively small company, I believed the company could be a viable part of our economy. I wanted to create jobs for people with a strong work ethic and develop a professional track for technicians, engineers, and management alike.

The first few months I spent listening. I scheduled countless "lunch for bunches" throughout California to meet every single employee in the company. I elicited their feedback and suggestions. Most were not shy in expressing their disappointment and anger with prior management practices—yes, red-in-the-face, *mad* employees. I wasn't in a position to judge what was valid or not. I could only listen. Mistrust was the common thread throughout the company. No one had any idea what was going on with the company and even if they were going to get their next paycheck. I looked for the implicit leaders—those key individuals who garnered the respect and following of other employees. I've always found those individuals to find the common ground with and challenge their colleagues on what can be done better and then get it done. I tagged them for subsequent meetings.

Next stop for me were the customers. Again, I spent a lot of time listening. In our virtual world, I still find face-to-face a really good place to start in building relationships if people are available. Fortunately, most customers welcomed my visits, since they had a lot of unpleasant feedback regarding our company performance and leadership to share with me, most of which was valid. Ouch.

Honestly, after those lunch for bunches and customer visits, I really did some soul searching on whether or not the better alternative was to just shut the company down. Performance metrics were nonexistent, and bitterness was rampant. When a company and its customer base have that much bitterness and anger at every level, it is hard to come back. Anger at every level breeds apathy and sabotage. However, in this case, I felt I should rebuild this company and take it to new heights.

My Aha Moment: Build the Company

In 2005, I chose to rebuild the company, becoming CEO and part owner. My first Aha! I really underestimated the people churn that was needed to move our organization from being an underperformer to a high-performance machine. I kick-started the process by firing the senior vice president and the chief financial officer due to some of their egregious actions.

Developing our leadership required growing and investing in my management team. Over a three-year period, we had 80 percent management turnover and then some; some self-selected out, while some were nudged out. I remember coming home from work one night and my then ten-year-old asking me "Who got fired today?" Another technical term I use to describe those couple of years: *yuck*. But I refused to give up.

I learned culture isn't dismantled and rebuilt overnight. I worked closely with our implicit leaders and pulled them together with the existing management team, and we created our first company strategic plan. Most of the team didn't understand what a strategic plan was and had never been through the process—most of the team had never been together in the same room before that day. I was thrilled! What a great opportunity to build our future foundation! We established our vision, mission, and values, and equally important, our yearly and quarterly action plan with metrics.

Today, we continue to create a three-year rolling strategic plan and include folks beyond our immediate management team. The values we rallied around then are still the values we rally around today: customer experience, industry relevance, and employee professionalism and engagement. Our daily challenge continues to be figuring out how we keep our employees engaged and how to stay relevant in a rapidly changing industry.

During our transformational phase, tensions grew in every department, and my level of stress remained high. A wise man taught me about self-care. He often reminded me that if I didn't manage my level of stress, I would find myself as tightly wound as when I first started taking care of my mom, or worse yet, find my health starting to deteriorate. He also offered feedback that stress can block creativity, listening for solutions required to lead. I was committed to offset the level of stress with a recommitment to running and my yoga practice. The management team and I then shifted our company focus from tactical fires to strategy.

In 2006, we moved all our office locations. All the leases were up, and we needed new space, and we had a proverbial fresh start in each of our geographic locations. That year, I felt that we turned the corner. In addition to rebuilding our company's reputation as an industry leader, I continued to build my reputation as a leader in our industry and community through board service and volunteer work. We continued to create jobs for people with a strong work ethic.

Our company began receiving regular unsolicited positive recognition from our customers. The fabric of our employee base had evolved! Internally, we implemented a rigorous quality management system. Our management team engaged individuals on their teams to help them understand the levers of success for profitability and to understand the importance of quality and safety throughout our supply chain at the beginning of the process, not just at the end. Employee performance improved immensely. People were proud of their work and day-to-day accomplishments.

From the onset, I've always operated with an open-door policy. Employees were approaching me with unsolicited feedback on how much more they were enjoying being part of a team, not just a company. Another program that came out of employee engagement was fifty-two things in fifty-two weeks. Each week for a year, we addressed a laundry list of issues through action. Some of our fifty-two things included trucks for the field, new hand tools for the techs, better laptops for all employees, and spontaneous recognition awards. Some programs the employees loved, some not so much, but all were well understood. We continued to rebuild our balance sheet and profitability.

By 2012, our company started exploring how to become greener. At the same time, we were working on breaking down some barriers that were reappearing between our installation and warehouse folks. Again, the team's creativity kicked in and developed a recycling program that involved the efforts of both groups. Without all the gory detail, we challenged the teams to hunt for recyclables within the company's job sites. Any monies from the collective effort were directly credited to an account for a company party. Since 2012, we've improved our emissions footprint and funded awesome all-company parties where we bring all the employees together and their guests, including hotels, dinner, dancing, cool goody bags, money cards, prizes, photo booths, and more.

Let me be clear. Our industry is tough, and working in the state of California is quite demanding. We have challenges every day. We're still challenged with how we best help our employees know and feel they are valued and appreciated. You know the old adage, "A customer only remembers your performance from your last job." This is also true with employees' memory of management. They are more likely to remember recent events and how we support them today than efforts of yesterday. Our management team is in lockstep in finding ways to achieve that balance. I'm so proud of our team. Thanks to the team's creativity, we've developed programs to figure out how to best support both sides of the equation. Like with my mom in search of the perfect club sandwich, we didn't settle for one solution; we looked for and implemented the next best one!

The year I spent with my mom also reinforced the importance of taking the time to be thoughtful and kind. So often the workdays can be stressful and task-oriented throughout the company, and the human side of managing can get lost. It's important to me that our employees feel recognized for their accomplishments at work. We recognize folks regularly with thank-you e-mails. I write birthday cards for each person and enclose a small token of appreciation. Sometimes it is a Starbucks card or movie tickets. This year every employee receives a real birthday card redeemable for a day off on or near their birthday to celebrate their special day. We instituted 401(k) matching, yearly merit increases, and employee profit sharing. We also have yearly "blue bird days." Blue bird days are extra holidays given throughout the year. One year it was a red, white, and blue ticket for an extended Fourth of July weekend. Another was a golden ticket for the holidays.

Also, on a personal level, it's important to me to support employees with compassion going through family hardships. I've had employees struggle with cancer or their child's cancer, family deaths, money issues, and domestic violence. I've learned I can't solve problems in an employee's personal life, but I can listen and check in on how they are doing. Life outside of work is important, and often the lines are blurred between work life and life outside of work.

The daily challenges of our economy, customers, and employees can easily push a leader to give up on a given direction. I choose to lead with unconditional commitment to each of our customers and employees. It continues to pay back by creating a positive work climate. On one of my birthdays, an employee surprised me with the most beautiful and delicious homemade sheet cake. Sheer joy! Being surprised with that cake really is the only time I've cried at work. With three kids and her husband also working full-time, she carved out the time to make it for me. I can't even make brownies out of the box without getting my finger caught in the blender!

I'm still choosing to build and create jobs. Last year, I bought out my business partner and am excited to continue the journey as the sole proprietor of the company. After ten years, I'm now building my business with a fabulous team of professionals that value our employees' talents and contributions. We operate from the perspective of abundance and kindness. It's been tough at times but worth finally getting here. Our team continues to use "help or hinder?" now as a litmus test for decision-making. And we continue to search for that perfect club. Love you, Mom. You gave me back my mojo!

Biographical Comments by the Lead Author

Cecelia leads PTI Solutions, a 100 percent woman-owned company of telecom connectivity professionals providing integrated network services for enterprises, government, and telecommunication providers—keeping businesses and people connected. As a first-generation American, Cecelia experienced the dichotomy of two parental styles, a hot-tempered Hungarian and a kind, charitable Scot. The contrasting styles influenced Cecelia's approach to life and helped shape her entrepreneurial spirit. Her parents started and built a metal spinning company, and Cecelia grew up cutting sheet metal. The oldest of four, Cecelia figured out quickly that life is about choices. Help or hinder? She chooses to always be in the help space, whether it's family, friends, colleagues, or business. She also recognized education as a key foundation to enable her in her life vision. Education quickly became a priority for her, and she became the first in her family to graduate from high school, college, and subsequently graduate school. With her BA from the University of California–Davis and an MBA from the University of Chicago, Cecelia happily tried to balance her life between family, career, and community. Of course, she recognizes that there is no perfect life balance, but she is all about always trying. Her passion for many areas continued to evolve and is still evolving. As an award-winning corporate executive, consultant, and business owner, Cecelia chooses to create jobs for folks with a strong work ethic and provides an environment for employees of all levels to thrive with a little levity and joy, and yes, profits! Cecelia, one of my former students and now my BFF, has been invited to guest lecture and share her leadership experiences to some of my other students. The simple key tenets of her leadership—"Never, never, never give up" and "Be kind"—set off a perfect example for others to follow. Cecelia and her husband, Pat, a surgeon, have three children. She continues to volunteer for schools and other organizations near her home and serves on industry and local community boards. She and I meet at least once a month to share a meal and explore ways to grow her company and discuss where her company is headed. I am proud of where she has gone and where she is going.

Chapter 34

When in Trouble, Take Charge

Amber Peebles

I am a Marine, and since leaving the service, I have been involved in the construction sector. My company, Athena Construction Group Inc. (Athena), is the nation's only HUB Zone construction company owned by a service-disabled veteran woman. As such, we engage in significantly sized federal construction projects, especially focusing on interior renovations. Construction is an inherently risky venture. Being a small business invites even greater risk.

Due to our unique status, large prime general contractors often pursue us to help them meet the federally mandated small-business utilization requirements. Failure to do so adversely impacts a prime contractor's performance evaluation, and the federal government can assess monetary fines to them as well.

A number of years back, we encountered an entrepreneur's most hellish moment, one that could have killed our company. In this particular instance, a nationally known prime contractor, call them company X, whom we had worked with previously, approached our company about an opportunity for work at a flagship military medical center to provide and install over one thousand doors and the corresponding hardware that consisted of over seventy thousand pieces. However, in order to do this work, we would need to partner with a large business, as the scope was simply too large for us to handle exclusively.

Another reason for partnership is that subcontractors are required to provide what is known as a performance and payment bond. In simple terms, a bond is a guarantee of financial performance. The owner of a company signs the bond and puts all his or her personal assets on the line should the company fail to meet its contractual obligations. In other words, you simply can't walk away from a job because you are in over your head or are losing money. Well, you can, I suppose, but the surety that provided the bond will take your 401(k), your cars, your house, your savings, and your cat if they think it has any value. You get the picture.

Company X introduced us to a specialty door, frame, and hardware company—I will call them Y—and he encouraged us to partner together in order to be awarded the work. I flew out to their headquarters, toured their facilities, had dinner with the president, and visited some ongoing jobs being performed by them. By all appearances and in light of this, they seemed to be a solid company.

Subsequently, Athena and Y partnered together on three major construction projects in Maryland, Texas, and New York, with a total contract value of over 7 million dollars. Because of its larger size, Y obtained the necessary bonds for the respective jobs. I cosigned the bonds, assuming very little risk as the primary signature was the president of Y. He and his company were on the hook.

The contracts we had together were in various stages of performance and seemed to be on schedule. Then I got "the call" at 0700 on Monday morning. Y had closed its doors and walked off from all its jobs throughout the country. Frankly, my company, Athena, was faced with total and complete financial collapse. The principals of Y would not return calls, and I was advised by an employee of Y that the owners had fled the country. To make matters worse, during the next two days, as a result of further digging, we found that the president of Y was a convicted federal felon and had served time in a federal penitentiary. He had been convicted of RICO violations, money laundering, mail fraud, and bribery of a public official. Athena had been had by unsavory characters that had been to this rodeo before.

And of course, company X did not want us on the job at this point, because they determined Athena was too small for the job, and they did everything possible to make us want to quit, including withholding payments on work already performed. We were being choked to death.

I soon realized Athena only had two choices: quit and let the chips fall where they may or find a way to finish these contracts. I took this simple proposition to my co-owner and vice president of Athena, Melissa Schneider, who is also a Marine Corps veteran. When I relayed our options, her response was simple and direct: "Amber, Marines never quit."

Realistically, our chances of turning this thing around were nonexistent, and we would be viewed as running a fool's errand. However, that declarative statement affirmed why she was my business partner, and it was the answer I was hoping for. If we were going down, it was going to be in a blaze of glory. We laughed (for the first time in days), did a fist bump, and then said, "F—— it, we've got nothing to lose. Let's go."

And so we went and replaced fear with action. Melissa started to personally run every job, and I called in every favor ever owed to me by anyone. I called American Express and told them to standby because I had to blow up my credit card and I needed them to be there for me, and they were. We recruited a retired construction professional and convinced him to forego golf and fishing to handle our San Antonio location. I worked out a deal with the surety for our New York job and ensured that the job stayed on schedule. We robbed Peter to pay Paul, and Melissa worked fourteen-hour days for months on end. I haggled with suppliers, got into screaming matches with company X's project executive, and fended off the vultures who wanted to prey on a company that was deemed vulnerable. And when I wasn't in a screaming match or slamming down the phone to drive an agenda, I appealed to people's better instincts to focus on the bigger picture of building a hospital for the war wounded.

We were hanging on by a thread as we successfully completed each contract. However, while we were fighting for survival, something else was occurring. The world of construction was watching us, and they were impressed. Our story had become legendary, and people and companies reached out to us. The thought being that individuals that displayed this level of character and resolve were people with whom they wanted to do business with. Our leadership and tenacity were being noticed.

Athena was recognized for this extraordinary achievement and was the recipient of the American Express Government Contractor of the Year Award. We received additional recognition from the American Subcontractors Association, and I became an in-demand speaker at various events. My story gave other small business owners insight and inspiration. I made deep and lasting friendships. Our reputation and exposure brought us more business.

More importantly, having survived this crisis, our company became more resilient, and so did we as owners and individuals. We have survived the worst and are empowered to successfully confront any potential crisis that affects our business. Our confidence level has created new opportunities. We have *mojo*, really *team mojo*!

Our mojo story has many simple truths: You always have a choice, and when your choice is consistent with your values, you come out a winner. Your lowest moments oftentimes bring forth your greatest achievements. Once the decision is made to prevail, you can always find a way. We are now proud that in 2015, Athena was given an award by the American Subcontractors Association as "the outstanding general contractor who has aided the subcontracting industry by outstanding administration, efficient field supervision and fair financial practices on a continuing basis and is emerging into a significant company in the construction industry."

My hope from telling this story is that any reader gains new insight into understanding that owning your problem, no matter the circumstances, is a life-affirming commitment. When you and you alone hold yourself accountable for results regardless of the situation, you achieve a permanent level of mojo that leads to a continuously rewarding life. Be a Marine!

SemperFi.

Biographical Comments by the Lead Author

Amber is the President of Athena Construction Group Inc., the nation's premier HUB Zone construction company owned by a service-disabled veteran woman. Athena is the recipient of the 2012 Small Business Government Contractor of the Year Award in the American Express Victory in Procurement Program. Amber is a United States Marine Corps veteran and a graduate of Park University with a BS in human resource management. Amber also holds a master's level certification in paralegal studies from George Washington University and project management certification from Villanova University. She served four terms as chair of the Construction and Utilities Business Council for the Prince William Chamber of Commerce and other leadership positions. I met her when she was part of AT&T's Operation Hand Salute in early 2012. It was my pleasure to serve as her mentor as she developed plans for her company. In 2013, the SBA awarded Amber the Veteran Business Advocate of the Year recognition for the Commonwealth of Virginia. In March 2015, Amber was awarded the Emerging General Contractor of the Year Award by the American Subcontractors Association. In August 2015, Amber was also awarded the SmartCEO's Cornerstone Award in recognition of Athena's impact on Prince William County. While we are two thousand miles apart, I continue to enjoy talking to her on the phone and sharing her successes and concerns. I am a fan of Amber and believe she will continue her success path. Her articles have appeared in the Washington Post *as well as numerous construction periodicals, and she has been featured in various magazines highlighting her leadership in a challenging industry. I love to hear about her continued success, as it could not happen to a better person.*

Chapter 35

The Little Red Engine That Could

Jennifer Schoenhofer

My Grandma

I Think I Can, I Think I Can, I Know I Can, I Know I Can was the first book my German grandmother ever read to me. She believed that optimism and perseverance were the key ingredients to success. She believed in the little red engine that could. It was the beginning of her teaching me that I can do anything if I put my mind to it! I never really connected the dots of how all my early life's lessons molded me to what I have become today at fifty-seven. My grandma was my greatest influence that has served as my beacon throughout my life. She inspired me by her own accomplishments. Her story would be an entire chapter by itself, but watching her with the eternal optimism, hard work, kindness, and fullness of life truly went into the heart and soul of who I am today.

I told her I wanted to be the first woman astronaut and drive a little red sports car, and she wrapped her hands around my face and she said, "Dream big, don't let anyone say you can't, because you can accomplish anything. If there is a will, there is a way." She told me that as a woman, the road will be more difficult but that I should never let that fear of difficulty interfere with accomplishing my dreams. During those years, I didn't realize those lessons were the building blocks of my sometimes-overpowering personality. She grew a confidence in me of following my heart, praying to the heavens, having faith, and finding the sunshine in everything. She would say, "Follow the light, and blessings will be waiting."

My life has been complex. I have lost both of my parents, and after twenty-seven years of marriage, we failed, but there are five points that my grandma taught me that are still true to this day and guide my every day of entrepreneurship. They are (1) never fear, (2) have integrity, (3) be tenacious, (4) keep your passion flame going, and (5) aim to leave a legacy. These teachings still guide me today.

Never Fear

I went to work, went to school, got my MBA, and at age forty-four, moved from working for a corporation to starting my own company. I had no idea the ups and downs that such a transition would entail. As I embarked on building my business, my most difficult task was trust, honor, and respect. You have to seek the needle in the haystack—the partners that have the same value-based virtues as you do. "Birds of a feather flock together" has meaning. If you aim to make a difference, then you have to create a community where all of you have that common goal. In my company, I aimed to build it such that no one was a number—a company where everyone would walk the walk. It is not as easy as it seems at all. My mantra has been, if you have your values straight, you don't need to fear!

Integrity, Tenacity, and Passion

Integrity, tenacity, and passion are my foundational principles. I have hung on to them for dear life! You have to be true to yourself. I have come across people with chisels, hammers, fists, videos, and words to try to break me. I'm not saying I didn't have many moments of feeling sorry for myself, crying like a blubbering baby, ranting, raving, and cursing, but in the end, these values saved me. Starting a business from nothing can be scary, but to be honest, that never crossed my mind. All I wanted to do was provide a service that makes a difference. My passion was anchored by the "pay it forward" concept. I saw the world at times being overridden by greed, and I felt my business needed to be a reflection of me, a person of complete integrity.

Legacy

Legacy—it's an interesting and powerful desire. To my way of thinking, I want my business and my life to leave an indelible and positive legacy in this world, to my children and grandchildren.

Putting it together

Here are five quotes from those that can make words flow better than I can that exemplify my grandma's five gifts to me:

1. Never fear

There are two basic motivating forces: fear and love. When we are afraid, we pull back from life. When we are in love, we open to all that life has to offer with passion, excitement, and acceptance. We need to learn to love ourselves first, in all our glory and our imperfections. If we cannot love ourselves, we cannot fully open to our ability to love others or our potential to create. Evolution and all hopes for a better world rest in the fearlessness and open-hearted vision of people who embrace life. (John Lennon)

2. Integrity

In looking for people to hire, you look for three qualities: integrity, intelligence, and energy. And if they don't have the first, the other two will kill you. (Warren Buffett)

3. Tenacity

Never, never, never give up. (Winston Churchill)

4. Passion

A person can succeed at almost anything for which they have unlimited enthusiasm. (Charles M. Schwab)

5. Legacy

The greatest legacy one can pass on to one's children and grandchildren are not money or other material things accumulated in one's life, but rather a legacy of character and faith. (Billy Graham)

Biographical Comments by the Lead Author

Jennifer has been growing companies for twenty-five years, spearheading also their increased profitability. At Bell South, Jennifer took the Brite Wichita Call Center from start-up to a $20 million annual operation over a five-year period. At TeleBase Network Services, she increased overall company growth by 43 percent. As the vice president of operations at Global IT Associates, she increased revenue by 200 percent and reduced operating expenses by two-thirds. As the CEO of Wireless Solutions International, Jennifer grew revenues by 400 percent. In the past thirteen years, Jennifer has concentrated on building her own company, Axis Teknologies, from the bottom up into a multimillion-dollar, certified woman-owned engineering firm. Axis has been on the Inc. 500/5000 list of fastest growing privately held companies in the USA for three years in a row; Forbes *magazine named Axis Teknologies as one of America's Top 100 Most Promising Companies of 2011; the Women's Presidents Organization named Axis as one of the 50 Fastest Women-Led Businesses in North America for two consecutive years; and Jennifer was also named 2012 Female Entrepreneur of the Year (Gold) by the Stevie Awards. Jennifer holds an MBA degree from Kennesaw State University in Georgia. Both Jennifer and her daughter, Jillian, who is also an executive at Axis Teknologies, are graduates of the Institute of Entrepreneurial Leadership, and it has been my pleasure to mentor them and serve as an adviser to their company. Their tenacity will continue to take them places, and their kindness will serve as an example to others.*

Section 6

Make Room for Giving

I have one life and one chance to make it count for
something . . . My faith demands that I do whatever I can,
wherever I am, whenever I can, for as long as I can
with whatever I have to try to make a difference.

—Jimmy Carter

Significant Reflections on the Impact of Gratitude

When you have a good friend that really cares for you and tries to stick in there with you, you treat them like nothing. Learn to be a good friend because one day you're gonna look up and say I lost a good friend. Learn how to be respectful to your friends, don't just start arguments with them and don't tell them the reason, always remember your friends will be there quicker than your family. Learn to remember you got great friends; don't forget that and they will always care for you no matter what.

—Marilyn Monroe

True happiness is to enjoy the present, without anxious dependence upon the future, not to amuse ourselves with either hopes or fears but to rest satisfied with what we have, which is sufficient, for he that is so wants nothing. The greatest blessings of mankind are within us and within our reach. A wise man is content with his lot, whatever it may be, without wishing for what he has not.

—Seneca

Let gratitude be the pillow upon which you kneel to say your nightly prayer. And let faith be the bridge you build to overcome evil and welcome good.

—Maya Angelou

Gratitude is not only the greatest of virtues, but the parent of all others.
—Marcus Tullius Cicero

Piglet noticed that even though he had a Very Small Heart, it could hold a rather large amount of Gratitude.

—A. A. Milne

Chapter 36

Following Your Heart—Igniting Your Passion to Serve

Mary Tuchscherer

The first stories I heard were narrated by my sturdy, hardworking Norwegian ancestors as they gathered around the kitchen table to feast on my mother's homemade Scandinavian sweets, drink from her bubbling coffee pot, and reminisce about homesteading on the remote plains of North Dakota. I was the attentive, quiet, little listener who absorbed the tales about the agrarian land that was shaping me.

Their stories were an invitation into their world, and I loved hearing their vivid tales of chasing vagrant cattle through the wheat fields and delivering mail in a blinding snowstorm. At the same time, I felt the longing toward something more. Inside my toe-headed top, I dreamed of creating a story beyond the prairies. I peered out of my bedroom window and longed to be a passenger in an airplane flying across the empty horizon.

I had no idea as a young girl that I was developing a passion for storytelling as a way to connect people and inspire change in the world. I had no inkling that one day I would sit around a fire in an African village and hear stories of women stigmatized for menstruating. I was clueless that the ability to read and write could be considered a luxury for a girl. I didn't know that someday my inspiration would be borne out of a desire to prompt and share the stories of girls and women never told before.

Now as a writer and facilitator of writing workshops, I have learned that there are extraordinary stories all around us. These accounts shape the way we see the world. Our narratives unite us—from the smallest details of our personal lives to the global issues of the world. Our stories are the bridge builders between cultures.

I live in the moment. So when my friend, a Malawi native, invited me to spend Christmas 2007 with him in his African village, I immediately said yes! Although at that time the trip seemed like a detour, I responded to my heart's desire and the intuitive voice inside that beckoned me. I chose to step outside my comfort zone, face irrational fears of insufficient capacity, and taste the unknown. Undoubtedly, I sensed there was something or someone calling me. I simply needed to trust I would be present when the summons arrived.

Less than twenty-four hours after landing in Malawi, I was among a circle of women—four from Malawi and four from the United States. As we dined on a traditional meal of chicken and rice, nsima, and cassava greens, we inquired about one another's interests. We were surprised to discover we all recently read the same international bestseller, *Eat, Pray, Love*.

As we shared our favorite reading lists, I was eager to ask where to find books written by Malawi women. I was curious to observe bewildered eyes glance from one to the other, as if in search of an answer that didn't exist. I wondered if this *mzungu* (white person) had perhaps asked an inappropriate question when I heard a small voice say, "There are none."

In that thunderous silence between the words, my heart split open. I envisioned writing workshops expanding from California all the way to Malawi, Africa. I imagined women gathered at the water well, in schoolrooms, in churches, and under a baobab tree. I saw global and cross-cultural connections emerging, and I knew that if we chose to work together, we could bring the female voices of Malawi into the light.

As I traveled from city to village and back, a sense of urgency to shatter the silence of female voices transformed from a flicker to a flame. My commitment to linking women in North America with their sisters in Malawi amplified. I wanted to underscore what we all have in common and to crumble the barriers that separate us. I promised to return to Malawi in eighteen months with a group of eight women and to offer an opportunity for us to write and share stories together. The first step was cemented. I trusted that through the power of love and connection, the rest would work out.

When I answered yes to an enticing invitation, I honored one of my earliest and deepest desires—to expand my world and be a loving force for change. What evolved has been a collaborative enterprise and a mutual affection that is eight years old and expanding now to Kenya. It doesn't matter if it's a fifty-year-old village woman who writes her name for the first time, a journalist who publishes an article educating people about their human rights, or a young student who writes one line of poetry, the thrill of witnessing the spark of a new voice once ignited never diminishes.

Although I have no way of knowing when the tipping point will come, I know this is my gift to the world. My vision for the women of Malawi to be seen and heard is well in motion.

Voices from Malawi

Today, I am proud to head a nonprofit, VoiceFlame, which has sparked the voices of over eight hundred women and girls, ages six to seventy-six, and trained thirty-four people to facilitate writing workshops in schools, churches, villages, and more. We published one anthology, and a novel has been written and is being edited. Girls who have never before spoken in front of their classrooms are now some of the first to raise their hands. Children, teens, and adults are eager to pass on their newfound assurance to others who remain too shy to read and write. When we educate one girl, we truly educate a village.

In 2014, Chikondi Lunguzi Njawala, our Malawi VoiceFlame program coordinator, experienced the power of writing and reading within the safety of a nonjudgmental group. She was thrilled to learn that writing could be so liberating, fulfilling, and joyful. Eager to expand her vocabulary, she began reading more books and established a library for children in the preschool she founded. Receiving positive feedback about her stories increased her self-confidence, and she soon discovered a desire to share her passion for writing with others.

After being trained by VoiceFlame to lead Amherst Writers & Artists classes in Malawi, she wasted no time before initiating a writing group for girls in her neighborhood. These girls, elated to be able to use their voices, helped Chikondi start another group in a nearby village. Secondary school groups followed, and now hundreds of girls are expressing themselves and discovering that their voices matter. Following are pieces written by Chikondi and some of her students. When you read these, you must understand that in Malawi, a very large number of the girls can't read or write.

The Voice of the Unseen
Chikondi Lunguzi Njawala

The joys of my soul—
I followed my heart,
God touched me, held my hand
I took the challenge with a positive mind
With my fears I followed

Their unseen beauty waved my attention
Their innocence captured . . .
I smile
As I wipe tears of joy in their eyes
As we sing songs together

Poverty is defeated,
No more sorrows, no more pain—
The chance to dream is here

Her face was down
Her finger in her mouth

Sounds of fear as clear
As the sound of the trumpet
Her heartbeat so loud
Her legs trembled
As her paper shook, her pen dropped

Not any more I say.
No more fears—
Only confidence—
The chance to dream is here

The sky is no longer her limit
Her eyes see great things,
Overlook past disappointments
Her body shakes as she dances
Her beauty revealed,
And her smile

I see the African queens
The girls with a dream—
Hope is found
The chance to dream is here.

Friendship
Monice Mapira, primary school student

Friendship can be confusing, nice, sad and very, very important. How do you become a friend? Everyone has these questions but what are the answers?

My Friend
Twambilire Kamwaza, primary school student

I have a friend and her name is Natasha. She is a good girl. She is short in size, bright and beautiful. She loves the colours pink and blue. Her birthday is on March 7. We are in the same class and also we are all short in size, and we help each other with homework. She lives in area 47 sector 2. She is a Roman Catholic. My best friend.

Among the first group of women we trained in Malawi to lead writing workshops, we had a student named Akossa Mary Mphepo. She was fortunate to grow up in a home surrounded by books and parents who encouraged her to read. At the age of five, Akossa and her friends created their first book club and began writing fairy tales together. She followed her dream to be a writer and graduated in 2006 with a degree in English literature. Now Akossa can teach other women, expanding her circle even more. A piece she wrote is a favorite of mine, and it is called "Not Once" and has been published in volumes XXVIII and XXIX of *Peregrine*.

Not Once
Akossa Mary Mphepo

It's seven in the morning and I open my window
To see golden sunlight filtering through the curtains,
Rain gently falling onto lush green grass,
Pink and purple petunias startling in their beauty—
Proud warriors standing up against the rain,
Taking it with bravery,
Letting it beat down their thin selves
And wash them clean,
Never bowing, never failing.
Not once.

I see myself in that rain, head held back in laughter
Hair all wet, shoes kicked off, mascara running
Down my face, lipstick smudged, foundation melted,
White work suit thrown off and trampled under my feet
As I do a crazy dance of victory
In God's shower of clear blessings.
Uninhibited, wild, happy, strong—
Beautiful black woman.
Proud warrior standing up against the rain,

Taking it with bravery
Letting it beat down my voluptuous self
And wash me clean,
Never bowing, never failing.
Not once.

I am excited and deeply humbled that by working with Malawi women, we have been able to ignite a flame that gives voice to women who represent the true heart of this impoverished and disease-ravaged nation, providing a voice that reflects a culture previously unheard. This ignites my passion and makes me crave for more.

Biographical Comments by the Lead Author

Mary Tuchscherer is the founder and CEO of VoiceFlame Inc., a nonprofit that believes in the power of words, voice, and connection between people of various cultures and backgrounds to effect positive change in the world. Growing up in the homogenous environment of rural North Dakota, Mary dreamed of a world beyond the familiar and wondered at the stories and voices that remained untold and unseen. The very absence of contrast in her physical and spiritual environments fueled her passion for difference, connection, and self-expression. In 1981, Mary traveled to Seoul, Korea, where her world exploded with the splendor of difference. Since then, she has shared stories with refugees, exchange students, foreign adoptees, and women of many cultures. She learned that beneath the color of one's skin or the language spoken, there is something we all share—our humanity. During a trip to Malawi, Africa, in 2007, Mary's heart burst wide open when she learned that less than a handful of Malawian women had ever been published, and her passion for serving those who have been silenced was ignited. This same energy continues to provide the mojo for her work today. Mary is certified as an Amherst Writers & Artists workshop facilitator and trainer and is an adjunct faculty member at John F. Kennedy University in Pleasant Hill, California. She holds a master's degree in spirituality and culture from Holy Names University in Oakland, California. Mary is a two-time recipient of the Soroptimist Ruby Award, Women Helping Women, given for her work with disenfranchised women in Malawi, Africa. She is the author of one anthology of cross-cultural women's voices, Nda Ku Ona: I See You with My Heart, *where I was able to participate by writing some introductory words. Mary was a participant in my Institute of Entrepreneurial Leadership programs, and I was pleased to serve as her mentor. We have worked together and stay as BFF. The San Francisco Bay Area is home to her and Jim Galinsky, her partner of ten years. Mary is a true example of someone focused on doing good for humanity.*

Chapter 37

Let Gratitude Lead You to Your Calling

Randy Haykin

My college friend Dick Lynch has been both an enigma and an inspiration to me. Back in our days at Brown University, Dick was intense—he combined the looks and charm of a *GQ* cover model, the toughness of a star defensive end in varsity football, and the disquieting charm of an effective fraternity recruiter. But few people at Brown realized Dick's background: he had come from an impoverished family in Cincinnati and worked hard in high school, receiving scholarships to pay for nearly his entire education, and came to Brown to find a way to rise above his upbringing.

After Brown, Dick returned to Cincinnati but followed a path unlike many other Ivy Leaguers—he honored his roots. He found something he was passionate about and eventually created a nonprofit that has impacted thousands of US veterans around the country. Instead of taking the typical consulting or investment banking route following his Ivy League education, Dick searched for a way to express his gratitude by giving something back.

Dick chose a target for his gratitude that was something that bothered him, moved him, and touched his heart: wounded veterans. In 2000, while most of his college buddies (including me!) were trying to figure out how to take advantage of the ballooning economy and economic and technology bubble, Dick set out to create an organization that would assist wounded veterans and make them a top priority in the minds of many other people. He used his entrepreneurial skills to create an organization called Impact a Hero.

His general idea was to create an organization that would inspire others to express their gratitude for what American soldiers have given in order to defend our country abroad. Focusing on post-9/11 veterans, Dick grew the organization by involving people like former president George Bush and his wife, Barbara Bush, football star Christian Okoye, and many NFL team owners.

In short, Dick had a sense of gratitude that was instilled by his family upbringing at an early age and heightened by the privileged lifestyle that he observed some of his friends at Brown living. Dick used his entrepreneurial intuition, creativity, and firepower to help others. He aligned his interest in business with his desire to give back to those less fortunate than himself. It was his gratitude for what these veterans have done for our country that drove him to develop his organization into a leading effort today that serves thousands of veterans across our country.

In my thirty years in the business world, I have noticed that some of the most impactful leaders—the ones with the most mojo—are those who act from a sense of gratitude for what they've been given.

What Does It Mean to Be Grateful?

The word *gratitude* stems from the Latin *gratitudo*, which means "pleasing, thankful." The word is also related to the term *grace,* from the Latin *gratia,* meaning "elegance, poise, and balance."

A person whom we would say is grateful is a person who recognizes the good in others, appreciates others, and is generally thankful for what they have been given.

In the context of Wall Street and Silicon Valley at the confluence of the investment world and entrepreneurship, it is sometimes difficult to see where gratitude enters into the picture, although in recent years, you more and more hear about wealth creators, such as Bill Gates, who donate a major portion of their fortune, as well as their creative talents, to improving living conditions in the poorest nations in the world. In fact, I have observed that in Silicon Valley and Wall Street, the more we have, the more we take for granted and the less grateful we seem to be. Instead of being grateful for what we have, those luxury apartments and massive homes seem to instill a focus on getting more and a never-ending cycle of expectations and entitlement.

My Story

My own path is different from Dick's, but my story is the same: gratitude led me to my current calling.

I grew up in Parsippany and Leonia, New Jersey. I was very blessed to have a family that was upper-middle class and quite able to provide all the luxuries of young life, including typical Little League baseball, musical instrument instruction, summer exchange programs to France, and a high-end education system. Unfortunately, what I had in the way of amenities became a replacement for lack of a family. I grew up the product of a divorced family and lacked confidence in myself to be a leader at a young age. By high school, I was focused on what it takes to be ultra-successful (success defined by money, power, and rank) and was constantly pushing myself to succeed and excel—good grades meant good college, good college meant good job, good job meant happiness, right?

It wasn't until I got to the Silicon Valley as a young employee at Apple Computer that I began to think about and focus on what areas of the working world I would most enjoy. Early on, I realized entrepreneurship was something that I could relate to: the creativity, the passion, the rigor, and the risk taking of successful entrepreneurs were extremely alluring. Fortunately for me, I was able to craft a career at Apple and, beyond that, aligned my interests and passions with what I was being paid to do.

In more recent years, I have noticed, as a professor at the University of California at Berkeley, that all too often young minds chase what their parents, friends, or society tell them will lead to success. They follow the path to medical school, law school, engineering, etc., only to find out that their real passions or calling doesn't align with their chosen field. In the end, if they are lucky, they can align passion and career, but 80 percent of those that I have met don't seem to have this lucky outcome. They end up in careers that may enrich them but leave their souls unsatisfied.

Following my focus on entrepreneurship and technology, I ended up being part of the founding team at Yahoo!, Overture, and NetChannel and then moved on to assist other companies and was soon offered money (in the form of a venture capital firm) to invest for other people as well in the burgeoning economy of pre-bubble Silicon Valley. With a partner from Brown and Harvard, we created a venture fund called Outlook Ventures, which went on to fund thirty-five start-ups. During that time, I learned a lot about the venture capital business: it is driven by financial returns, greed, and often pure luck. In short, it was not a field that I would say rewards gratitude for anything. I was beginning to sense a misalignment of my occupation with my calling.

During my venture capital days, my wife and I also began to spend time and money supporting a great cause called Opportunity International. That organization allowed us to see how high-net-worth families could donate dollars that would positively affect impoverished families around the world. Opportunity International had a great business model by providing micro-lending and micro-insurance for the poorest countries in the world. The organization raised money from wealthy families and gave money to impoverished families, who then used their entrepreneurial spirit with those funds to create jobs for themselves and bootstrap themselves out of poverty.

What to Do Next?

After deciding to ramp down my venture capital work, due to the misalignment I was feeling, I was faced with the question of determining my true calling and moving into something new.

Through an event that Opportunity International held, I heard Bob Buford, the author of *Half Time: Moving from Success to Significance*. He had mentored some of the great Christian leaders around the world.

He invited me to visit him and his team in Dallas and invited me to participate in his HalfTime Institute. Going through that program, our small class of fifteen executives learned how to strip down our strengths and weaknesses, identify our callings, and envision a future where we could each make impact in the lives of others. Bob was smart—his staff printed out booklets for each of us after the event, charting our progress and learnings and documenting our decisions. He also had each of us draw a picture of what we saw as our image of the future we wanted for ourselves and branded it into a piece of wood.

This diagram, which I drew on a large piece of paper at the peak of my HalfTime experience, came from the deep sense of gratitude that I felt was the calling for the rest of my life. I drew a hand at the bottom of the picture, which depicts my life, God, and me—all in one. The hand is holding a set of items, each item is spawning other items, and each of those items is spawning other items. The diagram reflects my desire to set an infrastructure, or platform, in place that will indeed help others help themselves, especially through entrepreneurship and mentorship.

For several years thereafter, I had regular mentoring calls with Bob Buford, and eventually found other equally powerful mentors to work with me on the vision for what I now call the Gratitude Network.

The epiphany for my calling finally came when speaking with my friend, Guru Singh. He asked me what impact I'd most like to have, and I told him about my vision from Bob Buford's training—the idea of leveraging my background in venture capitalism and entrepreneurship to affect a chain reaction of others to accomplish a positive effect in the world. I mentioned to Guru Singh that I had the idea for a social impact company that would affect hundreds of entrepreneurs all over the world, enabling them to come up with solutions that would in turn affect millions of lives of the marginalized.

"That thing you just described to me," said Guru Singh on one phone call, "that thing is your calling!"

The Gratitude Network Was Born

In the early days of my calling, I spoke with a lot of people who were already doing impact work. One memorable meeting was with my Brown friend and colleague, Diana Wells, president of Ashoka, who cheered me on and suggested ways to get my vision. Another wonderful encouragement came from Kimberly Dasher Tripp, who had been a student of mine at UC Berkeley and who worked as a program director for the Skoll Foundation. Both Diana and Kim encouraged me to use the thing I had already established a name in—mentorship—and to apply it to companies that were in a ramp-up or scaling stage, rather than just those in the concept or seed stage, as this would likely produce bigger and quicker positive results.

At first, using the knowledge I had from venture capital, I crafted a proposal, which I shared with Bob Buford and his staff, for a venture-like entity that would take private funds and invest them in social impact start-ups. However, in the process of doing this, it became clear to me that the missing component for most businesses is not only money but also more importantly knowledge and know-how for how best to grow a particular company.

I kept trying things out to perfect a model for the next step of my life. Then, on my fiftieth birthday year, I decided to declare 365 Days of Gratitude. The idea was simple enough: to focus myself each day on something I was grateful for and to blog an image and a description for each thing that made me grateful. One topic per day, for 365 days. At first, it went well. But coming into day 30, I started to run out of things I seemed to be grateful for. Then, during the next 335 days, I had to actually look around and notice what was going on around me and find delight in even the smallest of things. As the days passed, this became easier and easier. The finished product at the end of my fiftieth year of life was quite something—a slide deck of sorts, with 365 images representing the things in my life I was most grateful for.

During my 365 Days of Gratitude, I learned a lot about myself, and I also had an epiphany: what about focusing the efforts of my new calling to help impact entrepreneurship through a global mentorship network and a sophisticated process for problem-solving?

The result of that epiphany, of course, was the organization I have named the Gratitude Network, and today the Gratitude Network serves impact entrepreneurs all over the world through a trained team of mentors.

The Gratitude Network success is based upon three cornerstones:

1. *Entrepreneurship.* We aim to use entrepreneurship to empower others who are less fortunate—helping one entrepreneur at a time, who can then impact hundreds, thousands, or millions.
2. *Mentorship.* We involve others who have talents that can help socially impact entrepreneurs and allow them to express their gratitude by sharing their talents in a meaningful way.
3. *Gratitude.* We provide a platform for those of us who have done well, and we wish to empower others in the world that have been less fortunate through our time, treasures, and talent.

Finding Your Calling

The concept of gratitude for me is now best summed up in a famous quote from the Bible in Luke 12:48:

> *From everyone who has been given much, much will be demanded; and from the one who has been entrusted with much, much more will be asked.*

Like many of you reading this chapter, I am indeed quite fortunate—fortunate to have been afforded a good upbringing, fortunate to be living in America, where (compared to the rest of the world) there are fewer restrictions and many opportunities, fortunate to have had a great education, financial success, and a great supportive family.

If you too are feeling fortunate about your upbringing or your current circumstances in the grand scheme of things, then perhaps you too will take some time to consider how you can use your gratitude to chart a course for yourself that contributes to others.

If you've already found your calling, you are truly blessed. Keep at it and remind others that they can find their calling as well.

If you haven't found your calling yet, then I ask you to consider focusing on the things you are grateful for and planning your life instead to recognize where you can be of help and become a giver. You may find, like me that your gratitude also gives back to you probably more in awesome feelings than you ever imagined.

Biographical Comments by the Lead Author

Randy Haykin pirouettes between roles as serial entrepreneur, angel investor, venture capitalist, philanthropist, artist, singer, and educator. In 1997 Randy cofounded Outlook Ventures, a $200 million early-stage tech fund, investing in thirty-five early-stage companies. In 2006, Haykin Capital was formed to provide "mentor capital" to early-stage entrepreneurs, funding over thirty angel deals to date. In 2011, Randy cofounded a philanthropic venture group called the Gratitude Network and launched the Intersection Event, which brings together global thought leaders in innovation and social impact. Prior to his investment career, Randy served as founding VP of marketing and sales at Yahoo! and played early senior roles at Overture, NetChannel, Electric Minds, and AOL's Greenhouse program, a successful venture incubator. He has also held management roles at Apple Computer and Paramount/Viacom. Since 2006, Randy has taught courses on innovation, entrepreneurship, and finance at the Schools of Business at the University of California Berkeley and Cambridge University. He holds a BA in organizational studies from Brown University and an MBA from Harvard. He lives in Pleasanton, California, where he and his wife Patty raised their three daughters. His favorite hobby is singing (bass) in Voices in Harmony, which has performed across the United States and in Russia. Randy and I share similar goals in our friendship, including mentoring budding entrepreneurs. We have enjoyed brainstorming and enjoying the fruits of his Entrepreneur Wines brand, which are used to help fund the Gratitude Network.

Chapter 38

Finding Your Own Road: Turning Away from Entitlement and Toward a Life of Service

Summer C. Selleck

Fearless or *crazy*—it's usually one of those two adjectives that people use to describe me. The problem with that reasoning is that although those two words may be viewed as dissimilar by many, I do not believe they are mutually exclusive. Nor do I think that the intricacies of a person can be summed up in a single word. The spaces in between the simple explanations are really where the best stories lie. I feel as though that is the truth in my own story and the story of my greatest hero, my mother.

Many people can probably relate to that general statement: *My mother is my hero.* The reasoning for each person's admiration likely stems from a distinctive place. My reasoning is no different. However, if one takes into account that I've had the good fortune to meet some of the world's most respected scholars, entrepreneurs, and icons—and yet I can still say with certainty that my mother is my all-time greatest hero—well, I believe that beckons a story.

My story begins in an upper-middle class family in the San Francisco Bay Area. I am the youngest daughter of my father, a very intelligent doctor, and my very active stay-at-home, jack-of-all-trades mother.

Growing up, my mother was not afforded the luxury of attending college. Her parents were not wealthy, and her stepfather believed a woman's place was only in the home. Indeed, her lack of formal education was what she perceived to be her biggest obstacle in life until her death.

During my childhood, I remember my mother's constant embarrassment when helping me with school projects. She would almost always end up in tears and tell me to wait until my father came home because *he* could help me. I could tell she felt deep sadness about this, as if having no higher education made her voice less loud and her ideas less important. She tried not to let her sorrow show, but her regret was undeniable. Her insecurity in this area was likely the impetus for why she demanded from me that my own voice and ideas be developed through my education.

My father, on the other hand, is very well educated. He has his own dental practice, which he started over forty years ago. Like many of my peers, I could have probably taken over the family business. I could have easily had handed to me what my father built. I probably would have led a life of great privilege, as if that privilege was a birthright. I could have lived practically with no adversity, little effort on my part, and with very little discovery of my own independent identity.

However, that would have been, in my perception, not earned and therefore not in my nature. Not to say traveling on the same path as your parent is not noble. It can be noble to many; it just simply would not have been in my case.

I'm thankful for my upbringing. I think anyone would agree that when a person starts out on a path paved with opportunity, it is easier to achieve one's goals. My mother and father both worked hard to give me the best start in life possible, and that fact is not lost on me, and for that, I am thankful.

However, what I'm most grateful for in my upbringing is not my formal education or all the opportunities I had, but rather witnessing my mother's trajectory through life. I'm grateful to have observed not only her insecurity and her losses but also her triumphs. She felt limited by her lack of education, but that perceived limitation never stopped her from being the most quick-witted, street-smart, and well-read person I know. In her short fifty-three years, she touched more people than some do in one hundred years. She opened her own business. She managed my father's dental practice. She was wildly brilliant with people, artistic, and the funniest person in any room. She always had a project going. She was always creating something, always moving toward a goal, and always giving to others. She was both intuitive and painfully kind, which made her the right mixture of both head and heart.

I learned how to adapt to my perceived weaknesses from my mom. While I was growing up, my mom would dazzle me with stories about her own childhood. For instance, how she was on the cheerleading team in high school and was voted homecoming queen. She was active in many different areas and tried to make up for her academic shortcomings by being physically active and outgoing. She always had a book in hand and was constantly trying to learn and better herself through self-study.

In her early twenties, she was in an accident that restricted her to a body brace. She underwent countless back surgeries to correct the injuries she sustained. By twenty-five, she could barely exert herself physically the way she once had. She made up for this physical setback by trying to learn more, develop her mind, and create artwork.

She was physically disabled by the time I was born, so she had a good amount of experience feeling different. People would stare at her when we would go out in public, as she limped most of her life, and then finally transitioned to a walker and then a motorized scooter. When someone would stare, she would simply wink at them or wave or say hello. With all her physical ailments, she never would have considered herself disabled or handicapped physically. She merely believed that her impairments meant she needed to work harder and get stronger to counter her failing body and mind.

Then, when I was in seventh grade, my mom had her first stroke, which led her to lose her ability to read and write in her beautiful penmanship. For many people, losing first your physical ability and then your mental composure could end their will to live, but my mother worked tirelessly to relearn and recreate herself once again within the confines of her remaining abilities.

Even through all her challenges, my mother was still always compassionate and grateful. She never asked "Why me?" or grew resentful of her life. I recall one time when I was a child, she took me to sit with her as she gave blood. It was no easy feat getting her out of the house due to her disabilities, so when we arrived at the blood bank, I asked her, "What are we doing here? Why are *you* giving blood?" Her response was simple: "If I have it, and someone else needs it, then I will give it." That was her in a nutshell.

Looking back, I can tell my mom had a lot to do with my path in life. I do not actively choose to take the road less traveled. The path of least resistance is not by any means less noble. It's just that the divergent path is what I know. For example, while growing up, it became quite clear early on that I had extensive learning disabilities. I tried to hide this fact from my peers, but it was impossible to do. My grades were horrendous; I had trouble reading and comprehending concepts as quickly as other students. However, at a certain point, I realized that if I wanted to succeed, I would need to spend time working harder than anyone around me. I was the student that most teachers could not imagine finishing college, let alone continuing on to graduate school. That is why the proudest days of my life to date were when I was accepted to UCLA as an undergraduate, when I was admitted to law school, and then when I passed the California State Bar on my first attempt, all without any learning disability accommodations.

My mother's path is why I cherish every one of my experiences in life, even all my precious failures. Where some people might find my personal struggles—such as nearly failing out of law school, being the victim of discrimination, or the loss of my mother at an early age—a reason to fail, I see opportunity for growth and understanding in each of these.

I believe I learned patience and perspective from my mom. Yes, I struggled in law school. I was dealing with an intense depression caused by my mother's sudden death the week of law school orientation. Yes, I struggled teaching in Orange County. I was told many times I needed to look more feminine and not make waves if I wanted to be a successful educator. Did I let that obstacle or any obstacle stop me from finishing what I had started? Never! I have ingrained in my soul that fear of failure can't be an option if one intends to achieve anything.

My mother never made it to my law school graduation. She died at fifty-three at home, alone. I will never fully heal from that. Quite simply, her body just gave out. But her spirit lives on in my mind, and her will drives my heart. She is the reason that no pain, no sickness or fatigue, no preconceived notions of what life owes me will ever allow me to slow down or stop working. As long as my heart beats, I will strive to help others. I will help build my community, and I will make sure her work ethic lives on through me.

Today, I'm a lawyer running my own law firm. I'm working in a county that is conservative, and when I go to work, I'm the only person who looks like me. I'm a lesbian. I wear men's suits to work. I'm tattooed. I'm butch. I'm also smart as hell and unapologetic about who I am.

If anyone stares at me, I simply just wink or wave or say hello. No one in court ever seems to believe I'm a lawyer. When I meet people for the first time and tell them my profession, many have a look of total surprise, like "How could someone that looks like *you* be a lawyer?" However, I have never listened to anyone who told me to mute myself if I wanted to be successful. I did not pay attention when people told me I would never make it as a professional or that I was not smart enough or feminine enough to succeed. No one and nothing can take away a piece of my intelligence and, even more importantly, my strength. I am true to who I am. That's all I know how to be. That is what my mom taught me to be. That is why believing I am simply crazy or fearless does not do me justice.

I have been met in life by many people plagued with the failures that accompany a feeling of entitlement and privilege. Some people feel entitled to family money, to their birthright, to physical beauty, and so on. I believe where we come from and what we are born into should not dictate where we can go or who we can become. Some of the emptiest people I know have squandered their privilege, and some of the best people I know came from nothing. The real success story is written when people can create their own pathway to success.

Although my mom never felt badly for herself, I spent a lot of my youth feeling really sorry for her. Her body, and at times her mental capacity, always limited her. I did not understand how someone with so many problems could feel like they led a complete life. Unfortunately, it was not until after her death that I finally realized what an exceptional life she had led. People loved her. She changed lives in big and little ways. Her legacy and the influence she had on so many people are immeasurable. So her final lesson to me was simple: if someone with so many obstacles was able to make such a difference in such a short amount of life, then what could possibly be my excuse, with all my privilege and opportunity, to not do the same or more?

What even is privilege? I can only say what I think it should be: turning away from entitlement. No one should feel entitled to a successful life. No one should feel entitled to a healthy body, a strong mind, or absolute happiness. Things happen, and each and every person lives with their own individual struggles. I have worked to be successful in serving others with the tools I have, as well as my weaknesses. Through my service, I am privileged to find happiness and success. Until my heart stops, I'll keep living this way. I'm not saying it's the only way to be, but it is the only way I know how to be, because if I have *it* and someone else needs *it*, then I will give *it*. Whatever *it* may be. I will always give 100 percent effort to my success in life and help others as I can, just like my mom taught me. I will continue to promote tolerance and diversity in both the legal profession and the community and try to impact the lives of others through my community engagement.

Biographical Comments by the Lead Author

Summer is a lawyer in the San Francisco Bay Area. Since being admitted to practice law in 2013, she has practiced primarily in the areas of estate planning, probate, criminal law, and family law. Her deep passion is protecting and advocating for the rights of diverse classes, and she is deeply involved in her community while continuing to build her legal practice. Over the course of her life, she has worked zealously defending the rights of the lesbian, gay, bisexual, transgender (LGBT) community in numerous campaigns. She continues to promote tolerance and diversity in both the legal profession and the community and is massively impacting the lives of others through community engagement and outreach campaigns designed to build relationships, educate communities, and create a broader social impact. After multiple degrees, including her law degree, she jumped with zest into her law career and her service to the community. Three years after being admitted to practice law, Summer was elected to the board of directors of the Contra Costa County Bar Association in 2016 and is also on the board for California Women Lawyers as a co-affiliate governor. Summer continues to break walls for the underserved and the LGBT community. She was married in 2012 to Andrea, and they live in Martinez, California. I have known Summer essentially all her life. She served as a sitter for our younger son Michael, given that she lived two blocks down from us. My family mourned the terrible loss of her mother and joyed in seeing Summer succeed in her academic endeavors and seeing her marry Andrea. It was my pleasure to serve as a mentor to Summer at the Institute of Entrepreneurial Leadership. She is truly special to me.

Chapter 39

Creative Self-Trust
The Story of the Intuitive Writing Project

Elizabeth Perlman

You have treasure within you—extraordinary treasure—and so do I,
And so does everyone around us. And bringing
those treasures to light takes work
And faith and focus and courage.
        —Elizabeth Gilbert from *Big Magic*

I believe that we are all the creators, heroes, and heroines of our own life story. I believe that our stories are connected. Most of all, I believe in the power of working together, collaborating with the creative energy that is around us and inside us. It doesn't matter what you call it. All that matters is that it puts you in touch with the sacred, with that indescribable sense of Something Greater. When we can trust in our connection to Something Greater, then we can also trust ourselves.

Every creative process—whether we're planting a garden or building a business—follows the same archetypal structure, what the mythologist Joseph Campbell coined *"the hero's and heroine's journey."* You will find it in your favorite book or movie. You can also see it in yourself, in "the journey" that happens within a day, on a project, or across a lifetime. This chapter represents the very abridged version of my own self-trust process, in the creation of an educational nonprofit called The Intuitive Writing Project.

I designed and started the Intuitive Writing Project to facilitate writing-based empowerment programs for teenage girls, providing a safe space for girls to tell their story, discover their strengths, and realize their capacity for leadership. I have dedicated my life to this work because I believe in the power and wisdom of girls. But it is no accident that our mission was inspired by a girl who (once upon a time, when I was much younger) didn't believe in herself. Through my struggle, I found my service, and I found gratitude. Here is my story in steps:

1. "The Everyday World"—where all stories begin

For as long as I have been able to form letters on paper, I have loved to write. When I was a teenager—convinced that I was stupid, ugly, and worthless, and demoralized by the effort to please everyone—it was writing that saved me. When I wrote, I could actually hear my own voice, could hear my own needs and dreams, apart from the collective. The more I wrote, the better I understood myself. And the older I got, the more I saw the power of writing, the way writing creates clarity out of chaos, light out of darkness.

2. "The Call to Adventure"—the recognition that something is wrong, missing, or needed, and the beginning of the quest to resolve it

By the time I was in college, I knew I was interested in writing, personal growth, and intuitive development. But compared to all the conventional careers I was supposed to be choosing from, my interests just seemed weird and crazy. Although I actually wrote a two-page proposal for my dream job, something I called "Intuition Workshops for Girls," I was so crippled with fear and insecurity that I buried my dream in a box in the back of the closet.

3. "Refusal of the Call"—saying no to the quest because of fear

Instead of pursuing my passions, I went back to school to become a graphic designer, which would become my career for over a decade. Unfortunately, I spent most of those years feeling lost, empty, and depressed, staying awake at night, praying and crying the same thing over and over: "What am I doing with my life? Show me what I am supposed to be doing!"

4. "Meeting with the Mentor"—encountering the person who propels you forward

Looking back, what I was supposed to be doing was exactly what I *was* doing. In searching for answers, I found an amazing therapist who empowered me to read a lot of books, do a lot of writing, and spend a lot of time learning to listen to my intuition and surrender to "Something Greater."

5. "Crossing the Threshold to Another World"—the first step toward a new life

Because I was still afraid to take the leap into a more authentic life, coupled with an economic downturn, I went off the cliff. In 2008, I found it impossible to find the design work that I was living off, and I almost lost everything. But this time, when I asked what I was supposed to be doing, my intuition responded with the desire to get my Master's in Transformative Arts, the study of creative expression as a path for personal development. It was at the end of this rich three-year process that I was finally able to connect the dots. Suddenly, the prayer I had been praying for was answered, and the idea for the Intuitive Writing Project popped into my head, fully formed and flaming with life.

6. "Encountering Allies"—finding the resources you need to create something new

In order to make my dream a reality, I knew I needed time to write and design my vision for the program. I also needed to learn how to turn it into a viable business. This is what led me to Dr. Deju's Institute for Entrepreneurial Leadership (IEL). Starting in the fall of 2012, I spent the next year putting my ideas on paper, designing my curriculum, and writing my business plan while being mentored along the way.

7. "Descent into the Underworld"—getting pummeled by fear and resistance

Given the complexity of what I wanted to create and all I needed to do, I just assumed I would have to work all the time and give up everything else, sacrificing all my relationships and never letting myself rest—which is exactly what I did. I thought that if I just tried really, really hard, I could make things happen. But even when I had achieved my goals, developing a comprehensive empowerment program and detailed business strategy, I was once again frozen with fear, afraid I didn't have what it takes. The possibility of failure was paralyzing me.

8. "The Dark Night of the Soul"—when everything falls apart

For four long months after my IEL graduation, I abandoned my dream, buried myself in design work, and fell into another deep depression, angry at myself for being so afraid. And yet, it is always in our darkest moments that we are most willing to surrender—and the universe is quickest to respond.

9. "The Boon"—a moment of grace

The reason I froze up was because I forgot about collaboration. By myself, I didn't have what it takes. The only way to do something larger than ourselves is to consciously reconnect to "Something Greater" inside of you. First, I had to slow down and stop working. Then I needed to write.

What I wound up writing was a sort of manifesto of love for the Intuitive Writing Project, a love that was so much larger than anything I feared or had ever experienced. Through the process of writing, I realized that I would rather die declaring my truth than to spend another day in silence. This time when I prayed, I let go of the outcome. "If you want this organization to be created, I need more help!" I said. "I need *a lot* more help!"

10. "The Shift from Me to We"—putting yourself out there so others can journey with you

Within a few days, I was introduced to the creativity coach who introduced me to the extraordinary woman who would become my most trusted business partner and creative collaborator. Through her, more connections were made, more partnerships were formed, and the Intuitive Writing Project began to grow wings. Now, the girl had become a tribe. But of all the things we are creating together, I am most inspired by our shared belief in "Something Greater", the knowledge that we are working together in service to love.

11. "The Transformation of Self"—the growth that comes from experience

The Intuitive Writing Project is committed to fostering the evolution of creative self-trust for all people. This organization exists because of everyone who has resonated to its message, listening to their own wise and intuitive heart. Is it their love that now fills my heart? For me, the opportunity to listen to and support our girls continues to be the greatest happiness and the greatest privilege of my life.

12. "Return with the Elixir"—sharing what you've learned

When it gets dark, it's easy to feel defeated. But fear will always be part of the creative process. It's okay to be afraid, and it's okay to fall apart. All life begins in the dark. And we all have an inner knowing—an inner light—leading us forward.

Wherever you are on your journey, whatever you're working on or dreaming of or fighting for, please don't give up. The world needs every single one of us to bring our treasures to light. Through our struggles, we find our service, and through our service we learn to let go, to trust in the love of "Something Greater".

Through gratitude, you can accomplish so much and help so many people. Go forward in your journey.

Biographical Comments by the Lead Author

In pursing her passions, Elizabeth has followed a somewhat unconventional path. Yet through it all, her goal has always been the same: to tell and support inspiring stories, stories that heal, illuminate, and empower, especially women. As an undergraduate, Elizabeth studied women's leadership, art, writing, psychology, sociology, and ecology, before getting her BA in filmmaking, the one medium that seemed to encompass everything. But when her ideas for an inspirational environmental documentary proved less than practical, she decided to tell her stories on paper and went on to study graphic design at the Portfolio Center. From here, she spent the next ten years working as a designer and art director for global companies like BBDO, Nike, and West Elm. By the way, she is an awesome designer. It was during this time—stuck behind a computer—that she struggled with chronic depression. But it was precisely this pain that motivated her to pursue a rigorous course of therapy and spiritual seeking, which included studies at One Spirit Interfaith Seminary in New York, where she was ordained an interfaith minister in 2003. Still, it wasn't until the recession of 2008 that Elizabeth finally mustered the strength to take the leap and pursue the thing she had been secretly dreaming of ever since she was a teen. First, she enrolled as a graduate student at John F. Kennedy University, where she earned her Master's degree in Transformative Arts, the study and practice of creative expression as a tool for personal growth. Then, she enrolled in my program at the Institute of Entrepreneurial Leadership, where she learned the practical details necessary to implement her vision: the creation of The Intuitive Writing Project, a girl's empowerment organization where she serves (with great joy!) as the Executive Director. It has been my pleasure to mentor Elizabeth through various stages of this work in progress and to have seen her blossom into the person she is today. I consider her a BFF.

Twenty Rules to Keep Your Mojo and Succeed

(Based on a Bunch of Lives Well Lived)

Now that you have read all the previous chapters, you have seen the collective wisdom of thirty-five of my BFF in their own words. They are the most eclectic and phenomenal group of friends with all the mojo you can imagine, and they make my life most exciting every day. They represent every viewpoint, lifestyle, and set of priorities imaginable.

I thought it would be useful after reading their individual chapters to take the rules I have used to guide my life to this point and compare them to the recommendations for success that each of my BFF presented in their own written words. To do this, I parsed their written words, talked to all of them individually, and tried to use the results of this research to refine what I offer to you in this section as my new and improved "Twenty Rules to Keep Your Mojo and Succeed." *Success* is, of course, defined using my own definition (see the introduction to this book) as "being able to take the steps to lead a happy life on this planet, with comfort, moral support, true values, and a sense of accomplishment and fulfillment." To me, success essentially equates to a life well lived and not money and fame. I will let you be the judge when you put my twenty rules to work in your own life. Trust me, they work.

Rule 1

Values do matter. To succeed today, you need to
start by having a well-tuned moral compass.

Whether you learned your values from your mom, your dad, or your pastor, values do matter. Will Martinez (chapter 4) realized that as his dad lay wrapped in his favorite blanket a few weeks before his death, and Jackie Bhagavan (chapter 3) realized it seeing her mother as they escaped the Killing Fields of Cambodia, to the point where she still consults her mom today as an adult.

I got my moral compass from various sources, ranging from my grandmother to my parents to my friends (chapter 1). My list of values slowly evolved. Initially, it wasn't a list—it was just knowledge stored in a corner of my brain next to the Ten Commandments—but eventually I wrote things down. Don't be afraid if you don't get your list right the first time around.

Best-selling author Gary Hamel in his book *What Matters Now* points out that it doesn't matter where you get your values or how you get there, but it is important that you have them, since for one to succeed, one must begin by embracing the responsibility of the stewardship of our value compass. He enumerates five steps to get there, and I wholeheartedly agree with his list:

1. View your talents as a trust rather than to achieve personal gain;
2. On your road to success, be willing to put the interests of others ahead of your own;

3. Commit to always safeguard the future as you take advantage of the present;
4. Take responsibility for the systemic consequences of your actions; and
5. When you use a team to provide the "team mojo" needed to succeed (as rarely is success a singular accomplishment), distribute the rewards based on contribution to success, not rank or power.

Most of the folks contributing to the preceding chapters of this book clearly got their values straight early on, but your values may come later in your life and even if you are in your late forties, as was the case with Tom Gorham (chapter 29), who eventually found his set of values and used them to get out of homelessness and incarceration and into enormous life-changing success. Listen to your heart as well as your brain as you look around to define the value list for you, and the right answer will be clear.

Some like Nelson Mandela (chapter 12) used their values to allow themselves to get past the worst of times. Just like a compass will always point north and provide you direction, your moral values will help you succeed by moving you always in the right direction in alignment with your values. Success can only begin by having your compass of values pointed north. That is why to me, this is rule 1.

Can you succinctly define your values in an unequivocal way? Develop your list. Learn them and store them both in your heart and in your brain. They come in handy.

Kofi Anan, the former Secretary General of the United Nations, commented upon the death of Nelson Mandela, stating that "by showing us that the path to freedom and human dignity lies in love, wisdom and compassion for one another, Nelson Mandela stands as an inspiration to us all." So emulate Mr. Mandela! Set up the highest standard for yourself. You can do it. Even if you get 75 percent there, it is a great accomplishment.

Think high, stay positive, and remember success is a lifetime, not a destination. Keep the mojo going as you move forward through all the planned and unforeseen things life drops on your lap.

Rule 2

Your mojo will take you places, but team mojo will take you to the moon and back. To get your team mojo, you need to groom and nurture your BFF. You can't solo a climb to Everest or a trip to the moon.

In chapter 27, Larry Rockwell illustrates the spirit of team mojo during the last game of his softball coaching career. The magical, ever-engulfing nature of team mojo could not be clearer than in that example.

In my career, I have completed many acquisitions of companies and dealt with numerous entrepreneurs. In these dealings, I have repeatedly enjoyed greater success when the magical nature of team mojo infects an entire group focused on the single purpose of achieving a specific goal. When that happens, there is no way you can lose.

Other examples of team mojo in the book are sprinkled throughout. In chapter 24, Dina Finta had to rebuild her company's team mojo after Hurricane Katrina devastated her company, her employees, and her clients. Chapter 30 describes team mojo at work to help Anne Marie Taylor fight her cancer.

So how do you get team mojo going? It takes leadership and work. You need to change your style from that of a stern manager to that of a world-class coach. Here are a few things that will help you:

- Internally communicate with everyone in your team and keep the excitement high.
- Always thank your team members when something they do helps the team. Be a cheerleader.

- Keep no secrets, involve everyone, and listen to every idea.
- Let people excel and try to get out of their comfort zone without micromanaging on their heels.
- Don't kill people in your team when something fails—give them an A+ for trying and let them try again. Maybe this time they will hit a home run out of the ball park.
- Recognize that your team members have things to do outside the team. Give them time, and give them room.

In the end, when you and your team succeed, be prepared to celebrate and openly recognize each person's achievements. This gets your team ready for the next time they have to pull a big effort. Keep in mind the words in Will Martinez's chapter: "You can't solo Everest."

Rule 3

Accept that in today's world, "change" is the new normal. Pick things to do that align with your values and interests and shape them into Blue Oceans. Recognize that the future may be different than what you expect. Be prepared. It is awesome to spend your life sailing through the Blue Oceans you create.

Change is innovation, and innovation is responsible for our prosperity and, in fact, for our own existence. Don't forget about genetic innovation. We wouldn't be us without genetic changes. For instance, if six sigma had driven the process of genetic evolution (99.9999 sameness), today we would have slime and mold and not humanity! Our genetics have evolved by optimizing changes.

While change has existed since time immemorial, the speed of change has enormously increased in the last twenty-five years and will likely continue to increase. As we learn more about specific things, we can make quantum leaps that then foster even more changes.

The term *Blue Ocean* was coined by Professors W. Chan Kim and Renée Mauborgne, who described most of the business world as a Red Ocean where cutthroat competition leads to price wars and not much in terms of innovation. On the other hand, they proposed that companies should strive to create Blue Oceans, where there is no competition, and as such, new unique opportunities can then thrive. Cirque de Soleil is a classic example of a Blue Ocean. There were no circuses or theatrical experiences like them when they were started, and today they still dominate their unique form of entertainment.

Several of my BFF and I have thrived creating enterprises where competition is very limited or nonexistent. For example, every time I cross the new Oakland–San Francisco Bay Bridge, I am crossing over concrete supports that used a mix containing fly ash in lieu of cement. This mix uses recycled ash from coal boilers and is better and stronger than cement in the final concrete mix. The fly ash product is a Blue Ocean. That Blue Ocean led to the creation of a company called ISG Resources that my partners and I formed twenty years ago and today is part of a bigger company called Headwaters traded in the NYSE. Our company provided the tons of fly ash that are now part of the concrete in the Oakland–San Francisco Bay Bridge. When I fly on a Net Jet (a Warren Buffett company), I am also flying in a very unique company, another Blue Ocean.

My BFF and I have helped build many new innovations that we all enjoy today, and our life has been peppered by sailing through Blue Oceans where no sharks abound. Randy Haykin (chapter 37) was in the early team at Yahoo!, and Mark Thompson (chapter 12) was involved creating the behemoth Charles Schwab Corporation and a large number of tech start-ups, while Harlan Kleiman (chapter 14) gave birth to HBO, MTV, and Nickelodeon, as well as the early steps of pay TV. All of these started as Blue Ocean type companies.

While Tom Gorham did not know his Addiction Management Program was called a Blue Ocean until he and I met, his program is truly revolutionary and helps thousands of people every year. Who would have thought of using lifers at San Quentin to teach other prisoners how to get rid of addiction? God bless innovation. God bless Blue Oceans.

Once you become an innovator, it is hard to quit. Thomas Edison knew this. That is why he was granted 1,093 patents. My BFF and I are still sailing and uncovering new Blue Oceans and creating new successful enterprises. So can you!

As you create new opportunities, you also need to remember to keep innovating. You can't sit still. Adapting to a rapid pace of change will get your brain going. Look at Deborah Steinthal (chapter 18) and Betty Manetta (chapter 5). They are builders in constant motion. Their batteries never quit.

Nearly five hundred years ago, Niccolò Machiavelli, the Italian Renaissance thinker, recognized that change was difficult when he said, "There is nothing more difficult to take in hand, more perilous to conduct, or more uncertain in its success, than to take the lead in the introduction of a new order of things." We certainly know how difficult it is to harness change, yet change is the engine that drives humanity. In fact, President John F. Kennedy, who, over fifty years ago, was a true visionary, said it best when he said, "Change is the law of life and those who look only to the past or present are certain to miss the future."

So enjoy life and innovate. The only exception to this rule is, don't flip-flop on your values as you innovate. True values need no innovation. Values should be your constant.

Rule 4

Failures are nothing but learning steps.
Trials and tribulations will define your road.
Without failures, you won't appreciate success. The
challenges of getting there will make you stronger.

Even the most admired entrepreneurs have failed at one time or another. Steve Jobs only sold 175 units of the Apple 1, and the Lisa project got him fired from Apple before he came back. Sir Richard Branson, one of the world's most successful entrepreneurs, has had a number of flops such as Virgin Cola, Virgin Vodka, Virgin Clothing, Virgin Cars, and Virgin Digital. The key for both of these very successful entrepreneurs is that they both learned from their mistakes and figured out more things that work than those that do not. They never gave up. Among my BFF and me, we all have had failures, but we picked ourselves up and went on to achieve new successes.

Thomas Edison had 1,093 patents for different inventions, including the lightbulb, the phonograph, and the motion picture camera; however, his Edison Cement Company was a disaster, and you probably did not know it existed. Nonetheless, he did not give up and continued inventing. In fact, in his most famous invention, the lightbulb, it took him one thousand tries to get it to work. When asked about all these failed attempts, Edison said, "I didn't fail 1,000 times. The lightbulb was an invention with 1,000 steps."

In my business life, I have started businesses with certain business plans that I thought would be fantastic, but as we moved on, they proved to require adjustments to prevent a disaster. Remember rule 3, change is the new normal, and when you aim to develop a new product or service, failure is part of the optimization process, and you will have to adjust many times. Look at how many adjustments Harlan Kleiman (chapter 14) had to do to get the Long Wharf Theater off the ground.

Rule 5

Work hard, work smart. Never give up. Make a difference. Tap your BFF for advice.

One thing for sure, most of my BFF and I started poor, and we have seen hunger and lack of comfort, so we can appreciate what the bottom of the ladder looks like. We all have seen that education is the key to be able to live the American dream. Patricia Moore (chapter 7) is the classic example. She slept in a park when she was a kid and used their toilets as if it was her home. Yet she never gave up. When working hard wasn't enough, she worked harder. The same can be said of Jackie Bhagavan, Will Martinez, and Amber Peebles (chapters 3, 4, and 34, respectively). Of course, Amber can't quit or slack off, since she is a Marine and quitting is not in their vocabulary.

A word of advice to all of you is to check with your BFF when you are stuck. It is amazing, but a fresh look at a problem may be all that you need.

Rule 6

Don't be a victim. Sulking is a waste of time.
Sometimes laughter is better than drama. Resentment
is like drinking poison and then hoping it will kill
your enemies. Don't be imprisoned by bitterness.

(Please note that this rule is also tied to
rule 9, which deals with diversity.)

A number of us have suffered harassment, discrimination, and other forms of treatment that really give us every right to call ourselves victims, yet most of us took these as opportunities to show those trying to victimize us that they could not get under our skin. Diana Campoamor discussed discrimination in chapter 2; Betty Manetta, in chapter 5; and Deborah Steinthal, in chapter 18. I particularly like the approach Deborah Peacock (chapter 9) used to break the ice when she was an intern in a mine in Tasmania. Forty years ago, there were no women in the mines, especially in places like Tasmania. She shrugged off the fact that she was told she could not work in the mine when the new boss came in. Instead of accepting the decision, she won him by simply asking him for a dance.

The classic comment on not sulking is, of course, perfectly illustrated by Nelson Mandela. He never sulked, and he never held grudges. He knew when to move on. On one occasion, he said, "Wasting time and effort to fight for a failed idea is neither smart nor efficient." When you get involved sulking for something that was done to you, you forget that you can get out of that hole. If you let others turn you into a victim, you are digging a bigger hole for yourself and helping perpetuate discrimination.

Rule 7

Clothe yourself with humility.
However, be confident and stand tall. Don't be overly
dependent on gifts from government or others. Remember
to always stand on your own. You can do it!

Humility does not mean that you can't stand tall. The key to success is avoiding arrogance. When you look at my BFF, you don't see them wearing a sign that says, "I AM THE GREATEST." Actions speak louder than words. Keep your humility, and recognize that we are all the same when we are born and when we leave this earth. In between, we need to enjoy the ride and do good things to others. Bragging, badmouthing others, and in general showing off are just signs of weakness. Lack of humility generally also implies an inability to listen, and that can be a fatal flaw for success. You need input from everyone. Don't shut people out.

Winston Churchill puts it best when he said, "Courage is what it takes to stand up and speak; courage is also what it takes to sit down and listen." Be courageous, stand tall, but do not be arrogant. Be ready to listen intently at all times.

Rule 8

Practice continuous learning. Learn and evolve and then learn
some more. Remember, when you quit learning, you die.

Patricia Moore (chapter 7) has been learning all her life. She is so enthralled by new stuff that she is still going to graduate school to better herself and her family! However, learning doesn't require you to stay in school forever. Instead, it requires you to keep open your listening skills. The moment you shut down the listening input to the brain, you quit improving yourself, and you quit allowing yourself to be enchanted by new things and new ways. Can you imagine in today's world of ever-growing inventions not being curious to see how they work?

I have called the periods of time between new ventures in my life "semi-retirement phases," and indeed they are my periods to learn and evaluate what I want to do next. Retirement in full for many of us is just accepting that we are headed down and there is no future. When you do that, the excitement of life is over. To succeed, you need your mojo. To get your mojo going, you need lifelong learning. This means that you keep your mind open, and you continue to enjoy new adventures, read new books, and engage in new activities and so on. My BFF and I continually send texts or e-mails to each other with new ideas. We sit down and mentor each other. We have lunches. We keep life interesting. In fact, almost every week, I can count on getting a pleasant surprise from one of them that keeps my brain going.

Albert Einstein puts it best in as few words as possible when he said, "Once you stop learning, you start dying." He also added, "Education is not the learning of facts, but the training of the mind to think." Who knows, your continuous learning could lead to finding a new Blue Ocean you had not thought about. You don't want to miss that. As a Caribbean native, that is the ultimate trip, nothing but blue waters around you with the wind taking you around.

Rule 9

Accept what you are and who you are. Stand tall and embrace others for what they are. Don't be a judge. Incorporate diversity into your team mojo. Remember, diversity has been America's secret sauce. Respect multiple viewpoints.

Diana Campoamor (chapter 2) accepted her sexuality; Tom Gorham (chapter 29) accepted his addiction. I have accepted that I need to continually concentrate on balancing work and play, or I become a workaholic. We all need to be honest with ourselves and accept who we are. The world should accept us for what we accomplish, not for what we are. Otherwise, it is their loss.

A number of us have experienced discrimination on account of gender, ethnicity, or sexual orientation. Sometimes it is worthwhile going to bat and fight all the way; other times the road with less drama is appropriate. Much earlier in my career, I left a position because I had a better option that I wanted to pursue. At the same time that I made my change, a couple of other minorities had also left key parallel positions in the C-suite of the company, and a major newspaper interviewed the company executive responsible for human resources as to why three minorities in very key positions had all left at the same time. He responded, "Well, they left for no reason, but now we just have to hire more of them people." Well, as you can imagine, "them people" became the headline for a negative article on this Fortune 500 Company. The reporter then interviewed me a week later, and instead of getting mired in a battle, I said, "I can't understand the comment about 'them people,' but who knows. Maybe he meant that the company needed to hire some brainy people now, given that all three of us were brainiacs." By not getting into a battle, the issue ended there. The executive in question retired a month later (no reason announced), and the company truly got the message that they needed to focus on diversity big time—and they clearly have to this date. Sometimes the less obvious path is the best alternative.

The thing to remember is that in America, our secret sauce is diversity. We have every nationality and ethnicity represented in our country, and truly it is this diversity that is responsible for American exceptionalism. You will see my BFF are a most diverse bunch, and it is that diversity that makes our grouping unique, and that same diversity accounts for our success as a nation. Companies or countries that are monolithic do not have the breadth of experiences and outlooks of those that foster diversity.

Diversity expands the potential in our country for problem-solving that leads to economic growth. American entrepreneurship is enhanced by the diverse population that makes up our country and the character of our economic climate. Yes, there is some racism in our country, and yes, there is some gender discrimination and other forms of discrimination, and we must eradicate them once and for all and quickly. However, sulking and victimization are not going to solve the problem (see rule 6). The solution is to showcase what diversity accomplishes, and discrimination will ultimately go away and become insignificant.

Rule 10

Educate your heart. Just like feeding the brain is necessary, it is also essential to open your heart and feed it. This will provide balance to your life.

Your heart and your brain both need to be fed regularly. Your brain deals with ideas, and your heart deals with emotions. So often you hear about perfect products that are quite intelligently designed, but they don't make it in the marketplace because they don't make an emotional connection with a user. To succeed in life, we need to deal with both the brain and the heart.

If all you do is feed the brain and build businesses to enrich yourself, you miss an opportunity for well-being. Andrew Carnegie, the famous industrialist, said it best: "Wealth is not to feed our egos but to feed the hungry and to help people to help themselves." David Frost defined how love comes into success when he said, "Don't aim for success if you want it; just do what you love and believe in, and it will come naturally." In my case, I find that intellectual activities that deal with my own businesses serve to create wealth; however, I get more satisfaction when I use my knowledge and my wealth to mentor others and fund causes that are dear to my heart. It is such a balance of wealth creation and wealth donation that leads to contentment.

Rule 11

Success isn't just about me. Let gratitude lead you to your calling. Incorporate giving, mentoring, and helping into your daily life and make it part of your success. Find your epiphany. Remember Luke 12:48: "From everyone who has been given much, much will be demanded, and from the one who has been entrusted with so much, much more will be asked."

One of my BFF, Randy Haykin (chapter 37), has created the Gratitude Network, Mary Tuchscherer (chapter 36) created a nonprofit to teach literacy in Malawi, Africa, and I was the founder of the Institute of Entrepreneurial Leadership at John F. Kennedy University in the San Francisco Bay Area. What the three of us have in common is the wonderful personal benefit we have received from giving and mentoring. We actually get more for our heart than we give from our pocket.

How can you measure the smile you get when an African girl sees her writings in a published book? How can you measure the smile on a new entrepreneur leading a company that wins her first multimillion-dollar contract?

Share your success with others by earmarking profits for specific charities and mentoring specific groups to help them succeed. My BFF are very giving. You can be giving too.

Rule 12

Being persistent does not mean being inflexible. Use innovation to find a new door every time the last door slams shut. Be nimble.

Anyone who is busy innovating will fail on the way to success. Many of my BFF and I have seen failure and then more failure. People like

Will Martinez (chapter 4), Jill Osur (chapter 25), and Amber Peebles (chapter 34) have the tenacity and the passion to stay the course. We are all used to having doors slammed at our face, but then you get up and look for a new door.

If you are not careful, you can miss opportunities, as Alexander Graham Bell wrote, "When one door closes another door opens; but we often look so long and so regretfully upon the closed door that we do not see the one that has opened for us." The key is to learn why a door closed, and be nimble and smarter when the next door opens up. Being nimble is key to success in a world of constant change.

Rule 13

Perfection is the enemy of good.
You don't have to be perfect or lucky to have an
enduring impact. Your impact will happen when
you have the courage to stay focused on building a
better future rather than dwelling in the past.

Perfection is clearly the enemy of good. The pursuit of perfection will guarantee you failure and a great deal of frustration. When the first iPhone was developed, Apple's experts could not foresee the technology that would be embedded in the iPhone 6 today and the iPhone 7 soon. They couldn't even foresee that there would be an iPhone 6. What they focused on, instead of having a perfect phone, was having an excellent phone. The phone has gotten better in time as Apple has learned what people want and as technology has made more advances possible, but at the time the iPhone started, it was an excellent product.

So what do you do? Well, begin by pursuing excellence rather than perfection. Once you have developed a product or service that you feel is excellent, measure it through the eyes of a customer. You will learn a great deal whenever you use someone else's lenses to test products or ideas. Finally, accept that some ideas turn into home runs, and some are singles or doubles, but remember that singles win games. The pursuit of excellence should be a strong commitment in your life, and that pursuit will help you find success.

Rule 14

Just being smart doesn't cut it. Set goals. Be practical.
Chart a way. Get things done. You have no excuses.

Being smart is part of the equation that leads to success, but as Bill Hewitt points out in chapter 15, being organized is even more important. Successfully meeting objectives that you have established is a great tool to instill confidence. That self-confidence is critical to taking on whatever challenges you will face in your endeavors and accepting new challenges as opportunities.

Just like Bill, I keep a rolling plan of all the things I need to get done in the coming week, plus the following four weeks. This way I have already divided what I need to get done into bite-size chunks that I can more easily accomplish. It allows me to plan. If I am running late, I know that I have to make adjustments. If I hit a roadblock, I check with some of my BFF who may be able to help. To make sure things stay on track, I always use the following six steps:

1. Focus my energy on outlining what I need to get done and create a to-do list.
2. Identify the potential distractions and nuke them.
3. Schedule the specific time windows to get the task done.
4. Finish the hard stuff first. Then allocate windows of time to get specific pieces of the work to be done. I try not to be a perfectionist; I strive for excellence instead. I try to stay on schedule and avoid procrastination.
5. Review the work and get someone else to assess and comment on the work.
6. Revisit those parts that need adjustment, and then you are done. Stop. It is time to move on.

By the way, I always use these six steps. In fact, I used them to maintain this book on schedule while dealing with thirty-five coauthors, a couple of editors, reviewers, and a publisher. It definitely works.

Napoleon Hill, the author of a number of best-selling books in the 1930s and '40s, defined *goals* as "dreams with a deadline," and that is as simple as I can put it today. Brian Tracy, a famous business writer who wrote a best-selling book with Mark C. Thompson, one of my BFF, called goals "the fuel of achievement." Regardless of which definition you prefer, without goals, there is no achievement—there is no success.

Rule 15

Learn to communicate. Great success requires team mojo. Without communication, a team is doomed to fail. Incorporate empathy and trust into all your communications. Work at it. Communication is the Gorilla Glue that holds team mojo together.

Most tasks that we undertake are team efforts. The key on those is to move from your own mojo to team mojo. This requires excellent communication. In our discussion of rule 2, we talked about some things one can do to turn team mojo on, and they all hinge on how we communicate.

As a basketball fan and particularly as a fan of the Bay Area Warriors, an NBA team that had won about 90 percent of their games in the 2015–16 season, it is so obvious to see how their team mojo lets them move to the stratosphere of performance. Great success for this team is taking away the arrogance of many single NBA stars and replacing it with a team where everyone is a star, everyone contributes, and everyone respects one another. For you to succeed, you have to emulate the Warriors, plain and simple. However, I must note that in the second half of their playoff games in 2016, the Bay Area Warriors seemed to have had a deficit in confidence both as individuals and as a team, losing their team mojo and losing the championship. Here is a lesson for the future. Stay confident and communicate well with others. Without confidence and communication all teams fail.

Rule 16

Truly find your passion. Once you find your passion, use it to build your successes.

Everyone in my group of BFF is passionate. Most thrive on excelling and do not settle for second place.

Passion generally starts when you are a child, and it is now recognized that the most important thing in helping a child become passionate in life is to focus on what they can do rather than what they can't. Victimization is the worst enemy of passion, and as long as you are a victim, you can't succeed. So shed your victim title and move forward. I have never thought of myself as a minority. I always think of myself as being special, and for that, I am thankful.

If you don't believe you can do it, read a marvelous little book called *The Boy Who Harnessed the Wind*, a *New York Times* best-seller written by William Kamkwamba and Bryan Mealer, who came across the story while he was reporting in Africa, covering the war in the Democratic Republic of Congo. William was a very poor African farm boy born in Malawi, where Mary Tuchscherer (chapter 36) teaches literacy and writing to young women. William had read about electricity and became passionate about the subject and passionate about what electricity could do to his very poor family. He then found some science books in a local library, used some scrap parts, and built a generator and a windmill from scratch. His neighbors called him *misala*, or "crazy" in the language of Malawi, but he did build his windmill and singlehandedly was able to bring to his family both electricity and water using the power of the windmill. His passion never stopped.

In describing William's accomplishment, Nicholas Negroponte, the founder of MIT Media Lab and the founder and chairman of One Laptop per Child, said, "William Kamkwamba is an alchemist who turned misfortune into opportunity, opportunity beyond his own. The book is about learning by inventing. William's genius was to be ingenious."

Maybe a few of the young African girls that Mary Tuchscherer teaches to discover the world of written communication will follow the footsteps of William Kamkwamba and harness the fruits of their passion.

Sophia Loren, the actress, and for many years a symbol of passion to many, once said, "The two biggest advantages I had at birth were to have been born wise and to have been born in poverty." She definitely never considered herself a victim, and neither should you.

Rule 17

Listen and listen closely, for this is the most effective way to discover. Listening will provide you a way to define the right priorities for you and will help you get inspired.

When I visit a potential client with a business proposition, I always ask him to tell me what is important to him before I begin to make him an offer. Let the client speak first. That way you can see where his interests lie and what is important to him. What will close the deal? Listening is sometimes a forgotten skill, yet it is essential to success. When you listen to someone, pay close attention to what is being said, what is partially said, and what is left unsaid. Check the nonverbal messages. Pay attention and digest the information. You will then know how to respond and act.

Mark Twain tried to emphasize the importance of listening when he said, "If we were supposed to talk more than we listen, we would have two tongues and one ear."

Rule 18

As Helen Keller said, "Security is mostly a superstition. It does not exist in nature . . . Life is either a daring adventure or nothing. To keep our faces toward change and behave like free spirits in the presence of fate is strength undefeatable." Coupling such a culture with team mojo multiplies your chances to succeed.

I learned early on that financial security was a figment of imagination when I first came to the United States without my parents (chapter 1). Tom Deierlein learned it when he was shot by a sniper in the Middle East (chapter 13), and Dina Finta learned it when Katrina hit New Orleans (chapter 24). When you get hit by adversity, hit back and turn it into opportunity. If William Kamkwamba could build his windmill, so can you.

I have a picture in my desk that I bring out in times of adversity. It is a picture of Bugs Bunny, the cartoon character, saying, "That Means War!" The picture is simply a reminder to me that when adversity hits you, you must fight it and turn it into the greatest opportunity for you. Keep your face to the wind, accept change, and become undefeatable. If the adversity affected your entire team, your entire company, never fear; team mojo is here. Harness it and go on.

Rule 19

Believing gives you hope.
Without hope, success has no value.

Without a set of beliefs, it is difficult to have hope. You need to begin by believing in yourself, and without being arrogant, you need to believe in your abilities. Believe in your intuition and your support mechanism. Believe in your BFF. Find joy, peace, and strength in your beliefs. In my case, I also see hope from believing in a higher power, believing in my BFF, and believing in me.

Rule 20

BFF are to be enjoyed. Spending your life alone would be an awful experience. Turn your BFF into soul mates and ride life together.

My BFF are part of my life. We talk, we exchange ideas, we rejoice our successes, and we provide support when crises affect us. We serve as counselors; we hold each other. But we are friends, and friends enjoy each other. We balance our lives with the act of friendship toward each other.

I have one BFF that did not write a chapter in this book, but she is of utmost importance to me, and that is my soul mate, my wife, Shari Lynn. Over the years, my business life has taken me away to various places all over the world, sometimes on extended business trips. In all instances, we have tried to communicate as often as possible, but most importantly and to this date, when we are together, we create special little events for each other: date nights, special meals, special little touches that remind the two of us how special the other person is. My wife, my children, my in-laws, and my extended relatives are all family. Also, all my BFF are my family. With such a support group and some help from upstairs (maybe lots of help from upstairs), how can I fail?

Reducing the Message to Thirty-Six Words = Success

**Twenty Rules to Keep Your Mojo and Succeed
(The Success Equation)**
**Values + Team Mojo + Continuous Change + Learning
from Failures + Working Harder + No Sulking + Humility
+ Continuous Learning + Accept Diversity + Educate the
Heart + Gratitude + Innovation/ Persistence + Courage
+ Set Goals + Communicate + Be Passionate + Listen
+ Be Daring + Believe/Hope + Have Fun = Success**

Now that you have seen my new and improved rules, I want to leave you with my simple one-card equation in thirty-six words (one for me and each of my BFF) to remember how I keep my mojo. When you add these thirty-six words representing the twenty rules, you will definitely succeed. Enjoy the ride of your life and continue to change the world positively.

Index

Printed in the United States
By Bookmasters